American Medical A

Physicians dedicated to the health of /

D0189540

# Counseling
## the Alzheimer's
## Caregiver

## A Resource for
## Health Care Professionals

AMA
*press*

Mary S. Mittelman, DrPH
Cynthia Epstein, ACSW
Alicia Pierzchala, CSW

Counseling the Alzheimer's Caregiver:
A Resource for Health Care Professionals

**AMA Press**
Vice President, Business Products: Anthony J. Frankos
Executive Director, Editorial: Mary Lou White
Director, Production and Manufacturing: Jean Roberts
Director, Marketing: J. D. Kinney
Senior Acquisitions Editor: Barry Bowlus
Developmental Editor: Jane Piro
Copyeditor: Margaret Haywood
Marketing Manager: Reg Schmidt
Senior Production Coordinator: Rosalyn Carlton
Senior Print Coordinator: Ronnie Summers
Composition: David Doty Design
Printing: Sheridan Books

Internet address: www.ama-assn.org

Additional copies of this book may be ordered by calling 800 621-8335.
Mention product number OP120802.

ISBN 1-57947-262-1

Library of Congress Cataloging-in-Publication Data

Mittelman, Mary S.
  Counseling the Alzheimer's caregiver : a resource for health care
professionals / Mary S. Mittelman, Cynthia Epstein, Alicia Pierzchala.
        p. ; cm.
Includes bibliographical references and index.
  ISBN 1-57947-262-1 (alk. paper)
  1. Alzheimer's disease—Patients—Home care. 2. Alzheimer's
disease—Patients—Family relationships. 3. Caregivers—Counseling of.
4. Caregivers—Mental health.
  [DNLM: 1. Alzheimer Disease—nursing. 2. Caregivers—psychology. 3.
Counseling—methods. 4. Social Work, Psychiatric—methods. WT 155
M685c 2003] I. Epstein, Cynthia. II. Pierzchala, Alicia. III. Title.
  RC523 .M575 2003
  362.1'96831—dc21
                                                              2002008433

BP90:02-P-036:8/02

The material in this book is based on the longest-running and largest study of a psychosocial intervention for family caregivers ever to be conducted. The Spouse Caregiver Intervention Study at the New York University School of Medicine's Alzheimer's Disease Center began in 1987 and is providing counseling and support to caregivers of people with Alzheimer's disease (AD) to this day.

This book is designed to share the NYU protocol and the cumulative knowledge gained by its implementation with other health care professionals. The only requirement for its use is a caring professional who is dedicated to improving the quality of life for people with AD and their family caregivers. The book can be used in physicians' offices, social service agencies, hospitals, and other health care settings to create a counseling program that will provide support and guidance to family members and friends who are caring for a person with Alzheimer's disease.

The book is divided into 13 chapters that guide the reader through the counseling process. Chapter 1 provides health care professionals with an overview of Alzheimer's disease, its diagnosis, its progression, and the effects of caregiving on families. The book then goes on to describe the counseling process, including the assessment, individual and family counseling, ad hoc (as needed) counseling, and support groups, with suggestions for how to tailor the process to different settings. Finally, the book discusses the many issues that a professional will encounter when working with family caregivers. It includes practical suggestions that will help caregivers master the daily and long-term practical and emotional challenges of caring for a person with AD. The recommendations are based on the many years of experience of the professional staff counseling families at the NYU-ADC. End-of-chapter checklists are provided as a quick review of each chapter's key points.

The vignettes used throughout the book are composites of real people and caregiving situations and show how patient and caregiver well-being can be improved with counseling and support. The long journey a patient and caregiver must take as Alzheimer's disease progresses is brought to life by the story of Millie and her husband Ted, which serves as a case history from the time that he begins having symptoms of AD until his death and illustrates the counseling methods described in the text.

This book reflects the talents, intellect, hard work, and generosity of many colleagues and friends. We would like to express our sincere appreciation and gratitude to the counselors who implemented this protocol from its inception to the present. We start with Gertrude Steinberg, MA, and Emma Shulman, CSW, whose efforts to improve the lives of family caregivers were the inspiration for the NYU Spouse-Caregiver Intervention Study. The study would not have been possible without their efforts and those of Joan Mackell, PhD, Abby Ambinder, EdD, Helene Bergman, ACSW, and Sandy Hertz, ACSW, who also participated for many years as counselors, as did coauthor Cynthia Epstein, ACSW.

Our efforts to investigate ways to improve the lives of family caregivers and to write this book were encouraged and enhanced by the expertise of Steven H. Ferris, PhD, Executive Director, and Barry Reisberg, MD, Clinical Director of the NYU Alzheimer's Disease Center. We extend thanks to our colleagues at the NYU-ADC, James Golomb, MD, Emile Franssen, MD, Alan Kluger, PhD, Isabel Monteiro, MD, and Migdalia Torres, CSW, who provided valuable information and advice from the unique perspective of their respective disciplines. We also appreciate the contribution to our understanding of the issues involved in decisions about end-of-life care provided by Sandy Burke, Director of Patient Representatives at the NYU Medical Center. Janet Reichert deserves a very special thanks, as her organizational skills keep all our endeavors on track. We would also like to thank our editors, Barry Bowlus, Jane Piro, and Jean Roberts, for guiding us through the process of making this book a reality.

The NYU Caregiver Intervention Study has been supported by grants from the National Institutes of Health, and additional resources were provided by the NYU Alzheimer's Disease Center. At the heart of this book are the more than 400 caregivers who participated in the intervention study and shared their individual experiences so that many others could learn and benefit. We extend our sincerest thanks and admiration to them.

# contents

# INTRODUCTION

Alzheimer's disease (AD) has devastating effects on both patients and the families who care for them. It currently affects an estimated 4 million Americans, but that number is expected to grow to 14 million by the middle of this century, in large part owing to the aging of the Baby Boomer generation and longer life expectancies. Prevalence of the disease increases greatly with advancing age; research indicates that the disease affects 1 in 10 people over age 65, but the proportion increases to affect nearly half of those aged 85 and older. The cost of this disease is enormous, with the total annual cost of Alzheimer's care in the United States estimated to exceed $100 billion. So far, drugs produce only modest improvements, and the possibility of curing or preventing the disease still remains far in the future. It is no wonder that Alzheimer's disease is being called the health care challenge of the 21st century.

Most people with Alzheimer's disease are cared for by members of their family. Many of these caregivers become exhausted and overwhelmed as the illness gradually robs their relative not only of cognitive abilities but of functional abilities as well, ultimately leaving the primary caregiver with the task of providing or obtaining 24-hour care. Since the disease manifests itself differently as time goes on and may include behavioral disturbances such as agitation, caregivers often suffer significant psychological and emotional distress, particularly depression and anxiety. Often the stresses of caregiving can result in patients being placed in a nursing home sooner than necessary.

In the early 1980s, the staff at the New York University School of Medicine's Alzheimer's Disease Center began providing informal support and counseling to family members, individually and in groups, when patients came to the center for a diagnostic evaluation or to participate in clinical trials. The positive response to this support from caregivers led to a formal study of its effectiveness. The NYU Spouse-Caregiver Intervention Study began in 1987, through funding from the National Institutes of Health. More than 400 husbands and wives of patients with Alzheimer's disease enrolled in the study in the subsequent 10 years, some of whom are still participating today.

Using the kind of design usually reserved for trials of new drugs, we randomly assigned participants in the study to either a treatment or a control group after they had completed a comprehensive evaluation using a set of structured questionnaires. This evaluation is repeated at regular intervals for as long as caregivers participate in the study.

The treatment has two goals: first, to make it possible for spouse-caregivers to do what almost all of them say they want to do—to postpone or avoid placing their husbands and wives in nursing homes, and second, to reduce the negative impact of caregiving on the caregiver.

There are four components to the treatment: One component consists of two individual counseling sessions for the primary caregiver, within 4 months of enrollment, to address his or her specific needs. Because most caregivers would benefit from more understanding and help from their families, there are also four family counseling sessions with the primary caregiver and family members selected by the caregiver. Two of the components of the treatment provide ongoing support. Participation in a support group that meets weekly is required of caregivers in the treatment group. In addition, a vital component of the treatment is the availability of counselors to participants by telephone, which we call "ad hoc" counseling, to help them deal with crises and the changing nature of the patient's symptoms over the course of the disease and to supply resource information and referrals for auxiliary help, financial planning, and management of difficult patient behavior.

Each caregiver in the treatment group receives *all* components of the intervention and is given support for the duration of the illness. Caregivers in the control group receive the support that had been routinely offered to caregivers at our center, which includes resourcc information and help when they requested it, but no formal counseling.

We have shown, with this scientifically rigorous trial, that counseling and support of caregivers and their families is an extremely effective treatment. The program has had impressive results both in maintaining the well-being of caregivers and in delaying, and in some cases avoiding entirely, the necessity of placing the patient in a nursing home. Caregivers in the treatment group have been able to postpone placing patients in nursing homes for about a year longer than caregivers in the control group, with the median difference being 329 days (Mittelman et al, 1996).

The well-being of the caregivers also improved. While caregivers in the control group became increasingly depressed after they entered the study, caregivers in the treatment group did not (Mittelman et al, 1995). In addition, caregivers in the treatment group grew closer to their families and expressed increasing satisfaction with the emotional and practical support they received. This was not true of those in the control group. Moreover, caregivers in the treatment group were significantly better able to tolerate and manage the difficult behavior of the patients, which undoubtedly resulted in their providing the patients with a better quality of care.

The study showed, without a doubt, that counscling and support help families keep Alzheimer's disease patients at home. It is clear that the availability of long-term competent emotional support and referral to high-quality community resources can make a huge difference. This book is designed to help health care professionals achieve similar results.

# 1

# ALZHEIMER'S DISEASE: ESSENTIAL BACKGROUND INFORMATION

Everyone who offers counseling to caregivers of Alzheimer's disease patients should have a comprehensive understanding of the disease and the effects of caregiving on the families of patients. They should also be aware of the changes in cognitive functioning that are normal concomitants of aging, called *age associated memory impairment (AAMI)*, and the borderline stage, called *mild cogni tive impairment (MCI)*, which is neither normal nor dementia. This chapter provides an overview of the components of a diagnostic evaluation for cognitive difficulties and dementia associated with aging. The stages of cognitive decline are described in detail and illustrated with examples. Finally, an overview is given on the effects of caregiving and the benefits of intervention to the caregiver and the patient.

## Understanding Alzheimer's Disease

Understanding the differences between normal aging, mild cognitive impairment, and Alzheimer's disease (AD) is an important first step for a counselor giving help to patients and their families.

### Age Associated Memory Impairment

Many older people find that their memories are not as good as they used to be. The term *age associated memory impairment* describes cognitive changes that can be expected to occur in most people as they age. These changes are not necessarily harbingers of disease. They are part of the normal aging process and may be caused by a combination of biological and environmental factors.

Just as skin, hair color, bone mass, and vision change with age, so do brain structure and function. Research suggests that slowing of processing speed is central to this decline. However, vocabulary, the ability to learn, and general intelligence do not normally decline as one ages.

Physical impairments, such as uncorrected hearing loss, may make an elderly person appear to be cognitively impaired. In addition, medical conditions such as an underactive thyroid may cause cognitive impairment that is reversible. That is why a person who is experiencing cognitive changes should always have a complete diagnostic evaluation.

## Mild Cognitive Impairment

*Mild cognitive impairment* is a term that describes an intermediate stage between normal aging and dementia that has long been recognized in research settings, but has only recently, since the advent of pharmacological treatments for Alzheimer's disease, been diagnosed in clinical practice. MCI is characterized by decline in cognitive abilities (memory, concentration, orientation) and functional abilities (difficulties completing complex work-related tasks and daily activities) that corresponds to pathological changes in certain parts of the brain. In order to be given a diagnosis of MCI, a person must have subjective complaints of memory loss that are confirmed by an informant, objective evidence of memory loss on at least some neuropsychological tests, but have no deficits in routine activities of daily living.

These mild impairments often, but not always, represent a very early stage of a dementia disorder such as Alzheimer's disease. Many individuals diagnosed with mild cognitive impairment remain stable, and in a small percentage of cases, symptoms may actually improve. Although many people remain in this stage indefinitely and manage well on their own without need of assistance, the majority progress over time into Alzheimer's disease or other forms of dementia.

## Dementia

Dementia itself is not a disease but rather a group of symptoms that may accompany certain diseases or conditions, marking the deterioration of a wide range of cognitive functions serious enough to interfere with normal daily life or social interactions. In addition to cognitive impairment, symptoms may include changes in personality, mood, and behavior. Many different conditions and diseases can cause dementia. Dementia is not always irreversible. Potentially reversible causes include drugs, alcohol, hormone or vitamin imbalances, or depression.

It is a common belief that cognitive impairment is a necessary consequence of old age, and people frequently say things like, "Her memory is bad because she's so old, and you can't cure old age," or "He's senile, but what can you expect at his age?" But what is commonly called *senility* is not a necessary consequence of aging, and it is not true that nothing can be done. Such myths prevent older people from seeking medical help and obtaining proper care when their functional decline may be caused by a disease process rather than by the expected effects of age. Many people mistakenly believe the word *dementia* is a synonym for *crazy* and use the word that way. *Senile* is a general term that has commonly been used to describe all causes of dementia in the elderly.

## Alzheimer's Disease

Alzheimer's disease is the most common cause of dementia. It is a progressive neurodegenerative disease that develops gradually and is characterized by the destruction of nerve cells, especially in the areas of the brain vital to memory and learning. The pathological changes in the Alzheimer's brain include deterioration and loss of neurons (nerve cells) leading to brain atrophy (shrinkage), and the abnormal accumulation of proteins forming amyloid plaques and neurofibrillary tangles. In addition, neurotransmitters such as acetylcholine, dopamine, norepinephrine, glutamate, and serotonin are affected in Alzheimer's disease. While it is now clear that AD develops as a result of a complex cascade of events that take place over many years inside the brain, the cause (or causes) remains unknown.

The symptoms of AD usually only become evident after age 65; however, they may occur as early as age 40 (in rare cases, even younger). The risk of AD doubles every 5 years beyond age 65. The course of the disease varies from person to person. In some people the disease progresses quickly, reaching the end stage in only 5 years, while others may have it for as long as 20 years. The most common cause of death for people who survive to the end stage of AD is pneumonia.

The type, severity, sequence, and progression of mental changes vary widely. The early symptoms of AD are often dismissed as natural signs of aging. AD typically begins with forgetfulness, loss of concentration, and a decline in problem-solving ability. Confusion and restlessness may also occur. As the illness progresses, AD destroys cognition and ability to function and changes personality.

In contrast to the milder signs of memory loss associated with normal aging and mild cognitive impairment, changes in memory associated with AD and the other primary dementias are more pervasive, affecting orientation, mood, behavior, language, speech, movement, and coordination. These changes differ from normal aging and mild cognitive impairment in quantity and quality.

Many people believe that AD does not affect physical functioning. It is now known that AD begins to have subtle effects on motor function, muscle tone, and balance even in the earliest stages of the illness. If people survive until the late stages of AD, the illness affects all areas of their brains, so that they ultimately become incapable of performing even the most basic physical functions. This makes AD perhaps the most devastating disease of the elderly.

A commonly believed myth that prevents people from seeking a diagnostic evaluation even for severe memory problems is that there is no point going to a doctor because nothing can be done. In fact, there are many ways to relieve the suffering of people with AD and their families. Drug treatments are now available to manage some of the symptoms of AD. While no currently available drugs can prevent or halt the underlying disease process, advances in understanding Alzheimer's disease may lead to such treatment in the future. In the meantime, researchers and clinicians are working to enhance the quality of life for both patients and caregivers by developing ways to improve behavioral management and caregiver skills.

Psychosocial interventions can reduce the impact of AD on the patient and the family. For people in the early or moderate stages of the disease, medication has become available that may alleviate some cognitive symptoms. In addition, some medications may help control behavioral symptoms such as sleeplessness, agitation, wandering, anxiety, and depression that are frequently seen in the middle stages of AD. This makes it even more important to have a thorough diagnostic evaluation by well-trained medical specialists when someone seems to have significant changes in cognitive ability.

A common fear is that AD is inherited, and family members of patients are frequently concerned about their risk of getting AD themselves. Although geneticists are beginning to find chromosomal mutations in some families in which there are many cases of AD, these families are very rare—genetic factors are the sole determinant in fewer than 2% of the cases of AD. A variant of the ApoE protein called ApoE-4, located on chromosome 19, appears to increase the risk and lower the age of onset of AD. Nevertheless, while about two thirds of the cases of AD have at least one copy of this form of ApoE, almost one quarter of the normal elderly population do also.

Researchers today are actively searching for ways not only to increase longevity and disease-free aging but also to improve the quality of life of the aging population. Owing to the increase in life expectancy in modern societies and the fact that the risk of AD increases with age, many people currently face the prospect of suffering from dementia. A major focus of ongoing studies is to postpone, ameliorate, or prevent the onset of debilitating illnesses such as AD and to develop improved ways of helping the families of those who are afflicted.

## *Other Possible Causes of Dementia in the Elderly*

Diseases other than AD can cause dementia; most, but not all, are irreversible. While this book is about counseling caregivers of people with AD, much of the information will also be helpful when counseling caregivers of elderly people with dementia caused by other illnesses. It is important to be aware of the distinctive qualities of each of these illnesses to help both the caregiver and the patient understand the symptoms and adjust to them at the time of diagnosis and in the future.

In the absence of significant gait, balance, and coordination difficulties, older adults experiencing a slowly progressive decline in global cognitive function over a several-year period will be found on postmortem examination to have AD far more frequently than other conditions causing dementia. While many diseases can cause dementia, clinical considerations such as time, course, associated medical illnesses, and the absence of motor system abnormalities will usually serve to eliminate alternative diagnoses. For example, infections, cancers, or toxic explanations for dementia typically result in rapid clinical deterioration (although notable exceptions might include syphilis, AIDS, chronic alcoholism, and malnutrition). Dementia due to diseases such as liver or kidney failure and endocrine disturbances such as hypothyroidism are also easily diagnosed because of obvious concomitant medical abnormalities.

Stroke can cause dementia (vascular dementia), especially if the symptoms of dementia began shortly after abrupt onset paralysis, dyscoordination, or loss of speech fluency. In many patients with Alzheimer's disease, strokes can exacerbate the dementia and accelerate its course. Gait and other motor abnormalities early in the course of dementia are common in patients with hydrocephalus, Parkinson's disease, Lewy-body disease, corticobasal degeneration, or progressive supranuclear palsy. Because CT and MRI scans are able to identify strokes, hydrocephalus, blood clots (eg, subdural hematomas), and brain tumors, these abnormalities can usually be detected as potential explanations for dementia. Brain scans may also be of use in the diagnosis of fronto-temporal dementia such as Pick's disease, but accompanying clinical features including marked personality changes of disinhibition or apathy, stereotyped behaviors, and loss of language can be diagnostic clues. In general, when computed tomographic (CT), magnetic resonance imaging (MRI), and basic medical tests are negative in patients with a history of slowly progressive cognitive impairment, the most likely diagnosis is AD. A postmortem examination can confirm the differentiation of AD from other primary brain pathologies.

## Diagnosing Alzheimer's Disease

The early symptoms of Alzheimer's disease are ascribed by many people to old age rather than to an illness. It is only when a series of events occur that are difficult to ignore, such as getting lost or having an accident while driving, losing things and accusing others of taking them, or confusion over date and time, that a family member may seek a diagnostic evaluation for an elderly relative.

There are two generally accepted sets of guidelines for the diagnosis of Alzheimer's disease: the NINCDS-ADRDA guidelines (National Institute of Neurological and Communicative Disorders and Stroke—Alzheimer's Disease and Related Disorders), and the DSM-IV guidelines (*Diagnostic and Statistical Manual of Mental Disorders, 4th ed*). A summary of the NINCDS-ADRDA criteria for diagnosis of AD includes the following:

■ Dementia established by clinical examination and documented by the Mini-Mental State Examination or similar examination

■ Deficits in two or more areas of cognition (ie, language, memory, perception)

■ Progressive worsening of memory and other cognitive function; as disease progresses, patient experiences impairment in activities of daily living and altered behavioral patterns

■ No disturbance of consciousness

■ Onset between ages 40 and 90, but most often after age 65

■ Absence of other systemic disorder or brain disease that may account for deficits in memory and cognition

A diagnostic evaluation can rule out causes other than AD for the symptoms of dementia. Some of these causes of dementia are transitory and reversible, whereas AD is neither. Treatable causes of dementia such as depression, thyroid or heart disease, reactions to medications, alcoholism, malnutrition, head injury, or an eye or ear problem have to be ruled out before determining a person has Alzheimer's disease. These conditions may, of course, coexist with AD, and treatment may lessen the severity of symptoms. It should be noted that in a very elderly person, a stressful life event, such as hospitalization, relocation, or death of a spouse, may temporarily cause symptoms that can be mistaken for dementia.

There is no single test to identify AD. A comprehensive examination, conducted by a physician, will include a detailed history of symptoms, a thorough personal and family history, and a complete health history, including medications currently being used. A neurological evaluation, a mental status assessment, neuropsychological and psychiatric evaluations, a comprehensive physical examination,

other tests, including examination of blood and urine and an electrocardiogram, and a brain imaging exam such as CT or MRI will
help rule out causes of dementia other than AD. Physicians are now
able to accurately diagnose 80% to 90% of people who show symptoms of AD. A definitive diagnosis is possible, however, only through
the examination of brain tissue at autopsy.

The majority of people with AD receive the diagnosis from a primary care physician. In those situations where the general practi-
tioner is unsure of the diagnosis or attributes all changes to aging, a
specialist consultation from a neurologist or psychiatrist or a special
geriatric evaluation program should be requested. Diagnostic evaluations can also be performed at a memory disorders center at a university hospital such as New York University School of Medicine's
Alzheimer's Disease Center (NYU-ADC). There are 30 federally designated ADCs across the United States. These centers are ideally
positioned to offer evaluations and have access to the most up-to-
date information about differential diagnosis and treatment. At
ADCs, specialists administer a comprehensive diagnostic evaluation
that includes the following:

- *A psychiatric evaluation.* This part of the diagnostic evaluation
  involves assessments of cognition (memory, concentration, and
  orientation) and how it affects the person's ability to function in
  daily activities. It also includes assessments of behavior and
  mood, which may cause memory problems, as well as information about the person's past medical and psychiatric history.

- *Psychometric testing.* Psychometric tests objectively measure
  cognitive performance—the accuracy, speed, and quality of various aspects of mental processes. These include tests to assess
  functions such as immediate and delayed memory, attention, language, executive function, and problem solving.

- *A neurological examination.* A neurological examination assesses language, gait, coordination, reflexes, and sensory perception
  as they are affected by changes in brain function.

- *A physical examination.* A complete physical examination is performed and includes an electrocardiogram and blood and urine
  tests. These tests determine the presence or absence of conditions that may be related to (causing or aggravating) memory
  deficits. Such conditions include thyroid conditions, vitamin $B_{12}$

deficiency, electrolyte imbalances, high blood pressure, and heart arrhythmia (rhythm disturbances).

- *An MRI or CT scan.* An MRI or CT scan provides an image of the brain that helps in the diagnosis of Alzheimer's disease, mild cognitive impairment, or age-related cognitive decline by ruling out such conditions as stroke, brain tumor, or hydrocephalus, all of which can cause cognitive impairment.

At the NYU-ADC, several clinicians meet to review the results of the evaluation and reach a consensus diagnosis. A physician then discusses the results of the tests with patients and their family members, presents and explains the diagnosis, and provides appropriate recommendations. At a research center such as the NYU-ADC, possible participation in studies of new pharmacological and nonpharmacological treatments will be discussed.

After the conference with the physician, a counselor meets with one or more members of the family. The counselor discusses the family's reactions to the diagnosis and any care issues about which the patient or the family expresses concern. Since they sought the evaluation because they suspected something was wrong, many patients and families are not surprised by a dementia diagnosis. Some are shocked, refuse to believe it, or become depressed. Others are actually relieved to have their suspicions confirmed. When a patient is given a diagnosis of dementia, the counselor also helps the family decide who among them will be primarily responsible for the obligations the patient can no longer fulfill and, ultimately, the care of the patient. Finally, the counselor recommends resources in the community that can provide appropriate services and support. The counselor and other members of the clinic staff maintain contact with the patient, or with the family member who is the primary caregiver if the patient has dementia, to monitor the progression of the disease and provide support as needed. The counselor will also respond to requests for counseling and support from other members of the family. Thus, both patients and caregivers always have psychosocial and medical resources available to them.

Many family members are concerned that hearing the diagnosis will be devastating for someone with Alzheimer's disease. According to guidelines issued by the Alzheimer's Association, the individual with

Alzheimer's disease has a moral and legal right to know the diagnosis. Some patients may be too far along in the disease process to be able to comprehend the diagnosis. In these cases, a family conference may be held without the patient, and then an effort will be made to have the patient understand, if possible. By helping both patient and family understand the implications of the diagnosis, clinicians can help support healthy open discussion about the family's future and ensure that all family members have access to the care and support they need.

The process of working with a family over the course of Alzheimer's disease will be illustrated throughout this book by following Millie and Ted through their struggle with the illness.

Millie and Ted G, both in their 60s, were beginning to think about what they would do when they retired, even though they didn't plan to stop working for about 5 years. They were looking forward to traveling and their leisure years together.

In December, Millie started talking about what she would wear at the annual holiday party at Ted's office. For the first time, Ted seemed determined not to go. Millie worried that something was wrong at work. She began to think about Ted's behavior over the last few months and realized that he had not been the same—he came home late quite a bit, he would sit in his study working all the time, he would snap at her over the smallest thing, and he had been a bit absentminded lately, misplacing things and repeating himself.

One Saturday, Ted told Millie not to bother him because he had a report to write for work. He sat in his study for 3 hours. Later that day she went into the office to vacuum and couldn't help but look at the papers he had been working on. She couldn't believe her eyes. The whole document was incoherent. She sat down in shock, staring at the papers in front of her. A few minutes later, Ted walked into the study. Millie, trying to control the panic in her voice, asked what was happening. Ted said he didn't know, but he thought he was working too hard. Millie told Ted she thought he should see his doctor. Maybe something was wrong.

First Ted went to his own doctor and then a neurologist. After a thorough diagnostic evaluation, the neurologist reviewed the test results with Ted and Millie. He told them his evaluation suggested that Ted's symptoms were due to Alzheimer's disease and that he was in the mild stage, which could last for some time. The doctor said Ted should consider retiring sooner than he had planned and probably shouldn't drive any more. They left the doctor's office in silence. On the way home, Millie tried to talk about what the doctor had said, but Ted just said, "Leave me alone." A few days later, Millie brought up the subject again, and Ted said, "I told you, I'm just working too hard. You'll see, once this project is over, everything will be fine again. And please don't tell the kids. They'll just worry unnecessarily."

## The Stages of Cognitive Decline

In this section, we provide a brief overview of several scales used to measure cognitive capacity from normal to mild impairment and dementia. We then describe one of these scales, the Global Deterioration Scale (GDS), in detail and the pertinent counseling issues at each stage. Throughout this book the GDS stages are used as benchmarks for cognitive decline in Alzheimer's disease.

### *Scales to Measure Cognitive Decline*

Several scales may be used to track the course of cognitive decline in the elderly. The most widely used are the Global Deterioration Scale, the Clinical Dementia Rating (CDR), and the Functional Assessment Staging (FAST). Dr Barry Reisberg of the NYU-ADC developed the GDS and the FAST. The GDS is used to track the course of cognitive decline in AD and to define its stages, including the boundaries between progressive dementia and the "benign" memory loss of old age. The FAST describes functional decline in greater detail in the more severe stages of AD than does the GDS.

***The Global Deterioration Scale***    The Global Deterioration Scale is used to track the course of cognitive decline from normal aging to the dementia of AD. It consists of descriptions of seven major clinically distinguishable stages from "no cognitive decline" to "very severe dementia." The first two levels are associated with apparently normal cognitive functioning. GDS 1 indicates neither objective signs nor subjective complaints of cognitive decline. GDS 2 indicates that the person has subjective complaints of memory impairment that cannot be substantiated by objective evidence of memory deficit in a clinical interview. People in this category will not show deficits in employment or social situations. The complaints of someone with a GDS score of 2 are most frequently about forgetting where he or she has placed familiar objects or forgetting names he or she formerly knew well. GDS 3 is the first stage that describes clear-cut deficits that can be corroborated with objective tests, although these deficits are generally considered insufficient for a diagnosis of dementia. GDS 4 through GDS 7 define progressive stages of cognitive decline associated with dementia (mild, moderate, moderately severe, and severe dementia).

*The Clinical Dementia Rating*  The Clinical Dementia Rating is another commonly used global rating scale. The CDR describes five degrees of impairment in performance in each of six categories of cognitive functioning, including memory, orientation, judgment and problem solving, community affairs, home and hobbies, and personal care. The five degrees of impairment are: none (CDR = 0), questionable (CDR = 0.5), mild (CDR = 1), moderate (CDR = 2), and severe (CDR = 3). The ratings of degree of impairment obtained on each of the six categories of cognitive function are put together into one global rating of dementia (ie, 0, 0.5, 1, 2, or 3). The CDR is administered by a clinician using a semistructured interview of both the patient and an informant. Some researchers have used a score of CDR = .5 to denote mild cognitive impairment. CDR 1 to 3 denote increasing severity of dementia.

*The Functional Assessment Staging (FAST) Scale*  The FAST, which was derived from the GDS, measures functional deterioration associated with cognitive decline and Alzheimer's disease. The FAST scale is scored primarily on the basis of information obtained from a knowledgeable informant and/or caregiver and is especially useful in assessing functional capacity at the severe extreme of Alzheimer's disease. The functional equivalents of the last two stages of the GDS are subdivided into 11 substages that reflect the loss of specific basic functions.

## The GDS Stages of Cognitive Decline and Their Implications for Counseling

In this section we describe each stage of the Global Deterioration Scale in detail, from mild impairment (GDS 3) to the most severe stage of dementia in Alzheimer's disease (GDS 7). These descriptions are followed by sample counseling notes that might accompany an interview with a family caregiver of a person at that stage of cognitive decline. These notes highlight some of the most salient issues that caregivers face at each stage and provide examples of counselor recommendations that will address their needs.

***Mild Memory Impairment (GDS 3)***   In this stage, there is clear-cut evidence that the person's level of confusion and decline in function exceed the norm for someone of his or her age. Nevertheless, the person is not sufficiently impaired to be given a diagnosis of dementia. Objective evidence of memory deficit can be observed only with an intensive interview. Someone at this stage will have word and name finding deficits that are apparent to friends and family members. The person may read a passage or a book and retain relatively little material. The person may demonstrate decreased ability to remember names upon introduction to new people and may forget names of associates or clients at work. Someone at this stage may lose the train of thought during conversation, lose a word or expression, or misplace an important item. The person may have gotten lost when traveling to an unfamiliar location. There will be decreased performance in demanding employment or social situations. Co-workers may become aware of the person's relatively poor performance. At this stage, people tend to deny that there is any problem, although mild to moderate anxiety often accompanies symptoms. This early confusional stage can last about 7 years. (See Table 1 for a list of these symptoms and a comparison with later stages of AD.)

Recent studies suggest that as many as 75% of people who have cognitive difficulties sufficient to be categorized as GDS 3 develop AD. New pharmacological interventions are currently being tested that may delay further decline in people at this stage.

**TABLE 1**

Global Deterioration Scale (GDS) Stages of Alzheimer's Disease

| Stage | Symptoms/Behaviors | Assistance | Duration |
|---|---|---|---|
| **GDS3** | Word and name finding deficits<br>Loses train of thought in conversation<br>Misplaces important item<br>May get lost in unfamiliar location<br>Decreased performance at work<br>Reads material but may not retain much of it | None | 7 years |
| **GDS4** | Decreased knowledge of current events<br>May not remember events in personal history<br>Deficit elicited in serial subtractions (counting back from 40 by 4s)<br>Difficulties traveling to unfamiliar places<br>Difficulties handling finances<br>Repetitive questioning<br>Cannot perform complex tasks<br>No trouble recognizing familiar faces<br>Oriented to time and place | Minimal | 2 years |
| **GDS5** | Cannot recall aspects of personal life, such as names of close family, or address and telephone number<br>Can be confused as to time and place<br>Cannot perform serial subtractions<br>May need help preparing meals, selecting clothes<br>Wandering and pacing, restlessness<br>Shadowing (following) caregiver<br>No assistance needed with toileting, eating | Assistance/<br>supervision<br>required | 1½ years |
| **GDS6** | Unaware of recent events and experiences in their lives<br>May forget name of spouse upon whom they are dependent<br>No ability to dress or bathe themselves<br>May have loss of social inhibitions (cursing, sexual)<br>May have delusional behavior, hallucinations, paranoia<br>Obsessive symptoms (repeating same activity)<br>Disturbed diurnal rhythm (awake at night, asleep during day)<br>Starting but not completing anything<br>Anxiety, restlessness, agitation, violence<br>May have difficulty counting back from 10 by 1s<br>Incontinence<br>Can distinguish familiar from unfamiliar faces | Some<br>assistance<br>with activities<br>of daily living | 2½ years |

| Stage | Symptoms/Behaviors | Assistance | Duration |
|-------|--------------------|------------|----------|
| **GDS7** | Limited vocabulary, eventually all verbal abilities lost<br>Cannot recognize anyone, including self<br>No toileting abilities<br>Will lose ability to chew and swallow<br>Ability to walk is compromised or lost<br>Vulnerable to muscle contractures and bedsores<br>Vulnerable to infections and organ system failure<br>Decrease in agitated behavior | Total assistance for all activities of daily living | 7 or more years |

*Source:* Barry Reisberg, MD, New York University—Alzheimer's Disease Center.

## Counseling Notes

*Setting:* Alzheimer's Disease Center
*Counselor:* Agnes G, PsyD
*Counseling notes:* Mr and Mrs M

Mr M and his wife were informed that Mr M had a GDS of 3 and that his diagnostic evaluation indicated that he had mild cognitive impairment. Mr M said that he had been aware of having some problems remembering appointments and was taking more notes than usual on the articles he was reading to prepare for the classes he had been teaching for over 20 years, but all his colleagues joked about "senior moments," and he was no different from the rest of them. Mr M seemed to think the test results showed that he was normal. Mrs M was upset by the diagnosis and concerned about possible decline to Alzheimer's disease. She was upset that her husband didn't remember what he had been told. She said the doctor had recommended that he enroll in a clinical trial of medication that might prevent the progression of the memory loss. At this point, Mr M became anxious, was eager to terminate the interview, and said that he needed to leave to attend a meeting. Mrs M remained behind to talk further with me. I told her that a significant percentage of the people diagnosed with MCI did go on to develop AD and encouraged enrollment in the clinical trial as well as maintaining a good exercise, nutritional, and stress reduction program. I suggested another meeting to discuss legal, financial, and health care planning considerations such as health care proxies and living wills.

***Mild Alzheimer's Disease (GDS 4)***  GDS 4 is the first stage of cognitive decline at which a person can definitively be diagnosed with dementia. At this stage, a clear-cut deficit can be detected in a clinical interview. A person at this stage will have trouble remembering current and recent events and may not remember all the events of his or her own personal history. A person who is categorized as GDS 4 may find it difficult to travel to unfamiliar places or handle finances. However, a person at this stage will generally have no trouble recognizing familiar people, will be oriented to time and place, and will need no assistance with activities of daily living. A person who is at the early stage of dementia will frequently deny that there is anything wrong. The person is no longer able to perform complex tasks and will often avoid challenging situations. This stage generally lasts about 2 years.

---

### Counseling Notes

*Setting:* Memory Assessment Clinic
*Counselor:* Stephanie K, PhD
*Counseling notes:* Silvia J

Silvia J, 70, reported that her husband, Harold, age 74, who was recently diagnosed with Alzheimer's disease, has gotten lost several times when doing errands and has repeatedly forgotten to turn off the stove. She also reports that he has become irritable and she cannot talk to him about his problems. She says she feels helpless and doesn't know what to do and is afraid that "the house will burn down or some other terrible thing will happen." She appears anxious and slightly depressed. While Mrs J said she was relieved that his problems had been diagnosed, she had limited knowledge about AD. We talked about the different stages of the illness and I gave her reading materials and resources for further information. We discussed ways that Mrs J could make their home safer while allowing Harold to be as independent as possible. I also suggested enrolling Mr J in the Safe Return program at the Alzheimer's Association. Until now, Mr J had handled all the finances and legal matters; we discussed how Mrs J could begin to take over these responsibilities without hurting his self-esteem. I introduced the idea of long-term financial, legal, and health care planning, and Mrs J said she would try to find out about what plans had already been made.

*Moderate Alzheimer's Disease (GDS 5)*   At this stage, a person can no longer survive without assistance. A person who is categorized as GDS 5 will no longer be able to recall his or her address or telephone number. While patients at this stage will invariably know their own name and generally those of their spouse and children as well, they may forget the names of other close members of the family such as grandchildren. They will recall many major facts about themselves and others, although they will no longer remember some facts from the past, such as the name of the high school or college from which they graduated. Frequently people at this stage will be confused about where they are and what the date, day of the week, or season is, etc. They need no assistance with toileting and eating but may need help preparing meals or choosing the proper clothing to wear. This stage typically lasts about a year and a half. While many people continue living in the community at this stage, they can survive only with the support of someone who provides some assistance and helps keep them safe.

## Counseling Notes

*Setting:* Community social service agency
*Counselor:* Brian N, LCSW
*Counseling notes:* Thomas and Simon K

Thomas K, 82 years old, presented problems he was having caring for his brother, Simon K, who is 81 and is in the moderate stage of Alzheimer's disease. Simon lives alone on the third floor of a walk-up apartment building. Thomas K, Simon's closest living relative, lives in the same building but has health problems that keep him from being actively involved in his brother's care. Thomas K reported that his brother can no longer properly cook, shop, clean, or do laundry for himself and either sleeps or watches television most of the day. Several of his neighbors have complained that he has falsely accused them of stealing his mail. I advised Thomas to talk to the neighbors and explain that Simon has an illness that causes him to behave that way. Since Thomas would like to have his brother continue to live in his own apartment, the following services were recommended for Simon: home health aide—4 hours a day—and a community meals program for weekends. I recommended adult day care for social and recreational stimulation three times a week with transportation to and from the facility. Thomas K has power of attorney and will remain in charge of Simon K's finances and health care. Simon K will be routinely monitored, and the care plan will be adjusted as needed.

***Moderately Severe Alzheimer's Disease (GDS 6)***  People in GDS stage 6 are largely unaware of all recent events and experiences in their lives, although they almost always remember their own names and may still be able to distinguish familiar from unfamiliar people. They also may still have some understanding of where they are. People at this stage cannot remember a thought long enough to plan a course of action. They will need assistance with activities of daily living. People at this stage of AD no longer have the ability to dress or bathe themselves. At this stage, people may become incontinent. There are personality and emotional changes at GDS 6. Patients may lose their social inhibitions; delusional behavior (accusing the husband or wife of being an impostor, talking to imaginary people or even themselves in the mirror) is also common. Obsessive symptoms, such as continually repeating the same simple activities, are not uncommon. Diurnal rhythm is frequently disturbed so that patients can sleep much of the day and remain awake much of the night. Anxiety, agitation, and even violent behavior may occur. This stage of AD lasts approximately 2½ years.

**Counseling Notes**
*Setting:* Group medical practice
*Counselor:* Joan A, RN
*Counseling* notes: Melissa Z

Melissa Z, age 45, married with two teenage children, took her mother, Alison L, age 70, a widow who is in the moderately severe stage of Alzheimer's disease, into the family home 2 years ago when it became clear that Mrs L could no longer live alone. Melissa Z says that, although it has not been easy to have her mother in the home, the situation had been manageable until now. She reports the following difficulties: Mrs L wanders around the house at night waking everyone, has become increasingly agitated and aggressive—she hit one of the children on two separate occasions—and is experiencing hallucinations. Her behavior is frightening to the family. Melissa Z reports exhaustion and fear that she will not be able to continue to care for her mother in addition to the rest of the family. The following care plan was suggested: Mrs L would be seen by the physician, who would assess her behavioral and sleep problems and the possibility of treatment with medication. I gave Melissa Z a list of adult day centers and suggested that she begin to include her family in the care of her mother and in sharing the household chores, so that she could get some respite. I also recommended that Melissa Z join a caregiver support group.

*Severe AD (GDS 7)*   All verbal abilities are lost over the course of this stage. Early in this stage, words and phrases are spoken but speech is very limited. Later there is virtually no speech at all—only unintelligible sounds, although occasionally a patient will say a word or phrase. A person at GDS 7 is incontinent and requires assistance with toileting and feeding. Over the course of this stage, basic psychomotor skills such as the ability to walk are lost. The brain appears to be no longer able to tell the body what to do. Generalized rigidity and developmental neurologic reflexes are frequently present. GDS 7 can last 7 or more years.

**Counseling Notes**

*Setting:* Patient's home
*Counselor:* Betty S, RN
*Counseling notes:* Alfred C

Home visit to monitor the health status of Patricia C, 89 years old, in the severe stage of Alzheimer's disease, who is bedridden, no longer speaks, and takes food only in liquid form. Patricia C has had several bouts of pneumonia in the past year and is very weak. Her husband, Alfred C, 92, said he needed to talk to me about a disagreement with his children about how to care for his wife. Alfred C reported that he wants to continue to take all measures possible to keep his wife alive. His children believe that she is suffering and that she should be enrolled in hospice. Mr C feels he still has a connection with his wife even in her current state. He massages her and they listen to music together. I referred Mr C to a family agency where Mr C could get counseling that would include his children so they might resolve their conflict about Mrs C's care.

**Note:** A patient at an advanced stage of Alzheimer's disease may occasionally seem more cognitively intact (interactive, attentive, and focused) than one would believe was possible. Caregivers should be made aware that this can happen and realize that it is only temporary and does not signify improvement in the patient's dementia.

## The Effects of Caregiving on Families

Alzheimer's disease poses unique difficulties for many families. Adjusting to having a relative with the disease and coping with its symptoms and the patient's ongoing need for care are made more difficult by the fact that the illness is progressive. Redefining oneself as responsible for the well-being of a person in a new way is part of the process of becoming a caregiver. People come to identify themselves in this role at different points in their relative's illness depending on the severity of the symptoms and how they are perceived. Some people never regard themselves as caregivers even though they are performing this role, because it is seen as a normative part of family life that does not warrant a specific designation.

As the cognitive and functional ability of the patient with AD changes from stage to stage, so does the impact of the illness on the caregiver and the family. In the later stages of AD, patients become dependent on others to satisfy their most basic daily needs and are increasingly incapable of communicating these needs. The burden of care falls largely on family members who become increasingly responsible for their relatives' well-being while watching their cognitive and functional abilities deteriorate.

A family caregiver of a person with Alzheimer's disease is likely to experience considerable emotional distress. Some of the most common effects of caregiving are depression, anxiety, anger, stress, sadness, and grief. The magnitude of these effects will vary from one caregiver to another, depending on individual circumstances and characteristics. The amount and quality of social support available and the caregiver's understanding of the patient's behavior can have a major effect on the impact of the caregiving experience.

### How Is Caregiving Like a Career?

There are several useful paradigms for understanding caregivers' reactions to the illness of a relative with AD. Some researchers are using the image of a caregiving career to describe the experience of being a family caregiver for a person with AD. This analogy serves to emphasize the fact that caregiving has an entry point, multiple stages, transitions and changes, and an end point. Also, caregiving is shaped by events in the past (individual history and family relationships) and spans a long period of time. It is also like a career in that it can become central to the life of the person upon whom it falls.

Unlike other careers, caregiving does not confer social class or status and there is no financial compensation. There are no formal expectations of a caregiver, and you do not get promoted for doing a good job. Unlike many careers, caregiving is generally unplanned and often is superimposed over an existing career. Because of the insidious nature of AD, family caregivers frequently adopt the role before (or sometimes without ever) considering themselves to be such. Other caregivers are forced into the role suddenly when another family member, who was previously playing that role, becomes seriously ill or dies, moves to a geographically distant location, or is unwilling to continue.

## *Progressive Losses*

The patient's decline can be thought of as many losses. While we can predict the general course of AD, we cannot predict when a new symptom will occur in any particular individual. Research has shown that unexpected transitions are the most stressful. For caregivers of a person with dementia, the "career" is marked with many small and unexpected transitions as the nature of the impact of the disease on the patient's cognitive and functional abilities changes. If the impact of a chronic illness on a patient were not expected to change, a caregiver could learn about the symptoms and how to manage them, and the knowledge would stand him or her in good stead for a long time. One of the reasons caregiving for a person with dementia is so stressful is that the progressive nature of the disease makes it difficult for the caregiver to maintain a sense of control. What the caregiver learns about managing the patient's current symptoms may not prepare the caregiver for the changes brought on by the next stage of the illness. When caring for a family member with AD, one can never be sure how long a period of relative stability will last or when one will have to face another impairment or new disturbing behavior. Each time the caregiver adapts to one change, he or she is faced with another.

The caregiving career is marked by losses of many kinds. As the patient's functioning and cognition deteriorate, the caregiver experiences the loss of the person as he or she once was. At some point, it becomes clear to the caregiver that he or she has lost the previous role in the relationship of wife, husband, daughter, and so on. This does not mean that they necessarily become emotionally separated from their ill relative. Rather, they detach from their original role with the person (wife, husband, daughter, etc) and take on a new role (becoming more like a parent than a spouse or child) as the person becomes more and more dependent. The new role can feel disrespectful and inappropriate to the age and former place of the patient in the family. The nature of the bond between the caregiver and the patient is altered by the cognitive decline that makes the ill person less and less emotionally accessible. While enduring the loss of the person as he or she was, the caregiver also loses the anticipated future with the loved one. In addition, in order to devote the necessary time and energy to caring for the ill relative, many caregivers must give up or reduce the time they spend in other life roles, such as paid jobs, social activities with family and friends, caring for other family members, and recreational activities.

## PERSONAL VIGNETTE

In August of 1996 I retired, and to "celebrate," I decided to drive up to Vermont with my husband, Henry, then in his 6th year of AD. It was a first for me, as he had always been the driver. The son of an old friend was getting married, and I thought it would be nice for Henry to show up for the wedding and see all his old buddies. I also had a hidden agenda: to stop at a special motel in Vermont that we had gone to many times, which was like a honeymoon spot for us, and to do the things we always loved, like swimming in the beautiful indoor pool and playing Ping-Pong.

The trip was a nightmare. His perception of space had worsened, and his language and understanding was getting progressively more limited. Every time we had to make a bathroom stop, it involved all kinds of complicated maneuvers (should Henry use the ladies' room or should I go into the men's room), and I wondered what had possessed me to attempt this. Seeing my friends at the wedding was not a good experience for me, as I felt continually hurt by the sense that we were invisible because people were embarrassed by not knowing how to behave toward him.

The motel was the final straw. He didn't recognize the place, needed help putting on his bathing suit, swam a little but sank and scared us both, could hit a Ping-Pong ball and go and get it, but not find his way back to the table. Any shred of denial, or memory of the past I might have been clinging to, vanished in the enormity of the change in front of my eyes. I felt like a parent, not a wife. It was then that a voice inside of me clearly said, "After 40 years, we're not a WE any-more." I accepted that intellectually but then had severe abdominal cramps that baffled my doctor and lasted for 7 weeks. I guess that shows that there are many degrees of acceptance.

Vignette courtesy of Lois Morton, EdD.

## *Ambiguous Loss*

The theory of boundary ambiguity was developed by Pauline Boss in the 1970s to describe the reactions of family members to having what was termed *ambiguous loss*. It was first used to describe the reactions of military wives to having a husband missing in action. She went on to extend this idea to explain the stress in families of having a member with AD. The patient seems physically intact, at least until the later stages of the disease, but is no longer emotional-ly available to the caregiver to the extent that he or she used to be. Also, there are moments of relative lucidity, which only serve to add to the ambiguity.

The role of the patient becomes more ambiguous within the con-text of the family. For example, where once the father may have had unchallenged authority, his position is altered by his limitations. In some cases, in spite of the patient's obvious decline, these families are reluctant to disempower him by assuming responsibilities that have always been his. Caregivers may not be sure what place the patient has in the family. When the patient behaves in unexpected ways, caregivers become uncertain about what this means about their relationship. Helping caregivers understand and accept the implications of the changing nature of the relationship may resolve some of the feelings of ambiguity. When a relative has AD, no formal or public acknowledgment of loss occurs and, thus, neither can the grieving process that takes place when a loved one dies. There is no bereavement in the traditional sense.

## The Stress Process

The impact that caregiving has on people varies considerably. Some people seem to be seriously adversely affected, while others are less so. To some extent, it has been found that the impact of caregiving can be ameliorated by *moderators*—social, personal, or material resources that can act as buffers against the impact of the main stressors. Psychosocial interventions such as the one described in this book are based on the theory that by improving certain moderators—social support and mastery over the caregiving task—it is possible to decrease the impact of caregiving on outcomes such as depression, anxiety, and inability to continue to provide care outside of an institution.

The stress process model that provides a conceptual motivation for the intervention described in this book was developed by Leonard Pearlin and his associates. This model suggests that caregiver well-being is affected not only by primary stressors originating directly from the illness and care of the patient, but also from secondary stressors (family conflict, constriction of social activities). Social support and understanding of the meaning of the patient's behavior can reduce the negative effects of the primary stressor—the illness.

## Benefits of Intervention

The unifying theme of our ongoing spouse caregiver intervention is that improving social support and reducing family conflict will improve the ability of the caregiver to withstand the difficulties of caregiving and prevent or defer the need for institutionalization of the patient. It is at least as important to improve the quality of social support as it is simply to increase the amount of social support available to caregivers. The focus is on enhancing the supportive aspects of family involvement with caregiving while diminishing the negative aspects. A priority is to improve the adequacy of social support for the caregiver by first helping the caregiver to have realistic expectations, and then to convey them in a way that is likely to evoke a positive response.

The intervention has a secondary benefit, through education and support, of changing the caregiver's appraisal of the behavior problems being exhibited by the patient, thereby reducing their impact. The NYU intervention also provides ongoing formal support, not only for the primary caregiver but also for other family members. This is accomplished by the relationship established with the counselor during the formal counseling sessions and the offer to be available as needed from then on. Helping caregivers to cope effectively and with some feeling of mastery will enable them to care for their relatives with AD at home longer if that is appropriate, or to accept the necessity of finding other supportive living arrangements for their relative, such as an assisted living facility or nursing home, if that is the better alternative for caregiver and patient.

*2*

# ASSESSMENT

An assessment provides the foundation upon which the counseling process is built. It identifies the context in which care is being provided and the unique characteristics of the caregiver as an individual and in relation to the person with Alzheimer's disease (AD) and other family members. In this chapter, we describe the assessment used in the NYU-ADC study, highlighting specific elements and why they are important to counseling a caregiver of a person with Alzheimer's disease. We also emphasize the factors that are suggested by research and clinical experience to have an influence on the response to the caregiving experience and the ability to provide care, specifically the benefits of social support and the reduction of family conflict. The chapter ends with a sample assessment that demonstrates the assessment process.

There are published scales that can be put together to create a comprehensive assessment instrument. Using scales can provide a clinician with a concrete way to measure the amount of change that may have occurred as a result of counseling. The scales being used in the NYU intervention study are listed in Appendix B as examples.

## Components of the Assessment

The assessment is an opportunity not only for gathering information but also for showing that the counselor can be helpful, understanding, and sensitive. Each counselor will have his or her own style of conducting the interview; some will be more structured and formal, while others will be more conversational. Whatever the style used, the objective is the same—to obtain information about the factors listed below. The assessment will also serve as baseline data that can be compared with future assessments to measure change.

In the course of eliciting information, the focus should be on the caregiver and the caregiving situation. This will provide an experience, reinforced by counseling, to emphasize the point that the needs of the caregiver are as important as those of the patient. Counselors need to resist caregivers' temptation to ignore their own needs in deference to those of patients. Caregivers should be encouraged to maintain their own well-being as a goal in and of itself, as well as a means of being better able to care for the patient. In order to keep the focus on the caregiver, the AD patient should not attend the initial caregiver assessment meeting. The assessment interview should therefore be held at a time and place that makes it possible for the caregiver to safely leave the patient.

The assessment used in the NYU intervention included the components outlined below. The intention of describing the assessment is to help the counselor focus on the characteristics to assess and the reasons for their importance in this type of counseling. Counselors can adapt this assessment to the setting in which they work. In some settings, a different assessment format may be used. In other settings it may not be possible to conduct such a comprehensive assessment. The responses to the assessment should serve as a guide for designing an effective individualized counseling plan. The NYU assessment was conducted in the context of a research study. In view of the findings of the NYU study, we recommend that social support and caregiver appraisal of the patient's behavior be included as essential elements to be evaluated and enhanced in the process of counseling.

Data that are routinely collected in most settings, such as age, gender, ethnicity, home address, level of formal education, employment status, marital status, family composition, finances, current health status, and medical history, are examined from the perspective of their impact on caregiving. Such additional information as family history of dementia, prior caregiving experience, and knowledge of AD that is specifically relevant to AD caregivers should also be assessed.

Each of the components of the assessment provides valuable information on its own, but their meaning and impact on the caregiving situation should be viewed in the context of all the information gathered. A significant amount of data is collected during the initial assessment, although additional pertinent information will emerge in the course of counseling.

A few weeks after Ted was diagnosed with Alzheimer's disease, he had an accident while driving. He came home and told his wife Millie that he had gotten lost in the shopping center looking for his favorite hardware store and swerved into a parked car. He was very angry and said that there are so many new stores you can't find any-thing anymore. Millie was frightened. Over the next few days, she pleaded with Ted to stop driving. He refused. Millie had also been trying unsuccessfully to get Ted to stop working. She realized she needed help, but who could she talk to? Ted had asked Millie not to tell the children about his illness, and she wasn't sure she could handle telling them at this time anyway. Millie remembered that when her friend had had a problem with her adolescent daughter, she had gone to the community health center, and the counselors there had been very helpful. Maybe she could get some advice without any-one knowing.

## *The Presenting Problem*

In the initial phase of the assessment, the caregiver describes the presenting problem. Why has he or she come for help at this time? What kind of help is the person looking for? Is the person here for help with caregiving? The assessment is geared toward caregivers, and it is understood that the person will have been previously screened or directed to this service because it provides counseling and support for family caregivers of people with Alzheimer's disease.

A caregiver may describe a very specific issue that the counselor will have to view within the context of the factors uncovered dur-ing the rest of the assessment. Common presenting problems include reaction to the diagnosis or symptoms of the illness, family conflict related to the illness, and a request for information about resources and referrals. If there is an emergency or crisis, it will have to be resolved before proceeding with the assessment.

"My husband Ted was just diagnosed with Alzheimer's disease. First I noticed that the reports he was writing for his job didn't make any sense, and then, a few days ago, he ran into a parked car in the shopping center. I'm scared of what will happen next."

## Demographic Characteristics

The counselor will need to inquire about the caregiver's age, gender, culture and ethnicity, religion, financial and employment status, and family composition. The reasons for needing this information when working with a caregiver are explained below.

*Age* The age of a caregiver can be used to determine eligibility for specific services or entitlements, or it can be used as a touchstone for exploration into many aspects of a person's life. When a person is elderly, counselors may want to be particularly sensitive to his or her physical health, energy level, and possible frailty; emotional health including possible depression; and social situation including the possibility of isolation.

Many elderly caregivers have a very traditional sense of familial roles—for example, wife as homemaker and husband as breadwinner and financial planner—and need assistance in feeling comfortable with the new roles they must take on as caregivers. Elderly caregivers may have different priorities and goals than they did when they were younger. They may have fulfilled many of their prior goals and not feel as constrained by the caregiving role.

Young caregivers may have multiple responsibilities in addition to caregiving, such as work or obligations to their spouses or children that may lead to role overload. A young caregiver whose spouse has AD may be struggling with the loss of a breadwinner and parent for their children as well as the loss of a companion. Younger caregivers may not be familiar with resources for the elderly, but they may be more comfortable using the Internet for information, resources, and even support.

Although age can provide some indication about how a person approaches the caregiving role and the issues he or she may be facing, there is much variability within each age group, and counselors should be careful not to subscribe to generational stereotypes.

*Gender*  Gender roles are influenced by age, culture, and values. For example, male and female caregivers who have traditional values may be accustomed to carrying out different tasks within the home (women may do the housekeeping, while men take care of the bills). Female caregivers may view the personal care of another family member as a natural part of their role, while male caregivers may not.

Some caregivers may adjust well to the new responsibilities they must take on and may even enjoy learning new skills. Others will have difficulties breaking out of their gender-defined roles to take on new responsibilities in caregiving and need assistance in becoming comfortable with their new roles.

The counselor's understanding of the caregivers' view of what is an acceptable task will guide suggestions about allocation of caregiving tasks. Some caregivers may have to obtain the help of other family members or use formal services if they are unwilling to take on roles they consider to be inappropriate to their gender.

*Culture and Ethnicity*  The caregiver's ethnic and cultural norms influence his or her perception of the symptoms of dementia. Although people of different cultures may accept the fact that a person has a medical diagnosis of Alzheimer's disease, they may attribute different meanings to its cause. Dementia, for instance, is thought of in some cultures as the imbalance between body and spirit; as the work of evil spirits; as punishment for sins against a higher power, family, or ancestors; or as an inevitable consequence of aging. The way in which the medical and cultural explanations are compatible will influence the counselor's work.

In many cultures, caregiving is not seen as a role that one assumes when a family member becomes ill but rather as a natural part of family life: "Of course, I help my family with whatever needs to be done." The responsibility or the tasks that certain family members assume may be determined by culture; for instance, adult children may be expected to remain in their parents' home and tend to the family's needs. If the younger generation has been assimilated into the mainstream American culture while the older generation has not, this can cause distress.

Culture may also determine the degree to which services are accepted and used by patients and their families. For instance, a family that believes strongly in natural healers may not readily see the need for Western medicines. Many families from other cultures, particularly recent immigrants, may not know where to seek help, how to use services in this country, or even that these services are available to them. In some cases, language will be a barrier to services or will create misunderstandings in counseling. If possible, and in accordance with the wishes of the family, an effort should be made to help the family find someone who speaks their native language and understands their culture. Counselors should try to understand the issues from the caregivers' cultural perspective and work within that framework or refer them to someone who is more familiar with their perspective.

***Religion***    Religion is a very important part of many people's lives and can influence how they approach Alzheimer's care. Religion may be a source of strength and comfort. Within the context of their religion, people may find meaning in the tragedy that may support them throughout the illness. These individuals may turn not only to counselors but also to religious leaders for guidance. It may be beneficial for counselors and religious leaders to work together in helping a particular client. Religion, for some people, provides a context within which caregiving may be perceived as less of a burden or less stressful. On the other hand, some caregivers may believe it is their religious duty to always be the perfect caregiver, and religion can then become a source of stress or burden.

Religious beliefs may determine the health care decisions that a family makes. Some religions have very specific guidelines about which medical procedures can be administered and when it is appropriate to withhold medical care.

Religious beliefs also may influence a family's decision to have an autopsy, which in the case of Alzheimer's disease is the only method by which a diagnosis can be definitively confirmed. Although most religions now make some provisions for autopsy, some people hold to more traditional views and believe that their religions do not allow the procedure. The decision to have or not have an autopsy can be a source of disagreement or conflict among family members.

*Financial Status* The care of a person with Alzheimer's disease is very costly, whether a person is cared for at home or in a residential facility. Knowing the family's financial situation will help counselors provide proper referrals that will enhance patient care without burdening the family with excessive cost. Families may be reluctant to reveal their financial circumstances. The counselor needs to explain that the purpose of asking about financial resources is to determine the type of service to which the family can be referred, such as adult day programs and community health centers, as well as benefits and entitlements for which the family is eligible, such as Medicare, Medicaid, and other government programs. Some caregivers may need to see an elder care attorney for financial planning.

*Employment Status* Employment status may affect the amount of time that a caregiver can spend on patient care. People may feel compelled to care for the patient and give up leisure or volunteer activities if they do not have a job. Caregivers who work may need help accessing home care or coordinating activities for the patient during working hours. Employment status may also have financial implications for the type and amount of resources that a counselor can recommend. Caregivers with low-income jobs or who do not have a steady income will need assistance in finding resources that adequately meet patients' needs. Counselors should be aware that caregivers may be at risk of losing their jobs, missing a promotion, or cutting work time in the interest of their caregiving responsibilities.

*Education* Level of education may determine the way a person understands the illness and the way information may have to be conveyed to him or her. Some caregivers will have the educational background to comprehend the illness in medical and scientific terms and may want to read professional journals for information, while others will be more comfortable with information at a layperson's level. People with limited education may need information provided in simple terms. Videotapes may be more appropriate than books for transmitting information in some cases. If a person is skilled at using technology, counselors may be able to suggest resources on the Internet.

*Family Composition* The number of family members and their relationship to the caregiver and patient help determine the potentially available support and the other obligations of the caregiver.

The spouses of married caregivers (caring for patients other than themselves) may have reactions ranging from supportive to resentful. Caregivers who have young children may have conflicting demands on their time, while those who have older children may be able to rely on them to share the caregiving tasks. Thus, counselors will want to obtain information about the marital status of the caregiver and the number of children, siblings, parents, and other relatives who have a close relationship with the caregiver or the patient.

## Relationship of the Caregiver to the Patient

In the United States, approximately half of all people with Alzheimer's disease are cared for by their spouses. About one third are cared for by their adult children. Other family members such as siblings and grandchildren may also provide care. The family relationship of the patient and caregiver has major implications for the caregiver's reaction to the illness and the caregiving role. For example, when a spouse develops Alzheimer's disease, this affects every aspect of the caregiver's life, whereas an adult child who does not live with the patient may be able to maintain more aspects of his or her lifestyle.

When working with spouse caregivers, special attention should be given to the length of the marriage, whether this is a first marriage or whether either partner was married before, and whether there are any children from the current or prior marriages or relationships. A caregiver who stayed married because he or she found the idea of divorce unthinkable may be angry that his or her spouse now has AD and needs to be cared for. A spouse in a happy marriage may be angry that the couple's happiness was cut short by the illness.

Adult child caregivers may disagree with their siblings or other family members about how the caregiving obligations should be divided, where care should be provided, and how to use financial resources that could be part of a potential inheritance. Decision making and division of caregiving responsibilities can be especially complicated in blended families.

The relationship of the caregiver to the patient may also affect the ability to access the financial resources of the patient, to apply for entitlements, and to make medical and legal decisions on behalf of the patient. The caregiver may also have other significant relationships and accompanying responsibilities that may determine the possible level of involvement with the patient and the amount of burden the caregiver experiences.

## Patient Information

Although the counselor's main focus will be the caregiver, there is essential information about the patient a counselor must have in order to understand the caregiver's role and responsibilities.

*Information About the Illness*  It is important to obtain objective information about the patient's stage of dementia. This can help the counselor to understand whether the caregiver's perception of the patient's abilities and limitations are realistic. Caregivers who overestimate or underestimate the patient's capacity will make inappropriate demands and have unrealistic expectations of the patient that may lead to mutual frustration. This information will also help the counselor work with the caregiver to develop a suitable care plan.

If diagnostic information is available from the patient's physician, it will provide objective data about the patient's cognitive status. Otherwise, it is possible to gain some understanding of the severity of the patient's dementia by asking the following summary questions:

- Does your family member normally have trouble remembering recent events, repeat the same question over and over, or lose or misplace things? If only this question is affirmative, the patient is likely to be in the mild stage of dementia.

- Does your family member normally need help, not due to physical disability, with paying bills, traveling alone, or using the telephone? If the answer to this question is yes, but the answer to the next question is no, the patient is likely to be in the moderate stage of dementia.

- Does your family member normally need help, not due to physical disability, with getting dressed, bathing, or eating? If the answer to this question is yes, the patient is likely to be in at least the severe stage of dementia.

It is also important to be aware of other illnesses the patient has, because they may exacerbate the functional disability and complicate care. When eliciting information about the patient from the caregiver, the counselor should be sensitive to any indications of possible neglect or abuse.

***Background Information***  In order to put the caregiving in context, it is helpful to have a picture of the patient's life, employment status, social life, other interests and hobbies, responsibilities, and role in the family. Questions may arise about his or her ability to continue with these activities. Alternatively, these activities may be an ongoing source of stimulation and self-esteem.

***The Patient's Home Environment***  The purpose of asking about the environment in which the patient is living is to assess whether it is safe, enhances the independent functioning of the person, and makes caring for him or her easier. Some considerations, including adequate lighting, unobstructed pathways from room to room, and avoidance of small area rugs, are relevant throughout the course of the illness. Other questions about the safety of the home should be geared to the stage of illness of the patient and include whether toxic substances and sharp objects are accessible, whether there are locks on the bathrooms and gates on the windows. Some questions will depend on whether the person lives in an urban or rural environment. Counseling may include suggesting changes that a caregiver can make to achieve these goals.

### Excerpts From Assessment Interview: Millie and Ted

Millie said, "I am 62 and Ted is only 65. We were both in such good health, until this happened. Ted was always so strong.

"I've been working for 15 years, but until the children grew up, I stayed home with the kids and only Ted worked. He works for an insurance company in the home office. I loved taking care of them and Ted. And he was always so wonderful about helping around the house—he could fix anything, he always had the bills paid on time, we never had to worry about the future. . . . Ted has a really steady job and he didn't want to retire for another few years. Now that he's been diagnosed with Alzheimer's, he's going to have to quit. Even though the neurologist said Ted's in the mild stage, he recommended that Ted consider retiring.

"I would say we are a normal American family. We really haven't traveled very much, and we still live in the house that we moved into when we married 41 years ago. I am very active in the church.

"I've been a secretary for the same law firm for 15 years now. I didn't really have to work, but when the kids grew up I was looking for something to do, and Ted said his friend needed a secretary, so I took the job. I really didn't need the job. Ted has always been such a good provider. Now I don't know what I would do without it.

"We have three wonderful children. Tom is 40 years old. He's married to a lovely woman named Diane and they have two teenagers. Our daughter, Carol, is 38 and has three young children. Both of them live close by. Matt, our other son, lives far away."

## *The Role the Caregiver Plays in the Care of the Patient*

The amount and kind of care a person provides to the patient will affect the issues for which he or she seeks help. If the person has primary responsibility for the patient and provides all the direct care, then counseling may involve education about the formal services available to augment the caregiver's own efforts. If the caregiver supervises others who are responsible for the hands-on care, he or she may need help communicating effectively with the aides and forming realistic expectations of them. Caregivers who do not live with the patient may need to travel long distances between work, their home, and the patient's residence. They will not be available for many of the hands-on care needs of the patient, but they will face the difficulties of supervising a home care attendant and coordinating, without being able to closely monitor, the tasks and daily activities in which the attendant will be involved. If the patient is living in a residential facility, the caregiver may need counseling about realistic expectations, frequency with which to visit, and interactions with staff.

Those who are caregiving from a long distance and cannot visit regularly need help to devise a system of oversight that will ensure the safety and well-being of the patient and minimize the need for crisis visits. Caregivers who are able to visit the patient regularly may need help in establishing a schedule that will not be overly demanding on their time, while ensuring that the patient is well cared for. All caregivers may need help developing a daily schedule for the patient and information about resources.

## Physical Health of the Caregiver

The counselor should ask about the caregiver's current illnesses; physical, visual, and hearing disabilities; medications; use of substances such as alcohol; and an overall subjective rating of current physical health. The last is important because subjective rating may be a better indicator of a person's ability to provide care than the actual number of illnesses they have.

The caregiver's level of physical health or illness may determine the amount of care and supervision he or she can safely provide. Caregivers who are physically ill, disabled, or frail may put themselves and the patient at risk if they do not obtain sufficient additional help.

Counselors should be alert to signs of self-neglect, since caregivers frequently defer their own health care to the needs of the patient. These caregivers should be reminded of the importance of self-care, including sleep, exercise, and attention to their nutritional needs, and should also be encouraged to make regular visits to their primary care physicians.

## Emotional Health of the Caregiver

A caregiver's emotional stability and resilience will facilitate responding to the demands of caregiving. AD caregivers bring their history of previous experience with difficult life events to the current situation. Some of these emotional reactions can contribute to undermining the physical health of the caregiver (through self-neglect, for example). They can also make the caregiver unwilling or unable to seek or respond to social support and offers of respite, creating the potential for social isolation of both caregiver and patient.

When emotional reactions are extreme and severely impair the caregiver's ability to function, these symptoms must either become the focus of treatment, or the person should immediately be referred to a setting in which they can be addressed. If the caregiver's condition puts the patient at risk, other family members need to be involved, or a referral may need to be made to protective services. Caregivers with a prior history of mental illness or a chronic mood disorder may be particularly vulnerable to the challenges of caregiving for an AD patient and may require additional support. Caregivers who express suicidal ideation or plans should be referred at once for appropriate treatment. Counselors should also ask questions to determine the possible abuse of alcohol and drugs. In extreme cases of caregiver emotional illness, counselors should facilitate alternative plans for care of the patient (eg, another family caregiver or respite in a nursing home).

Caregivers are at elevated risk for mood disorders such as depression and anxiety. Spouse caregivers are especially at risk for depression. Research has shown that counseling and support can have a significant impact on the number of symptoms of depression a caregiver experiences. Caregivers should be monitored for these disorders and counseling directed toward increasing social support and creating a realistic appraisal of the reasons for the patient's symptoms as a means of alleviating the symptoms of these disorders. Some caregivers will benefit from pharmacological intervention in addition.

## Caregiver Understanding of and Response to the Illness

*Caregiver Knowledge of Alzheimer's Disease* Some caregivers will have done a great deal of research about Alzheimer's disease before they come to counseling, while others will know very little. Some people may be afraid of knowing what will happen to their relatives as the disease progresses. The accuracy of the understanding of the impact of the illness on a patient can affect the caregiver's perception of his or her behavior and ability to make realistic plans for the future and provide appropriate patient care. In Chapter 4 we give a detailed description of the kinds of questions a counselor can ask to assess the caregiver's level of knowledge of the illness.

*Caregiver's Perception of the Patient's Behavior* It is important to the counseling process to know whether the caregiver's perception of the patient's abilities and impairments is compatible with the other information the counselor has been able to obtain about the severity of dementia.

The way in which the caregiver interprets the meaning of the symptoms is a major determinant of the experience of caregiving as stressful and of caregiver depression. For example, does he or she believe that the person is purposely behaving in a difficult manner? Does the caregiver believe the symptoms are a sign of aging? Does the caregiver say the patient always behaved as he does now? If so, counseling that addresses misperceptions about the cause of the patient's behavior can have a potentially powerful impact on caregiver well-being.

***Response to the Patient's Behavior*** In the course of caring for a person with AD, caregivers' reactions to the changes in memory and behavior that confront them will vary over time and will also be a reflection of their temperament and the number of other issues with which they are dealing. A caregiver whose relative is in the mild stage of the disease may become enormously frustrated by what will later seem like a relatively benign behavior. The same caregiver who was initially so reactive may later begin to take the symptoms of the disease more or less in stride. By understanding the motivation for the caregiver's responses, the counselor can determine whether interventions such as additional education about the disease, improving behavior-management techniques, reframing the meaning of the patient's behavior, or recommending respite will help the caregiver to be less distressed and to respond effectively to the patient.

> "The neurologist told us a little bit about Alzheimer's when he gave us the diagnosis. My neighbor's mother had AD, and she used to wander around and the police would bring her home. I can't bear to think of Ted like that.
>
> "I get so annoyed at Ted. He doesn't seem to pay any attention to what I say. Why does he keep asking the same question over and over again? It really gets on my nerves."

## Social Support

Social support may be provided by informal sources such as family or friends or by formal sources such as paid personnel or social services.

***Informal Support*** Social support has many dimensions: the number of people in the social network, who they are (children, siblings, friends) and their relationship to the caregiver, the kind of support each member provides (emotional, task related, financial), negative interactions among the members of the network, how satisfying the caregiver finds the support system, and how much support the caregiver feels he or she needs. The counselor will want to assess the quality of relationships in the caregiver's social network and, if necessary, will work toward enhancing the role its members can play in supporting the caregiver. Spouse caregivers may have previously relied on their husband or wife as a major source of social support that has now been lost as a result of the illness.

Caregivers who naturally tend toward isolation may be particularly uncomfortable reaching out and asking for help. It may be useful to share the research with them about how social support can reduce the burdens of caregiving, while appreciating that social interaction itself may be stressful for these people.

The family can be an invaluable aid to a caregiver, as well as a source of stress. Research suggests that reducing family conflict is at least as important as increasing family support in changing the amount of stress felt by the caregiver. At best, family members can be supportive of the primary caregiver and the ill relative, knowing when and how to offer help. At worst, family interactions can increase the caregiver's stress when family members misunderstand or have unrealistic expectations of each other or are critical or angry.

***Formal Support***   The counselor will want to know whether the caregiver has already accessed formal supports, such as paid help at home, day care, and other community resources, and the extent to which these services are adequately addressing his or her needs and those of the patient. It is important to know whether the patient is using the entitlements for which he or she is eligible, such as Medicare, Medicaid, Veterans Administration benefits, or disability insurance benefits.

"We're very close to all our kids and see Tom and Diane all the time. Even though Matt lives far away, we talk to him every week. How can you ask me about getting support from the kids? We haven't even told them anything. We have lots of good friends, but what are they supposed to do for me? I love to babysit for Carol's kids, and I used to babysit for Tom's when they were younger, but fortunately I've never needed to ask our kids for anything.

"Why would I hire someone to help with the housework? I do the cooking, cleaning, and shopping, and Ted is a great handyman."

## Quality of Life

In addition to each of the factors described above, it is essential to get a global picture of what each person considers important to quality of life. What are his or her values? What would need to change for the caregiver to feel that the quality of life has improved? Schools of thought that have come out of the medical tradition emphasize physical functioning and health behaviors as measures of quality of life. Currently, the concept has been expanded to include mental health and mental functioning, social activities and social functioning, occupational functioning, and religious activities (spiritual practice, meditation, prayer).

We have found that caregivers are very responsive to a one-item pictorial representation of quality of life on a centigrade thermometer in which "0" is terrible and "100" is perfect. It provides a context in which to discuss aspects of their lives that they consider meaningful. This measure, when repeated after counseling, can be a useful index of overall improvement. Caregivers who feel competent in their ability to care for the patient and have adequate support will generally report improved estimates of their quality of life (perhaps because of greater confidence, better sleep, and more effective expenditure of physical and emotional resources).

"If you had asked me this question a few months ago, I would have said I have everything I've always wanted. But now, it feels like everything's changed. I would say, on a scale of 0 to 100, my quality of life is 75."

## Clinical Impressions

While the counselor is conducting the assessment, he or she will also be trying to get a general sense of the caregiver's attitude toward the experience and the underlying threads that go through the narrative. These are clinical impressions that are derived from what is both stated and unstated, including body language, tone of communication, and the way the caregiver interacts with the counselor. Caregivers who are open to new ideas, good problem solvers, optimistic, and can see the humor in difficult situations will most likely have the internal resources to adjust to the caregiving role, given adequate support and information. Caregiving requires flexibility and a focus on the needs of another, which may feel like an excessive demand on those who tend to be rigid, have a low frustration tolerance, or are self-centered. Those who tend to have depressive personalities may have trouble mobilizing the motivation and energy needed to consistently carry out the caregiving chores over the course of the illness. People with a tendency toward anxiety may be troubled by the requirements of decision making and continually facing the unpredictability of the disease.

People who are more extroverted and thrive on social interaction may find the limitations imposed by caregiving distressing, because they may have discontinued relationships over the course of the illness of their relative. Those who are more introverted may find it difficult to ask for and accept help and may feel more imposed upon by having to interact with health care professionals and other service providers.

By understanding caregivers' personality types, the counselor can plan interventions that will maximize their strengths and minimize the impact of their limitations in the way they respond to the challenge of Alzheimer's disease. The counselor may also be able to anticipate the specific aspects of caregiving that may be particularly difficult or easy for individual caregivers. Throughout the counseling process, the counselor needs to be aware of caregiver characteristics that increase vulnerability to negative outcomes. The information gathered in the assessment will shape the counseling plan for each individual caregiver.

## Sample Assessment Summary

After speaking with Millie, the counselor at the community health center wrote up the following assessment.

Millie G is a 62-year-old female, married to Ted G, 65 years old, for 41 years. They are both Caucasian and members of the Lutheran church. One son, Tom, 40 years old, married with two children, 13 and 16 years old, lives 1 hour away from Millie and Ted. Another son, Matt, 34 years old, lives out of state. A daughter, Carol, 38, married with three children, ages 8, 6, and 4, lives half an hour away. MG is currently employed as a full-time secretary, in the same firm for 15 years. She and Ted have lived in the same two-story home in a middle-class neighborhood for their entire marriage.

MG came to counseling because her husband has recently been diagnosed with Alzheimer's disease. TG is otherwise in good health. MG is worried about her husband's job, his safety, and their future. She says she doesn't know what she would do without Ted, but MG will not talk about the illness with family until she decides how to approach the subject with them. MG consistently repeated that she does not want anyone to know about Ted's illness and asked if the information in the counseling session would remain confidential. I assured her that all information discussed would be kept confidential and explained under what conditions I would be obligated to present information about our sessions to outside parties.

MG is in good health. She stated that she has a good marriage; he was always a good provider, always saw to the bills and repairing the house, while she took care of the cooking and food shopping. MG stated that both she and her husband have a good relationship with their children. MG is friendly with some co-workers and neighbors, although many of their old friends have moved out of state. She keeps in close touch with her children. MG and TG attend church regularly.

MG is a very pleasant woman, soft-spoken, but appeared very anxious and has some depressive symptoms. She stated that she has been very stressed since she discovered her husband was having cognitive difficulties.

MG is a woman with many strengths and family supports. However, as a result of her husband's diagnosis, she appears unsure of how to proceed and overwhelmed by the change in him. She has a limited understanding of Alzheimer's disease and, at this point, appears unable to mobilize herself to seek further information. She has a significant work history that suggests a capacity to organize and solve problems and can benefit from counseling to reduce symptoms of depression and anxiety and access supports. Immediate issues include Ted's driving and job jeopardy and informing significant family members of diagnosis.

**In the next chapter, we will see the counseling plan that Millie and her counselor have agreed upon.**

# Counselor Checklist

### The Presenting Problem

☐ Ask the caregiver why he or she has come for help.

☐ View any specific issues in the context of the factors uncovered in the full assessment.

### The Assessment

☐ Explain why the focus is on the caregiver, not the patient.

☐ The AD patient should not attend the caregiver assessment interview.

### Demographic Characteristics

☐ Record the caregiver's age, gender, culture and ethnicity, religion, financial and employment status, educational background, and family composition.

### Relationship of Caregiver to Patient

☐ Assess the relationship (past and current) that this individual has with the patient.

### Patient Information

☐ In the absence of medical information, ask the three questions that can help you evaluate the severity of dementia of the patient.

☐ Ask about the patient's life, employment status, role and responsibilities in the family, and social life.

☐ Assess whether the home environment is safe.

### Caregiving Role

☐ Assess the role that this person plays in the care of the person with AD.

### Physical Health of Caregiver

☐ Record the caregiver's medical history, asking for a subjective rating of the caregiver's overall health.

☐ Assess self-care, including sleep, exercise, and attention to nutritional needs.

**Emotional Health of Caregiver**

☐ Assess the severity of emotional reactions and refer, as appropriate, to a setting where they can be addressed.

☐ Look for signs of excessive use of alcohol and drugs.

☐ Assess for suicidal ideation or plans in caregivers who are depressed and refer at once for appropriate treatment.

☐ In extreme cases of caregiver incapacity, facilitate alternative plans for care of the patient (eg, another family caregiver, respite in a nursing home).

**Caregiver Understanding and Response to Illness**

☐ Assess the caregiver's level of knowledge of Alzheimer's disease.

☐ Ascertain the caregiver's perception of the extent of the patient's abilities and needs for care.

☐ Identify symptoms that are most difficult for the caregiver to manage.

**Social Support**

☐ Assess the quality of relationships in the caregiver's social network (informal support).

☐ Assess the formal support already in use to see if these services are adequately meeting the caregiver's needs and if the patient is using all available entitlements.

**Quality of Life**

☐ Ask the caregiver to evaluate his or her current quality of life on a scale of 0 to 100, where 0 is terrible and 100 is perfect.

**Clinical Impressions**

☐ Assess the caregiver's personality type in order to create an individual counseling plan that will make use of the caregiver's strengths and work with his or her limitations.

# COUNSELING THE CAREGIVER

Caregivers may present themselves for counseling at any time in the course of the illness, from the point of diagnosis to bereavement. They may ask for help with a concrete problem, such as managing the patient's behavior, or express a more general need for support. The counselor's experience and knowledge of Alzheimer's disease (AD) make it possible to understand the stage of the patient's illness, what the caregiver may be experiencing, and what he or she needs to know to deal effectively with the current situation and to anticipate changes as the disease progresses. The counselor can help the caregiver adapt to transitions such as a new stage of the illness or nursing home placement.

There are many objectives in counseling the caregiver of a person with Alzheimer's disease. The most salient are to maintain and enhance the physical and emotional well-being of the caregiver; reduce the negative effects of caregiving, such as isolation, stress, and depression; and ensure that the patient is well cared for. Counseling can include education, support, referrals, and information about additional resources.

This chapter is a guide through the counseling process, from contracting with the caregiver, through planning and implementing the intervention, to evaluating the outcomes. It also includes counseling strategies and techniques that will enable the counselor to build on the caregivers' strengths and minimize the effect of their limitations.

## Conditions of the Counseling Arrangement

Each setting has its own procedures and requirements for providing services, which should be clearly explained to the client and agreed to before counseling starts. The client needs to understand the extent and limitations of the services that will be offered and what fees there will be, if any. In developing the contract, the counselor needs to address the issues of protocol (the number, timing, frequency, duration, and location of sessions) and, if applicable, who will participate in family counseling sessions.

### *The Protocol*

In addition to the assessment, the NYU study protocol includes two individual counseling sessions with the primary caregiver and four meetings with the caregiver and other family members within a few months after intake. (See Chapter 4 for a discussion of family counseling.) An essential part of the NYU protocol is what we call *ad hoc* counseling (see Chapter 5), the availability of counseling by telephone on an as-needed basis.

In response to the chronic long-term and progressive nature of AD, the NYU model provides support and counseling for the caregiver for the duration of a patient's illness. Due to changes in the patient caused by the illness, needs for new services, such as paid home care or day care, and unpredictable crises, such as hospitalization, caregivers may require support or assistance at any time. Coping with the nursing home placement can be as physically and emotionally debilitating to the caregiver as were the day-to-day issues when the patient was at home.

The extent to which a counselor will be able to replicate this protocol will be dictated by agency or health care provider policies, financial status of the client, and insurance considerations. For example, if providing counseling during the process of nursing home placement does not fit in with the mission of an agency, the caregiver should be made aware of other supportive services that are available to ease these transitions. It is essential that the caregiver fully understand the nature of the services that can be provided by the agency.

In scheduling meetings with caregivers, the counselor should try to be flexible. Working caregivers may need evening or weekend sessions, and frail or incapacitated caregivers, or those who cannot leave the patient, may need to have sessions in their homes. Caregivers may also need to arrange to have supervision for the patient in order to participate in counseling sessions and may only be able to come on specific days or at specific times. Again, the extent to which a counselor will be able to replicate the NYU intervention, in which the counselors went to the homes of caregivers' who were unable to travel to the NYU center and were available if necessary on weekends and evenings, will depend on the setting in which counseling is provided. It is desirable that every effort be made to schedule sessions to minimize caregiver stress.

## Participants

If the caregiver is agreeable and family members are available, the counseling plan should include some family sessions in addition to individual sessions. Research has shown that family support is crucial to the well-being of caregivers of people with AD. It is important, therefore, to emphasize to the caregiver the benefits of involving the family if at all possible. If the caregiver is reluctant to include other family members, the cause of this reluctance may be an issue to explore, and the counselor can, when appropriate, help the caregiver overcome the difficulties preventing family involvement. (Family counseling is discussed in Chapter 4.)

## The Counseling Process

The counseling process includes a review of the caregiver assessment, identifying goals, and developing a plan to achieve them. This process can occur repeatedly as previously set goals are met and new issues emerge. Throughout the process, the counselor will be providing emotional support, education, assistance with problem solving, and referrals for additional resources. The counselor begins to build a relationship with the caregiver from the first contact. The assessment, discussed in Chapter 2, is essential to the counseling process because it provides an initial opportunity to explore the areas that are important to caregivers and gives the counselor an opportunity to demonstrate interest and a willingness to help.

When counseling caregivers, clinicians should, of course, adhere to the basic principles of treatment and standards of behavior expected in any other clinician-client relationship.

## Steps in the Counseling Process

The five steps in the counseling process are discussed below.

***Step One: Review the Caregiver Assessment***  The assessment provides information that makes it possible for the counselor to develop an individualized plan for counseling and support that is based on the unique needs of each caregiver and patient. Counselors should review the results of the assessment prior to the initial counseling session and summarize what appear to be the most important issues to be addressed which, with the agreement of the caregiver, may become counseling goals.

If the counselor identifies severe medical or psychiatric problems affecting the caregiver, the initial task will be to either help the client accept an appropriate alternative referral or decide whether it is possible to work collaboratively with another health professional. In this case, the counselor and the caregiver have to clearly define:

■ Why certain issues are better addressed in other settings

■ The purpose of the referral to another setting

■ How the information gained at another setting fits into the counseling process

■ Whether the caregiver can return to this setting at a future date

***Step Two: Identify Problems and Issues***  During the assessment, the caregiver may have presented many problems. It may be that one problem can be readily identified as most distressing or that the number of problems is overwhelming to the caregiver. These problems may need to be clarified or put into language that makes it possible to develop a counseling plan. Assisting the caregiver to be clear and specific about a problem so that it is accessible to change is an integral part of counseling. Through the process of clarifying the problem, the counselor and caregiver may gain a greater understanding of what is troubling the caregiver. Caregiving is only one part of the caregiver's life and may seem especially burdensome because of other demands or problems. Helping the caregiver recognize this may give him or her a more realistic appraisal of the burden of caregiving.

There may be times when a counselor and caregiver have differing perspectives about the cause of a problem and the best way to remedy it. In these cases, if the issue is important to the well-being of the caregiver or the patient, part of the work of counseling may be to address the differing points of view. It is essential to the counseling process that the counselor and caregiver agree on the problem that will be addressed.

If any of the issues presented by the caregiver suggest that the caregiver or patient may be in danger, this will obviously become a priority for counseling. If the caregiver is not willing to address such a situation, then it may be necessary for the counselor to take steps to actively intervene to prevent harm.

Together with the caregiver, the counselor will determine the problems to be addressed and their order of importance. For example, the caregiver may find the repetitive questioning of a patient in the mild stage of dementia unbearable and think that stopping this behavior is the most important issue. This same caregiver may also doubt the veracity of the diagnosis since the patient is able to function relatively independently. In this case, the caregiver will have to understand that the patient is ill before he or she will become more tolerant of the behavior or be willing to find new ways of responding that will reduce the number of times the patient repeats the same question.

In addition to those identified by the caregiver, the counselor may want to bring issues to the caregiver's attention that he or she may not have considered or that the caregiver has not identified as most immediately important. Sometimes the problem the caregiver articulates may mask another issue that, when uncovered, will become a focus of counseling.

The counselor may be aware of some issues that he or she will not necessarily try to address with the caregiver at the start of counseling. These issues may become the focus of counseling later in the process, or they may be dropped when the counselor gets to know the caregiver better and decides that the initial interpretation of the issues was erroneous.

Millie had presented several problems during her initial assessment. She told the counselor that her husband, Ted, insisted on driving even though he had had a car accident and that he did not want to stop working despite his diagnosis and a recommendation from his neurologist that he stop these activities. She also said that Ted no longer wanted to go out with friends, nor did he come home with funny stories about work. He forgot to pick things up for her from the store, and he kept saying he had to mow the lawn, even though he had just mowed it the day before. Ted just wasn't the reliable person he had been. Together, the counselor and Millie explored the issues and came to agreement that there were two main problems that needed to be addressed first—the issue of driving, which posed a threat to Ted's safety, and the work situation, in which Ted could not appreciate that his job was in jeopardy.

***Step Three: Set Counseling Objectives***    Once the problems have been identified, the next step is to identify the desired objectives and the steps that need to be taken to achieve them.

A counselor may identify objectives such as improving a caregiver's understanding of the illness or helping the caregiver obtain assistance with caregiving tasks. Having obtained the caregiver's agreement that these are worthwhile objectives, it will be necessary to identify the steps by which they will be attained. For example, the caregiver may decide to read a book or watch videotapes to learn more about Alzheimer's disease. If the objective is to build a suitable care plan, a first step might be to ask family and friends to become involved in the care of the patient. With the counselor, each caregiver will define specific goals relating to his or her individual situation.

In order to maximize the probability that the objective will be achieved, the steps will have to be realistic and suited to the unique characteristics of each caregiver's situation. For example, if the caregiver is a member of a senior center, the counselor might suggest that he or she speak to the social worker at the center to explore its resources for caregiver assistance. If, through questioning, the counselor can enable the caregiver to identify a solution, the experience will be empowering, and the caregiver may feel a greater investment in solving the problem.

Millie and the counselor agreed that eventually Ted would have to stop driving, but for now, it would be a good idea for him to drive only during the day and only to familiar places that weren't far from home. Millie and the counselor discussed how she could approach the subject with Ted. The counselor asked Millie to tell her what had happened the last time she had tried to talk with Ted about driving. Millie said that one day she and Ted were getting ready to go to the movies. "Just as we were about to go out," she said, "I got up the courage to tell Ted I thought it wasn't safe for him to drive anymore. I said that I wanted to drive and that he should give me his keys. He refused and said, "Forget the whole thing. I'm not in the mood to go anywhere now."

### *Step Four: Select Modality and Therapeutic Approach*
Having identified the desired objectives, the next step will be to select the most appropriate modality and therapeutic approach with which to achieve them. Some objectives are more suitable to individual counseling and others to family counseling, support groups, a referral to another service, or educational lectures.

Each counselor will already be familiar and comfortable with certain therapeutic approaches and will want to draw on them. The approaches briefly described and illustrated later in this chapter have been used effectively in the NYU intervention. Some goals may be best achieved with a combination of methods.

Millie and the counselor decided they could work on the driving issue together but that it would be helpful to discuss the work issue in family counseling, where Millie could get the support of her children. That, however, would require Ted's agreement to tell the family he was ill. Millie said she'd rather work on one thing at a time, and they agreed that telling the family could wait until the driving issue was resolved. The counselor asked Millie if she would like to try role-playing with her to see if they could come up with ways she could approach Ted about driving. She explained that role-playing meant that each of them would try out being Millie and Ted. They experimented with this for the remainder of the session, and Millie said she would try again, using the strategies she had practiced. They agreed to have another individual counseling session the following week at the same time. The counselor also gave Millie a book about Alzheimer's disease, so she would understand more about Ted's illness.

***Step Five: Evaluate Progress***  Evaluation occurs throughout the counseling process, as well as at specific times determined by the counseling plan, because when one goal is achieved, another, which was less immediate, can be addressed. Alternatively, a new issue may emerge that becomes the focus of counseling. It is also possible for it to become apparent that the agreed-upon goal is not attainable at this time. If goals cannot be attained in the time frame permitted at the setting in which the counselor works, the counselor should refer the caregiver to another setting that can continue to provide the caregiver with the resources and support he or she needs. Evaluation is a collaborative process between the counselor and the caregiver, and they should both agree about whether the goal was attained. With the counselor's help, a caregiver should be able to recognize when a change or progress has occurred. Part of the evaluation will be to understand why a certain goal could not be achieved and identifying the obstacles, the overcoming of which may become a goal of counseling.

Millie did not come for her next scheduled counseling session, but when the counselor called her, she agreed to come the following week. When Millie arrived, she said she couldn't do any of the things they had talked about and would rather take her chances driving with Ted than hurt his feelings. He had always done the driving when they went out together, and it just didn't feel right for her to be behind the wheel. She wondered if she hadn't overreacted. "After all," she said, "everyone has accidents now and then." The counselor realized that driving was a symbol of Ted's role in the family and how much Millie would have to change her feelings about her role in the household in order to adapt to the changes in her husband. Helping Millie to deal with the emotional implications of Ted's illness then became the focus of counseling.

## *Counseling Considerations*

The counseling process begins with the initial contact with the caregiver and includes everything the counselor does to enhance that person's coping skills, social support, and ability to manage taking care of both his or her own needs and those of the patient. In the course of counseling a caregiver, as with any other client, the counselor can expect that issues that were addressed early in the process will come up again at a later time in a somewhat different form as the caregiver struggles to understand and accept the consequences of the illness. Of course, this is a normal part of a therapeutic process. Feelings of sadness, loss, anger, hopelessness, and guilt are reactivated by the patient's progressive decline, which demands that the caregiver continually make new adjustments.

People may not let go of their beliefs and hopes all at once, even if they claim to have accepted that the person has Alzheimer's disease. For example, a caregiver may become angry with the patient for behaving in a particular way (eg, not saying thank you) and feel personally offended, even though he or she knows that the behavior is caused by the illness. Caregivers may need counseling to help them accept the implications of the diagnosis. Caregivers who do not want to tell family and friends about the diagnosis may not get the support and assistance they need. Some keep the diagnosis to themselves for fear that people will withdraw from them.

If the person with AD is still in the early stage of the illness and the family is willing to openly discuss the implications of the diagnosis, they can plan together for the future, for instance, by preparing advance directives while the patient can still participate. Family members and the person with AD will need support and information to attend to these issues. The caregiver will also need to learn a great deal about the illness, especially the unpredictable nature of the ill relative's level of functioning.

During the early stage of the illness, the person with AD can benefit from participating in a support group for patients and in many normative community activities. When the person is in the moderate stage, caregiver concerns often center around dealing with the behavioral changes, need for more physical care, and use of services such as home and day care. In the most severe stage, caregivers have to provide complete physical care for their relative, or hire someone else to do so, and face end of life issues. Throughout the course of the illness, caregivers will need to learn how to provide health care for their relative, deal with possible hospitalization, and maintain their own well-being.

Effective counseling does not necessarily have to be continual but may be intermittent. Once a counseling relationship has been established, additional counseling sessions can be initiated by the caregiver when he or she feels the need for help or by the counselor if he or she thinks that the caregiver will not ask for help.

The need for additional counseling frequently occurs in response to a behavioral change in the patient or when a new issue is anticipated or has emerged. During periods when the patient is stable, caregivers often develop a level of comfort that is destroyed by a change in the patient or the care plan. When a trusted home care aide leaves, the caregiver will need to find and train a new person. This may mean becoming more involved with providing routine daily care after a period of relative freedom from these tasks until a new person can be hired. Similarly, feelings of sadness and grief, which may have been put temporarily out of mind while the patient is stable, are reawakened each time a new symptom occurs that represents further decline. With counseling and experience, the caregiver will bring more internal and external resources to coping with each successive crisis.

The way in which a counselor works with a caregiver will be a function of his or her own style and understanding of the needs of the client. The information the counselor obtained during the assessment—especially regarding the caregiver's strengths, which are a resource, and limitations, which may be mitigated by counseling—will be a framework upon which to build the counseling plan. In addition, the counselor always needs to be aware of the other aspects of the caregiver's life and the way in which they interact with the demands of caregiving. The needs of a sick child, other family responsibilities, or the caregiver's career may draw attention and energy from the caregiving role. Even though caregiving is the primary focus of counseling, its place in the overall context of the caregiver's life needs to be appreciated and other needs and goals supported.

Counseling is intended to provide emotional support and the opportunity to learn caregiving skills. In general, the counseling described in this guide focuses on attending to present caregiving-related issues. It does not seek to bring repressed or unconscious issues to awareness. Exploration of past events is limited and is only undertaken to find a way, if possible, to detach negative past experience from current concerns. This approach is not an attempt to minimize the impact of the past experience but, when possible, to create an opportunity for a new beginning. Parents may be reluctant to ask a child who has been estranged from the family for help, or they may not want to include relatives with whom they have had a falling out in the past as part of their support network. Sometimes the illness of the parent can provide a safe and acceptable reason to reestablish broken connections.

## Counseling Techniques and Strategies

Each counselor will work within the framework of his or her unique style. This style is developed from the counselor's training, work experience, personality, and comfort in using particular techniques and strategies. The following counseling methods have been found to be effective with AD caregivers at NYU: exploration, role-play/modeling, cognitive restructuring, behavior modification, visualization/use of imagery, and humor. The descriptions illustrate the use of these methods with family members of people with AD. Counselors may already be familiar with these methods and feel comfortable using them. These illustrations may help counselors who are unfamiliar with these methods to begin to explore new ways of working with caregivers. Counselors should not restrict themselves to a specific technique in a counseling session, but rather they should respond to issues, images, and themes presented by the caregiver and use them creatively to help the caregiver.

### Counseling Strategies

Alan S and his wife Marge had just come home from a long visit with their daughter Sally in Chicago. It hadn't been easy to be with Marge in what now appeared to her to be a strange house, but he had thought things would be better when they were back in familiar surroundings. Now that they were back home, it looked like the problem wasn't strange surroundings, but that she had progressed to a more severe stage of dementia. Marge didn't remember the trip to Chicago at all and kept calling Alan in the office asking when they were going to visit their daughter. She also called Sally repeatedly, but Sally had an answering machine that picked up her messages while she was at work. Marge thought the voice on the machine was her daughter and got very angry because Sally never answered her questions.

Alan made an appointment to see his counselor, hoping she could help him figure out what to do. Alan said, "The office used to be my haven, but now it feels like Marge is there too. I can't concentrate. I feel like I'm holding my breath while I wait for the next call from Marge. Now Sally is calling me every day begging me to stop Mom from yelling into the answering machine." The counselor said jokingly, "Holding your breath all day isn't good for your health. Why do you think Marge keeps calling?" "I guess she's lonely," said Alan. "But I can't stay home with her all the time. I'd never be able to take a breath." The counselor asked, "How can I help you get some air?" Alan answered, "Marge's sister has been offering to come over and spend a few hours every day with her, and I've been too proud to take her up on it. Maybe if I accept her offer, Marge will be less lonely and I'll be able to breathe more freely. If Marge stops calling Sally, then Sally won't be so angry with me and she and I can have a normal conversation again."

In this vignette, we see how the counselor listened to the language and tone of the caregiver's narrative, stayed with his expression of the experience, and worked with his image to clarify his need. In this way, she acknowledged his feelings and helped him reach his own conclusion about how to begin to get relief.

## *Exploration*

Exploration is a basic technique used in counseling. The counselor uses his or her own unique style of questioning and responding during a counseling session to explore an issue with the caregiver, including gathering necessary information, helping a caregiver gain insight into a problem, and processing thoughts and feelings about the issue. This may enable the caregiver to articulate feelings, look at the situation in a different way, and devise his or her own solutions to the problems he or she has raised.

## Counseling Strategies

William came to his counseling session with the following situation: He and his wife, Teresa, who has moderate stage Alzheimer's disease, received an invitation to a dinner party at their friends' home. At first, he was very happy to have received the invitation—it had come from their long-time friends, and although they didn't get together often, they always had a great time when they did. He described a few of the fun times they had had. William told the counselor that after thinking about the invitation for awhile, he wasn't so sure that he should accept. When the counselor asked what his concerns were, William said that Teresa had been tired lately, she didn't seem to enjoy going out anymore, and he really didn't want to put her through the trouble of a whole evening out.

The counselor remembered that just recently William had told her about a wonderful day at the park that he and Teresa had had, and she explored with William why his attitude toward going out with Teresa had changed. The counselor first touched on several issues raised by William's explanation: Had Teresa been feeling well? Had he noticed a change in Teresa's behavior in other areas of daily life? William answered no to all the counselor's questions. When the counselor explored further, asking William what he thought the evening might be like if they accepted the invitation, William hesitated. The counselor asked if William thought that it might be too stressful for Teresa to be at a dinner party. William hesitated again, "Not stressful, but . . ." The counselor gently pointed out to William that she felt he was trying to say something but couldn't bring himself to do it. William sat quietly for a time and finally said, "I love Teresa, you know that. I love spending time with her but this, well, she does things sometimes that, well . . . are . . . embarrassing. I mean, I know it's the illness, but there will be people there who don't know her. . . ."

In this example, the counselor's sensitive questions, bringing in the information the caregiver had previously shared with her, enabled the caregiver to feel safe enough to express his true concern, that Teresa would embarrass herself and him. The counselor did not challenge his early rationalizations but supported him as he continued to explore his feelings until he was able to articulate the real problem himself. It is not clear at this point whether Teresa should attend this gathering, but the counseling has created an opportunity for William to examine his feelings about the changes in his wife and the impact of these changes on their lives.

## Cognitive Restructuring

Cognitive restructuring is a therapeutic approach that attempts to have the person identify negative thought patterns and then reexamine problems in a more rational and constructive way. In cognitive restructuring, the counselor introduces alternative interpretations that show the caregiver that his or her view is not necessarily the only way to look at the situation or the only realistic interpretation of it.

### Counseling Strategies

Frank came to counseling because of feelings of low self-esteem and rejection that emerged a few months after his long-term partner Peter had been diagnosed with AD. Frank had never felt comfortable with Peter's family. He described a recent visit to Peter's parents, saying that Peter had not made any effort to bring him into conversations as he had in the past. Frank began to wonder if he had become less important to Peter and if he was thinking of ending their relationship. The counselor asked Frank whether Peter had behaved the way he used to with his family. Frank said, "Now that I think of it, no, Peter hardly said a word to anyone." Frank realized how little he knew about Alzheimer's disease when the counselor explained that it is common for people in the early stage of the illness to withdraw in social situations because they feel overwhelmed, are afraid of forgetting names, and generally feel less competent when interacting with others. This kind of behavior can actually be an adaptive response on the part of the person with AD and is not to be understood as a reflection of a change in his affection for his loved ones. Frank was relieved to find out that there was another way to think about Peter's behavior and felt he would react more appropriately in the future.

## Behavior Modification

Behavior modification uses the techniques of conditioning to control or change learned behaviors. While the counselor may not use a formal behavior modification protocol, its principles, based on the theory that a person will be motivated to use a new desired behavior if it leads to a positive outcome or reward, can be useful.

A caregiver who has known a patient for a long time is likely to have developed habitual behavior toward the patient. The caregiver's behavior may no longer have the same outcome as it did in the past, now that the person has AD. For example, caregivers will naturally continue to try to reason with a relative with AD in spite of repeated evidence that this is no longer possible. The counselor can help the caregiver to recognize the futility of maintaining accustomed ways of behaving and to learn new ways of relating to the person as he or she is today.

The counselor can help the caregiver to identify behavior that is no longer constructive or appropriate and possible alternative behavior toward the patient. It will be important for the caregiver to practice this new behavior and talk with the counselor about how it felt to behave in a different way. If the new behavior does not work as planned, it will, of course, be necessary to think of another alternative. The counselor's encouragement can help the caregiver to recognize the progress he or she has made.

In theory, the new behavior of the caregiver is, in and of itself, the reward. The counselor's approval and support can be emotionally rewarding to the caregiver as well and will encourage the caregiver to consider whether there are other ways in which he or she would like to behave differently in relation to the patient.

## Counseling Strategies

Deirdre complained that she almost always got into a shouting match with her husband, Tim, who was in the early stage of AD, when he refused to take his diabetes medication. She said she always started by trying to convince him to follow the doctor's instructions and ended up yelling out of frustration. Deirdre explained to the counselor that she got upset because she knew that Tim could become really sick if he skipped a dose of his medicine. Deirdre already recognized that her anxiety made her husband anxious, too. The counselor did not criticize the caregiver for her behavior, as they both understood it was an expression of her concern, but helped her to devise an alternative way of behaving toward her husband that was more likely to ensure that he would take his medication and that the atmosphere in their home would improve. The counselor asked Deirdre what Tim really liked and she said he always enjoyed taking a walk in the park. The counselor and Deirdre agreed to try an experiment. Deirdre would kiss Tim and say, "After you take this pill, I'll get dressed and we can go for a walk in the park." She definitely would try not to scream, get excited, or convince him to do what she asked. They decided to meet again in 2 weeks to see how she felt when she used this new strategy to get Tim to take his medication and whether he took it more often without a battle as a result.

## Role-Play/Modeling

In role-play, the caregiver is encouraged to take on a role that is not his or her own in a contrived situation in order to understand the role more clearly. The counselor and caregiver may reenact a problematic situation and then role-play alternative scenarios. Earlier in the chapter we discussed that Millie and her counselor did a role-play to help Millie find a way to approach Ted about driving. Here is a segment of their discussion when the counselor is acting as Millie to model an alternative approach. Rather than be critical of Ted's driving, they decided to put the focus on Millie.

### Counseling Strategies

*Counselor as Millie:*  Ted, you know, I was watching television yesterday and I saw this program that says women have to be more independent.

*Millie as Ted:*  Yeah, I agree, as long as they don't go too far.

*Counselor as Millie:*  Oh, Ted, be serious. I was thinking about ways that I could be more independent, and I thought that maybe you could teach me a little about paying bills, and maybe I could start driving some more when we go out together. The lady in the show said that her husband let her drive out on the highway for the first time ever, and she felt incredible.

*Millie as Ted:*  Yeah, it could be fun—watching you.

They then role-played the same situation with the counselor acting as Ted. This approach was very different from Millie's more direct style and made Millie more aware of alternative ways to change old routines.

## Visualization

Visualization can be very effective when the focus of counseling is to help a caregiver envision a new approach to a situation. This technique uses imagery to accomplish this goal. It can be used in modifying behavior, reducing stress, and increasing self-awareness. When used for the purpose of changing behavior, for instance, it can help caregivers envision themselves behaving in or feeling a new way, enable them to practice the new ways in their minds before acting them out, and help them to gain confidence and comfort with the proposed changes.

### Counseling Strategies

Millie has agreed to the scenario worked out in the role-play. To build her confidence, the counselor suggested that they do a visualization of what this might be like. The counselor asked Millie to close her eyes and picture herself behind the wheel with Ted next to her. "What do you see, Millie?" "I imagine him watching every move I make and just waiting to tell me what I am doing wrong." "And how are you feeling?" "I am nervous—wishing I hadn't started this." The counselor asks Millie to visualize a way out of the discomfort. "Let your imagination take over a bit," says the counselor. Millie sits for a moment and then says, "I say to myself, I have to keep this up." The counselor encourages her to continue. "What do you see happening next?" Millie burst into laughter. "I say to Ted, 'It isn't easy for you to be in the passenger seat, but that's where the driving instructor sits.'" Millie then says to the counselor, clearly pleased with herself, "Pretty cute, don't you think?"

## Humor

Humor may work best when the counselor and caregiver have established a working relationship and the counselor has some knowledge of the caregiver's situation and what he or she may find to be funny. This will allow the counselor to use humor with sensitivity, avoiding subjects that may be troublesome, humiliating, or painful to the caregiver and to reassure the caregiver that laughing at a particular situation is not the same as laughing at the person with AD.

Not everybody finds the same things to be funny. It is not recommended that the counselor come to the session prepared with a list of jokes. Sometimes, however, finding the humor in a situation or enjoying a laugh can reduce stress, strengthen the working relationship between caregiver and counselor, and allow for the expression of darker feelings.

## Counseling Strategies

After the counselor had commented on how well her husband looked, the caregiver "joked" that she was afraid he would live to be 100, far longer than she herself expected to. She then commented that his siblings had all died at quite a young age. The counselor asked if she attributed his healthful appearance to her good cooking. "Maybe." She smiled. "Or more likely to the fact that I hardly cook at all." In this situation a humorous approach enabled the counselor and the caregiver to touch on the common, but rarely expressed, feelings of ambivalence caregivers may feel toward the person for whom they are caring.

# Counselor Checklist

### Conditions of the Counseling Arrangement

☐ The counseling protocol is dictated by agency or health care provider policies, financial status of the client, and insurance considerations.

☐ The counseling plan should include family sessions as well as individual sessions, if possible.

☐ The counseling plan should include support for the caregiver over the entire course of the patient's illness.

### The Counseling Process

☐ Review the caregiver assessment prior to the initial counseling session.

☐ Assist the caregiver in clarifying and prioritizing problems.

☐ If any of the problems suggest danger to the caregiver or patient, make these issues a priority, and intervene if necessary to prevent harm.

☐ Identify realistic objectives and the steps needed to achieve them.

☐ Select the most appropriate modality and therapeutic approach to reach the objectives.

☐ Tailor the counseling to the individual situation.

☐ Provide emotional support and the opportunity to learn caregiving skills.

☐ Evaluate the progress made in attaining goals in collaboration with the client.

### Counseling Techniques and Strategies

☐ Express empathy when questioning and responding to explore issues and establish a relationship with the caregiver.

☐ Introduce alternative interpretations to the caregiver's negative thought patterns.

☐ Help the caregiver recognize unconstructive ways of behaving and learn new ways of relating to the patient.

☐ Use role-playing to help the caregiver experience new approaches to problem situations.

☐ Include visualization techniques to guide a caregiver in modifying behavior, reducing stress, and increasing self-awareness.

☐ Use humor, when appropriate, to reduce stress.

# 4

# FAMILY COUNSELING

The purpose of family counseling is to help family members provide emotional support to the primary caregiver, the family member who carries the greatest weight of the caregiving, and to help all family members adapt to the changes that Alzheimer's disease (AD) imposes on them. The theory of the stress process (described in Chapter 1) suggests that family support can play an important role in reducing stress on the primary caregiver, while family conflict has a strong negative impact on the primary caregiver. Counseling can maximize the positive contributions of each member to caregiving, prevent one member from carrying the entire weight of the caregiving role, and reduce family conflict. This chapter guides the counselor through the process of arranging and conducting family counseling sessions.

## Preparing for Family Involvement

During the individual session, the counselor will begin preparing for family counseling with the caregiver. The counselor will introduce the idea of seeking help from family members or friends and explain why this can be beneficial—getting support, lessening distress, reestablishing connections. Caregiving can bring a family closer together through sharing care for someone important in their lives—the patient. A family counselor can help them to work together effectively, with minimum disruption to the well-being of any member of the family.

Millie called her counselor and said, "I broke my promise to Ted not to tell our kids that he has Alzheimer's disease. I told Tom last night. I couldn't help it. I feel so overwhelmed by the illness, the driving situation, Ted's refusal to stop working, and most of all, the fact that I couldn't talk to the kids or anyone about it. I thought about everything we talked about in counseling and realized that for my own sanity I couldn't hide Ted's illness from the family any longer. I called our son Tom and told him the whole story. Tom said he had been waiting for the right moment to ask me whether anything was wrong with Dad. I realized that even if I didn't tell anyone, that didn't mean they weren't aware that Ted was having problems. I told Tom that I come and talk to you and that you had recommended that the family come in for a counseling session. He said he would really like to do that." The counselor said, "Are you ready to tell your other children?" Millie said, "Yes, I could really use their support."

## *Addressing Caregiver Reluctance*

It is not uncommon for caregivers to be reluctant to ask family members to participate. These are some of the reasons they give for their reluctance to involve their families:

- Hesitance to impose on other family members

- Fear of being forced by other family members to change the way in which care is being given

- Discomfort with disclosing that she or he has gone for help for fear of seeming incompetent

- Fear that the family will misinterpret counseling as psychiatric help

- Desire to hide the relative's AD from other family members

- Reluctance to have outsiders, including professionals, talk to other members of the family

- Unwillingness to reconnect with estranged family members

- Fear of being refused by family members

The counselor can try to shift the caregiver's perspective on the purpose and meaning of family counseling—that it is to help family members find a way to participate. Distinguishing between counseling in the context of caregiving and mental health treatment can reassure the caregiver that coming for counseling does not imply that he or she is inadequate or having psychological problems. If caregivers seem likely to respond to an emotion-focused rationale, the counselor can point out that they may feel less stress if other members of their family participate in counseling. If caregivers are more problem focused, a cognitive approach, referring to the research about the value of family support, may be more effective. It may help to explain that family counseling may improve the quality of life of the patient as well as that of the caregiver. The caregiver may appreciate the potential value of having the whole family learn about AD and caregiving issues from a professional.

## Family Counseling Techniques

George told his counselor that he and his brother had never agreed about anything. "I've been doing pretty well without his help. It will only be more difficult for me if he gets involved. Then I'll have to deal with him and Mom." The counselor said, "Well, George, maybe if we get together in a family session, we can find ways for your brother to take over some of the caregiving tasks without interfering with you. You keep talking about how exhausted you are. What if your brother would agree to take over the caregiving while you went on a vacation?" George said, "If you could convince my brother to do that, maybe it would be worth inviting him."

Asking family members for help can be particularly difficult for caregivers when there has been a divorce, separation, or other type of estrangement. For example, if the primary caregiver is the spouse of the patient, but not the parent of the patient's children, there may be resentment and conflict about who should be involved in providing care.

It should be noted that, while family counseling can be beneficial to most caregivers, there are situations in which bringing the family together to address AD-related issues may not be recommended. The relative with Alzheimer's disease may not be the highest immediate priority for other family members. Severe psychopathology in other family members can impinge on the possibility of effectively addressing the AD-related problems. For some families, cultural values might preclude disclosing private family issues or accepting help from outside the family.

It might be necessary to forgo family counseling, at least for the time being, if the caregiver does not agree to involve family members, is not ready to disclose the diagnosis to others or to accept support, or there is a situation that would take priority for others in the family.

## Who Should Participate?

We have recommended that the intake assessment include a discussion of the people in the caregiver's social network, their relationship to the caregiver, and their contributions to caregiving (see Chapter 2), as well as how satisfied the caregiver is with the assistance received. This information can be used as the basis for a discussion about who in the family should participate in counseling and suggest to the counselor who might be included in family counseling beyond those people mentioned by the caregiver. The counselor should encourage the caregiver to include as potential participants in family counseling sessions members toward whom he or she has ambivalent or bad feelings, because this person may still be interested in helping in caregiving.

It is generally preferable to have the same people participate in all family counseling sessions. In some cases, family members may be able to attend only some of the sessions, because of geographic distance or other restrictions on availability. They may be included in family counseling if the caregiver requests it. However, since consistent contact with the counselor enhances the ability of the participants to make needed plans and changes, the decision to change the composition of the group should be made with caution.

*How Is Family Defined?*  How a person defines family and identifies potential participants in counseling will reflect cultural norms and individual and family traditions. For some caregivers, godmothers, great aunts, cousins, long-time paid helpers, and friends are all potential candidates for involvement in the counseling sessions.

*Should People With AD Be Involved in Family Counseling?*
Caregivers often ask whether the person with AD should be involved in family counseling. This question raises sensitive issues and offers an opportunity for the counselor to help the family deal with the ongoing concern about how and when to involve the person with AD in other family matters. The intent of involving the

person with AD is to maintain his or her place within the family and to encourage his or her involvement in family matters. Nevertheless, it is also important to protect the patient from situations that may feel threatening or overwhelming and with which he or she is no longer able to cope because of diminished cognitive capacity.

Millie told the counselor she wanted all her children and Ted to come to the session. When she told Ted about the meeting, he said, "I don't need a meeting. There's nothing wrong with me. If you think you need help, you go." When Millie told this to the counselor, she explained that Ted's reaction was not unusual. It was his way of protecting himself by staying away from a potentially uncomfortable situation and acting as if everything was okay. Millie said, "Maybe it's better that he not be there at first."

There are arguments both for and against involving the ill family member. A patient in the early stage of AD retains many strengths and cognitive abilities and can contribute to making plans for himself and the family. Seeing the family interact with the person with AD can provide information about the way the family responds to the person that no amount of secondhand reporting can provide. A family's reasons for wanting the patient to attend might include the fact that they habitually include the patient in all family activities, wanting the counselor to witness firsthand how they are relating to the person with AD, or feeling guilty about talking about the patient "behind his or her back."

Other family members would prefer to exclude the patient. With the patient present, family members may not feel free to discuss the difficulties they encounter as caregivers. Caregivers and other family members may wish to have a safe place to discuss their reactions to the patient's illness, without worrying about the impact of the discussion on their ill relative. In addition, they may worry that the person with AD may be disruptive or upset by the discussion. They may want to talk about how to handle the patient's disruptive behavior or how to take over the patient's responsibilities and would be embarrassed to have that discussion in his or her presence. If the patient is no longer able to participate reasonably in a discussion and the family recognizes that this is the case, they may want to exclude him or her from family sessions.

It may be useful for the counselor to meet the person with AD before the decision about whether he or she is able to participate is made. Sometimes this can help to determine the extent to which it would be appropriate for him or her to be included. After the meeting, if the counselor thinks that the participation of the person with AD would not be productive, the counselor and caregiver can review the patient's strengths and impairments and the reasons for recommending against inclusion. The counselor may suggest trying the first session without the patient and then deciding about future meetings. A possible compromise is to include the patient in some family sessions and have other sessions without him or her.

## Inviting Family Members

Once the counselor has helped the caregiver identify family members and others he or she would like to have as participants in counseling, the feasibility of their participation should be reviewed. What would be the best location and time for the meeting to make it easiest for all participants to attend? If many of the desired participants live at a distance, a different format, such as a conference call, may need to be considered for at least some of the sessions.

In most cases the caregiver should be the person to invite family members and friends to the meeting. In the interest of time, if a caregiver is unable or unwilling to reach out to a family member but is committed to having the person at the meeting, the counselor may offer to initiate the contact on the caregiver's behalf.

If the counselor is initiating contact with a family member, he or she should review with the caregiver what information can be revealed. Family members may or may not be aware of the primary caregiver's participation in counseling or of the patient's diagnosis.

Family members may respond positively to the invitation to participate or may express reluctance. Some family members who have been estranged may welcome the opportunity for inclusion as a way of reconnecting with the family. Some may not want to attend for fear of being asked to do more than they want to do or may not choose to be involved with the caregiver or the patient. If potential participants express negative feelings toward another member of the family, the counselor may be able to persuade them to change their minds by explaining that the purpose of the meeting is to help support the caregiver and provide the best care for the patient.

## The Family Counseling Process

Calling a family meeting is a communication that something very important has happened in the family and may generate both relief and anxiety in the people who are invited to participate. The first meeting should provide an experience in which participants feel reassured that they will be understood and optimistic that they can get help and that a knowledgeable and evenhanded professional will maintain a safe environment. If this happens, the participants will be motivated to continue the process, which ultimately will provide the basis for their ongoing support for each other. As the first session has special meaning, so does the last, in which there is an expectation that they will carry on without the guidance of the counselor.

The counseling process should proceed in a way that ensures that what takes place within the session will have an impact beyond the session and beyond the time when the sessions end. Sessions should provide a model for future planning and problem solving. The counselor can convey the expectation that participants will learn and change and will be enabled, by the family counseling sessions, to improve their abilities to devise plans and coping strategies together over the course of the ever-changing illness. The way in which family members respond during the counseling sessions can provide all participants with information about each family member's capacity to collaborate in the care of the patient and in providing support for the caregiver.

The counselor should convey a realistic appraisal of each family member's level of involvement in the caregiving situation at all times. It is essential that the counselor be accepting of all feelings and experiences while neither condoning nor judging, even when family members reveal weakness, anger, pain, or behaviors of which they themselves or others disapprove. However, if a person describes behavior that is inappropriate, such as having lashed out at the person with AD, this is an opportunity for the counselor, while expressing understanding and compassion for the difficult situation, to suggest alternative means of coping with one's emotional reactions. The counselor's need to express positive regard for each participant does not preclude recognizing behavior that is not constructive, either in relation to the person with AD or to other family members, and exploring alternative responses.

The counselor's interaction with the family is always geared to understanding and meeting its needs, as well as to providing education and resources. All interactions with the family are therapeutic. Even the manner with which the counselor describes the protocol and gets feedback from the participants is an opportunity to model respectful communication and negotiation.

## The Initial Family Meeting

The initial family counseling session is an opportunity for the counselor to meet the members of the caregiver's family and to get a sense of how they interact and of how their relative's illness has impacted them as individuals and as a group. The counselor will provide the structure for the session but should have a flexible plan. A typical first session plan will have several components, including an introduction, exploration of family members' understanding of the impact of AD on the primary caregiver, identification of issues, tentative solutions and task allocation, summary, and agenda for next sessions.

In the course of this meeting, the counselor forms an impression that will guide the initial work with the family to ensure that it will be supportive of all the family caregivers, especially those who carry the greatest caregiving responsibilities, as well as the person with AD. The assessment of the family's interactions and the roles and contributions of the individual members to the family system is an ongoing process that builds on the information provided by the caregiver in the individual session. The counselor will continually refine the counseling strategies and adjust the content of the sessions as new information is obtained.

*Step One: Establishing Rapport*  The counselor initially establishes rapport with the family by introducing himself or herself, welcoming each individual family member to demonstrate respect for their individuality within the group. From the first contact with the family, a warm, accepting, but also clear form of communication will not only help to build an alliance in which they can trust that the counselor does not have a hidden agenda but also provide a model for communication among the participants.

> "Hi, I'm Gloria Sterling, and I've been meeting with your mother to talk about what it's been like for her since your Dad became ill. You can call me Gloria if that's comfortable for you. Please introduce yourselves, tell me what your relationship is to Millie, and let me know how you would like to be addressed. I know that you are all aware, as I am, that Ted is not here. I heard from your Mom that he didn't want to come to the meeting, and surely we'll talk more about that later."

This is an opportune time to clarify how each member would like to be addressed. For example, in some cultures elders are addressed in a formal fashion at all times, regardless of the setting. In other cases, it might be perfectly appropriate to refer to members by their first names or their familial role within the family (Mom or Dad).

***Step Two: Introducing the Protocol*** After the counselor and family members have introduced themselves, the counselor can explain to the participants that the main reason for the meetings is to be supportive of the person who has the primary responsibility for taking care of the patient and make sure that all participants are in general agreement with this agenda. The counselor clarifies the scope of the services the agency can provide, so that participants understand what they can reasonably expect, and then explains the guidelines for working together—the protocol, the ground rules, and the counselor's role. It is important for the counselor to assure the participants that what transpires in the meetings will remain confidential, unless they themselves agree to share the information with others, and that the opinions and needs of each person will be respected.

***Step Three: Getting to Know Each Person's Perspective***
The counselor can create an atmosphere of sharing that initiates the collaborative process by asking each of the participants to describe any changes they have observed in the person with AD and their understanding of the illness. This gives all participants an opportunity to hear each other's perspectives and may also make it possible for each family member to become aware of the difficulties faced

by the primary caregiver. It may, in fact, be the first time that these thoughts and feelings have been expressed in front of all family members in a group.

The counselor opened this phase of the meeting by saying, "I imagine that you have noticed changes in your Dad over the last year or so. As you all know, your father has been diagnosed with Alzheimer's disease. I understand this is the first time you have come together as a family to discuss what's going on. Would each of you share with us what you have observed and what you understand about the illness." Matt said, "You know, I've been worried for a long time, because Dad hasn't been calling me the way he used to, and when I call him, he gets off the phone as fast as he can, but no one said anything to me, and I didn't want to be the first to bring it up." Tom said he had noticed something was wrong and was relieved that finally he knew what the problem was so that something could be done. Carol said, "Relieved? Are you nuts? That means he'll be in a nursing home by this time next year." Her husband, Don, said they were exaggerating: "Of course he's changed; that's what happens to most people when they get old." The counselor made a note to herself that she would need to clarify some of the myths of aging that people often have.

After these initial comments, the counselor will guide the family toward the understanding of how their perceptions tie into the goal of these sessions, to help the primary caregiver.

"I see that each of you has observed the changes in Dad. Since it looks like Mom spends almost all her time with Dad, I wonder how you all think it's been for her?" Carol said, "Now that you mention it, Mom used to love to play with the kids, but now she complains that they get on her nerves." Millie responded, "I hadn't even noticed that. I can't get your father's problems out of my mind. I'm terrified that he may be fired. How could he live with the humiliation? And how will he feel if I continue working? I'm not ready to retire." The counselor encouraged the family members to express their feelings about what was happening to Ted and Millie.

***Step Four: Identifying Issues and Problems to Be Addressed***
Each family is unique in the way that it will approach the goal of
supporting the primary caregiver. In the process of discussing their
own perspectives on the illness, all participants will have indicated
a certain level of knowledge about the disease and have introduced
the issues they feel are important to resolve in order to provide support for the primary caregiver. They also will have identified issues
that are important to their own lives.

The counselor listens for both individual perspectives and needs
and the commonalities among them and can then share these observations with the participants in order to develop a basis for identifying and discussing the issues and problems to be addressed. The
counselor can help each family member understand the points of
view of the others and see the similarities among them.

> The family thought it was important for Ted to quit working before he
> got fired. The counselor pointed out that Millie would need support
> to broach this subject with Ted and to handle his reaction. Matt said,
> "I don't think there's any good way to tell him. What reason will we
> give?" Carol said, "What will Dad do all day if Mom doesn't stay
> home with him?" Her brothers said Millie should not have to quit her
> job because Ted quit his. The counselor said, "It seems like the most
> immediate problem is that something has to be done about Dad's
> job situation in a way that doesn't cause Mom to give up something
> that's important to her." She then commented that it's always a kind
> of balancing act to keep everybody's needs in mind.

In the discussion that follows, the counselor will help clarify the
issues and get general consensus about which ones will be
addressed and in what order. The counselor may have to introduce
issues that family members have not mentioned, possibly because
they are unaware of the necessity for thinking about them, or
because they find it too difficult or stressful to discuss them.
Medical, legal, and financial planning for long-term care are essential
issues to be raised.

In this phase of the discussion, past issues and unresolved family
conflicts may be disclosed. Once in awhile, family members have
different opinions about who should or should not have been

invited to the family sessions. The counselor can acknowledge their discomfort or displeasure and reinforce the fact that they came because they care about the person who is ill and the primary caregiver. The counselor can comment to the family that it is natural for old conflicts to be activated by a new stressful situation. However, the purpose of the meeting is to focus on the current situation and explain that past issues can be more effectively addressed at another time and place.

Occasionally, one or more family members will have a particularly severe reaction to the illness and need extra help. If this is beyond the scope of the family meetings, it should be addressed in additional individual sessions, either within the agency or by referral to appropriate additional services.

***Step Five: Starting the Process of Change***   The family may have identified many issues, some of which can be addressed over time and others that require immediate attention. To help the family begin to resolve these issues without overwhelming them, the counselor can help the family identify one or two objectives that are important to them and are also relatively easy to achieve before the next meeting and can help the family to allocate tasks.

Some of the problems and issues are of a practical nature and can be solved by accomplishing concrete tasks. Suitable tasks might include gathering all relevant financial documents, enrolling the person with AD in the Safe Return program of the Alzhiemer's Association, visiting a day care center, visiting with the patient, or calling the caregiver more frequently. Some tasks may have immediate impact, while others may set the stage for future planning. In addition to their obvious practical value, assignments give the family an opportunity to "practice" working together and to identify areas of difficulty that can be addressed in the next session.

It is the counselor's role to guide the discussion of task allocation, taking into account the needs, strengths, and limitations of each family member. Geographic distance, financial means, emotional capacity, conflicting care needs of their own nuclear families, and career demands all play a part in determining the ability of each family member to contribute to the care of the ill relative and provide support for the primary caregiver. Family members who are unable to provide hands-on care may be able to contribute to the care of the patient in other ways or be willing to pay for an aide to be hired. Each family member has to assess how much of his or her financial, physical, and emotional budget can be allocated to the care of the patient.

In addition to concrete issues, emotional needs and feelings may be expressed. Some family members may feel that their efforts are unappreciated, taken for granted, or misunderstood. In this environment, family members may reveal feelings of sadness, regret, and disappointment. By having the whole family together in counseling, each member may be able to give and receive support and be less alone with his or her feelings. A family member who is critical and unaware of it may begin to recognize the impact he or she is having on others. When feelings are explored, family members may come to understand and be more sensitive to each other and make an effort to change their communication style.

Everyone tried to think of steps to take to help out. Matt offered to talk to a friend of his who worked at the same company as Dad to find out about their retirement policy. Tom said he would talk to Dad about how great it would be if he had more time to spend on his favorite hobby, fishing. The counselor pointed out that they were choosing strategies to protect Ted from confronting the effects of his illness and asked them if that was their intention. They all said that they were uncomfortable talking to him about it at that point. She suggested that they discuss their concerns about what might happen if they spoke more directly to their father.

*Step Six: Concluding the Session*   In concluding the session, the counselor can summarize his or her observations of what has occurred. The counselor's comments should include appreciation of the willingness of the family members to attend the counseling sessions and foster support for the primary caregiver, recognition of the family's strengths as well as the interpersonal difficulties they may need to overcome, identification of areas in which further education is needed, and identification of issues and problems that will be the focus of ongoing work.

The counselor reviewed some of the pros and cons of talking to Ted about his illness that family members had raised. She said that it wasn't possible to predict how he would react and that they should take their cues from Ted and follow his lead. If he seemed to be open to a frank discussion, they could address work issues with him. If he preferred to talk "around" the issue or to deny that he was having any problems, they should not try to confront or convince him of the truth. The counselor said she understood that this was a difficult situation for everyone in the family and recognized the efforts they were making to support each other and to address Ted and Millie's needs. In closing, she said that they could continue to work on this issue next week. She also suggested some books they could read to learn more about Alzheimer's disease.

Sufficient time should be left at the end of the session to make plans for the next meeting. The NYU intervention strategy includes ad hoc counseling (described in detail in Chapter 5), which provides a form of ongoing support that can be accessed at any time the caregiver or family members reach out for it. If ad hoc counseling is a part of the protocol in the setting in which the counselor works, time should be reserved at the end of the session to discuss how this resource can be used and to assure the participants that they can contact the counselor between sessions. This resource can be of benefit, if used correctly, to offer additional support and information between sessions. The counselor should caution the family not to disclose information in ad hoc calls that they would be unwilling to share in the family sessions. The counselor should be careful not to allow an individual relationship with one member of the family to develop or to engage in private counseling about issues that should be addressed with the entire family.

## Ongoing Counseling Sessions

All counseling sessions include feedback on the previous session, the experience of carrying out the tasks participants agreed to try to accomplish, identification of difficulties—what worked and what didn't—making plans for continued efforts, new problems that have arisen since the previous session, and issues that can now be addressed because others have been resolved or relinquished.

Throughout the sessions, although the explicit discussion may be task related, the underlying theme is almost always the emotional meaning of caregiving and the illness of the patient. Education is an important component of all sessions and should be tailored to the knowledge level and needs of all members of the family.

***Step One: Reviewing the Previous Session***   At the beginning of each session, the counselor should briefly review what transpired in the previous session. The counselor can ask participants for reactions to the previous session and whether participants have continued the dialogue after the session to reinforce the concept of process. The responses will help the counselor gain further understanding of the family dynamics and make him or her aware of family members who may potentially support each other and share responsibilities. After they have each expressed their thoughts, the counselor may point out similarities and differences in reactions among the respondents.

***Step Two: Reviewing Previous Commitments***   In the previous session, participants may have agreed to undertake concrete tasks or to try to change their patterns of communication or behavior. The counselor should be sensitive to the fact that people will have had varying degrees of success in following through on their commitments. In addition, they may have reconsidered and decided against doing what, in the spirit of the session, they had said they would or realized that there were things that had not been mentioned in the session that were worthwhile doing. The counselor should introduce the discussion in a way that does not make family members feel competitive with each other but that focuses on the tasks that need to be accomplished.

The discussion should elicit answers to the following questions. Have the family members been able to make progress with the tasks they took on? If so, how did they do it? How did they feel when they accomplished the task or successfully changed their behavior, and what obstacles did they need to overcome? If the assignments were not fulfilled, were the impediments emotional, practical, or a result of conflicts among family members?

At the start of the session, Millie told the counselor that Ted had agreed to retire. The counselor asked how they had achieved this. Tom said that one Sunday after their usual family dinner he had taken advantage of a moment alone with Ted to ask him whether he was still enjoying work. "Dad said, 'What makes you ask?' I told him I had noticed he didn't talk about work the way he used to. Dad said, 'You know, your Mom said the same thing. When she said that, it made me think about retiring sooner than I had said I would.'" Millie said that later that evening, after the kids had left, Ted started talking about how nice it would be if he had more time to fish and garden and that maybe it was time to retire after all. Millie said that the following Sunday at dinner, Ted told the family that he had decided to retire. Carol said, "I told him I was glad he had made this decision, because now I could spend more time with him since neither of us would be working." Millie said she was relieved that the problem of Ted's working seemed to have been solved. Tom said, "We thought we were following Dad's lead by not talking directly about his illness with him. I hope we did the right thing." Carol said, "I know we did."

It is important to pay attention to the reactions of all family members to each other in order to build a mutually supportive team effort. Nevertheless, the reaction of the primary caregiver to the efforts of other family members is paramount, as it will serve either to reinforce their efforts on his or her behalf or highlight where misunderstandings or miscommunications still exist. Further discussion can lead the family members to a greater understanding of how to be more effective in their efforts to help.

### Step Three: Identifying Issues for Current Consideration

In the course of the session, it will become clear that as some issues have been resolved, others have taken on a higher priority. In addition, new issues, problems, and conflicts will emerge. These can be discussed in the same way as the original issues were in the first session. Family members can be helped to recognize any similarities these problems have to the previous problems and how approaches that worked in the past can be applied to solving the current problems.

Carol said that they had solved the problem of how Ted spent his days, so Millie could keep her job. Carol went to Ted's house after she dropped the kids off at school and kept him company while Millie worked. Don said, "This is all well and good and I know Millie and Ted need help, but what about us? We have three kids and Carol's never around anymore. She seems to be spending all her time with Ted. Why doesn't Diane do something? She only has a part-time job, and her kids are older." The counselor observed that, although the family thought they had solved one problem, there was now another: Carol had taken on too much. Tom said he didn't think Ted really needed someone around all the time at this stage of his illness. When she heard Tom say this, Carol reluctantly agreed that she was being overprotective, but she insisted that some steps had to be taken to be sure Ted was safe. Carol said, "He likes to go for long walks. What if he gets lost?" This gave the counselor the opportunity to talk about safety issues in and outside of the home. She described the Safe Return program and suggested that they enroll Ted.

***Step Four: Concluding the Session*** At the end of each session, the counselor can summarize and review the progress that has been made and the goals that remain to be achieved. Task assignments should be reviewed. The counselor should also discuss the time and date of the next session and who will attend. If the next meeting will be the last family session, then the family should be reminded of that fact so that it does not come as a surprise and they can prepare for the termination.

## The Final Session

The counselor should begin the session by acknowledging that this is the last session and giving the participants a summary of observations about the progress that has been made. The goal is to empower the family to continue on their own what was begun during these sessions.

This session will then follow the pattern of the previous sessions, including a review of the previous session and progress that has been made, and identification of new issues. In the last session, when new issues are identified, a greater emphasis should be placed on relating them to previously solved issues. It is hoped that the family will have understood the underlying principles of sharing responsibilities and providing support for the primary caregiver.

The counselor will then ask the participants to share their own observations and feelings about what has transpired. They can also be asked to reflect on what it means to them that this is the last family session.

The counselor reviewed the progress that had been made. She noted, however, that Carol looked worried. Carol said she was still concerned about Ted having to go to a nursing home, since she remembered visiting her grandmother at one and hating it. The counselor said she was sure that this must have been a very upsetting experience for her, but that the need for that kind of care would probably not happen for a long time and that that many people with Alzheimer's disease are cared for at home. Maybe we should talk about how Ted is spending his time now.

Millie said Ted spent a lot of time in the garden and had gone back to his stamp collection, which he hadn't touched in years. Carol said she picked Ted up a few times a week and brought him with her to her children's Little League practice. Tom took Ted fishing on weekends. Millie said she felt that Ted was less tense than he had been when he was working and thought she could keep her own job, at least for the time being. She said she had never wanted to bother her children with her problems, but now she realized how wonderful it was to have them helping out.

The counselor reminded the family that this was the final session. She told them that she was available by phone should they have any further problems. Everyone seemed glad to know they had someone to call. She also recommended that they join support groups in their neighborhoods for caregivers of people with AD.

If there is a system for ad hoc counseling, the participants can be reminded that this resource is available for ongoing advice and counseling, and the protocol for its use should be reviewed. The session should end with some final words of recognition of the progress that has been made, goals still unmet, and encouragement for the future.

After the final family session, in the NYU intervention protocol there is an individual counseling session with the primary caregiver to assess the effectiveness of the family sessions from the perspective of the caregiver and to make referrals as warranted by the current needs of the caregiver for resources, counseling, and support.

## Understanding the Family

Every family has a culture of its own with a style of communicating with each other and of relating to the outside world. The NYU protocol does not include a formal structured family assessment. However, the NYU counselors make an informal assessment of the way the family functions as a unit and the part each member plays by observing how they interact during a counseling session.

In working with families of a person with Alzheimer's disease, we have found that caregiver appraisal and reaction to the behaviors common in people with AD, as well as family conflict and degree of cohesiveness, have a significant impact on caregiver well-being and should be evaluated and addressed when appropriate in the counseling process.

If one views the family as a system, it becomes apparent that changes such as the emergence of a serious chronic illness in one member will reverberate throughout the system and be felt by every member of the family. The concepts described below, many derived from the family therapy literature, can provide a framework for organizing observations, selecting goals for the ongoing work, anticipating areas of difficulty, and evaluating the outcome. They can help to highlight areas of strength as well as potential roadblocks to responding to the crises that are part of the ongoing process of caring for someone with Alzheimer's disease.

### *Openness*

Families differ in their degree of openness to each other and to the outside world. When the family's traditions or norms preclude its members from interacting with outsiders beyond a narrowly defined range of contacts, it may be difficult for them to comfortably seek formal support, including counseling. Parents in such families may have strict rules about what the children can be told and how much is shared with people outside the family. For example, if parents voice the sentiment, "Don't wash your dirty linen in public," it suggests that problems are to be kept within the family. A member of such a family may be unwilling to disclose his or her feelings in front of other family members or an outsider if they choose to come to counseling at all. Families such as these are unlikely to publicly acknowledge that their relative has Alzheimer's disease and may feel ambivalent about seeking help. When an individual member of such a family does approach a health care provider, he or she will need a great deal of understanding and support from the counselor in trying to engage other family members in the counseling process.

When trying to engage the more closed family, the counselor needs to demonstrate respect for their style by not setting up the expectation that they reveal private family matters. It may be more useful to take a more objective informational approach to helping such families. The counselor can take a didactic approach, discussing what is known about Alzheimer's disease, and try to establish a dialogue about concrete facts and issues.

A family that is more open may express themselves more freely and use the counseling sessions to address their emotional reactions to their relative's illness and to accept help in dealing with them. When emotions are too intense, however, the counselor's task may be to help the family to contain them and focus their energy constructively.

## Relationships and Roles Within the Family

One purpose of family counseling is to educate the family about the ways in which AD has altered the patient's ability to function in his or her former role in the family. If the family has a clear hierarchical structure, roles tend to be clearly defined. In such a family, when the person who holds the power and authority becomes ill with Alzheimer's disease, the family may have difficulty reorganizing. They are losing an authority figure and may have neither prior experience nor confidence in their ability to take on his or her role. If the father was the primary decision maker and acknowledged leader of the family, it may be difficult for the wife or adult child in such a family to assume tasks formerly performed by the father. The problem is exacerbated when the person with AD is unable or unwilling to share or relinquish these tasks and family members fear confronting him or her. Counseling can help family members take on new roles while continuing to honor and respect the patient's place in the family.

One of the dynamics one observes within a family is the intensity and exclusivity of the relationships among its members. When alliances between specific family members exclude others, they may create polarizations and splits within the family that prevent the family from functioning as a unit. An intense bond between a spouse caregiver and one of his or her children, for example, may make it difficult for other siblings to be helpful and supportive of the caregiving parent. They may feel that their efforts are intrusive or unwelcome.

## *Coping Style*

The stress-process model suggests that the way in which stressors are appraised has an effect on the magnitude of the reaction. When family members understand that the behavior and functioning of their relative are caused by illness, they will react differently than if they believe they are purposeful. The response of each family member to the stress of caring for a relative with AD also depends on an understanding of the options and resources available to deal with the situation and the sense of control over it. If individual family members feel powerless, thwarted, and unsupported by the rest of the family, they will appraise the situation as more stressful than if they feel supported and encouraged in their efforts to cope.

The way a family responds to the demands of caring for a person with AD may have roots in previous experience with other stressful life events. If they mobilized their resources and worked together effectively in the past, the counselor can help them to identify constructive strategies they have used and suggest ways for similar coping mechanisms to be used effectively in the current situation. Families without a history of coming together under stress may discover that they have the necessary coping skills or may be open to developing them in the course of counseling.

Counseling can help each member of the family increase his or her abilities to help each other cope with the demands of caring for a person with AD. The counselor can get some idea of each participant's coping patterns by asking specifically about how he or she has responded to previous stressors. A caregiver's ability to adapt to stressful experiences may be influenced by social support, financial resources (eg, income and the ability to purchase needed services), and psychological resources or personality characteristics (eg, self-esteem, sense of control).

Some research suggests that a more problem-focused, information-seeking, rather than emotion-based, coping style may lead to better outcomes. The counselor needs to be aware of individual coping styles and how they relate to the overall family response and to mobilize the use of the most constructive methods.

## *Communication Style*

The counselor should be aware of both the content and the process of family members' communications with each other. Body language, amount of eye contact, and the degree to which members of the family are paying attention to each other or tuning each other out can give a counselor an indication about the style in which family members communicate with each other. Some family members may speak openly, while others may be more reserved. Some people are able to express their feelings directly and take responsibility for them. Others will either project their own feelings onto others or induce others to act or express their feelings for them.

Families differ in their level of comfort in discussing certain topics such as illness and death. In some families it is not customary for parents to discuss certain topics with their adult children. When families are reluctant to discuss their relative's illness, the symptoms it causes, and his or her personal care needs, the counselor should acknowledge that they may not be accustomed to speaking about some of the issues that they are now confronting. Nevertheless, they will need to find ways to meet the patient's needs and to communicate with each other about them. It may be possible to use the safe environment of the counseling session to practice overcoming these barriers. One way to encourage this is for the counselor to speak directly about a symptom such as incontinence, helping the family to tolerate the discomfort this may create.

The counselor has to attune himself or herself to the family's style of communication in order to work effectively with it. The counselor's ability to understand the meaning of the communication as well as the process can enable him or her to help family members to become aware of their feelings and needs and, if the environment is safe enough, to risk expressing their emotions and asking for help directly. The ways in which the counselor speaks realistically and empathically about Alzheimer's disease and the struggles families face can encourage family members to speak more openly and directly about their relative's illness.

## Culture and Religion

Culture and religious beliefs can influence a family's understanding of the meaning of Alzheimer's disease and determine its members' response to the patient's need for care and who will provide it. Religious beliefs and spirituality can also provide caregivers with a context within which to understand and accept the illness and their responsibilities for providing care.

A family's cultural values, ideas, beliefs, and behaviors can provide a structural framework for collaborating in support of the primary caregiver of a person with AD. On the other hand, cultural and religious values and norms may cause conflict across generations and within a generation due to differing levels of assimilation. Adult children, siblings, partners, and other family members may have assimilated into the dominant culture to greater or lesser degrees. This can create conflict among family members about what is appropriate support and care for the person with AD and the primary caregiver. Assimilated members from families with traditional views who are not meeting other family members' expectations might be viewed by them as rejecting their caregiving responsibilities.

If the family comes from a cultural background different from that of the counselor, especially if the family is not assimilated into the dominant culture of the community, the counselor's ability to be effective will depend on understanding a family's cultural uniqueness—values, expected role behaviors, historical experiences, language, and religious beliefs. If the counselor believes that a family can get the help they need more comfortably and effectively by using a specialized service, it is important that they understand why the referral is being made so that they do not feel rejected or that they have failed in any way.

## Assessing and Improving the Family's Knowledge of AD

It is especially important to assess the family's knowledge of AD and its current and future effect on the functioning of the ill person, and of treatment and care options. The extent and depth of the education the counselor will provide during family counseling will depend on what the family already knows and how its members apply their knowledge to planning for the future and to dealing with the day-to-day issues of caring for and relating to a person with AD.

Not infrequently, some family members will be more aware of the current knowledge about diagnosis, symptoms, and treatment of AD, while others have little knowledge or even false beliefs about AD and its effects. These differences can create conflicts about the cause of the patient's symptoms, appropriate treatment, or the possible options for care. They can also lead family caregivers to disagree about the patient's abilities and limitations. Those who have little knowledge about Alzheimer's disease may attribute intentionality to behaviors that are beyond the patient's control. Education in the family counseling session can help ensure that all participants have received basic information and avoid conflicts due to lack of reliable information.

The more knowledgeable the family members are, the better able they will be to assess the needs, strengths, and limitations of the person with AD and the primary caregiver, as well as their abilities to satisfy these needs. To be most effective, education about AD should be ongoing and integrated into the counseling process.

The counselor should find out how each member of the family prefers to receive information, for example, from written materials, seminars, or the Internet. The counselor can also provide or recommend appropriate literature, videos, or other resources that participants can review independently and, if they choose, discuss in a session. It is important to remind family members that not all information they obtain from the media is reliable, and they should try to refer to more than one source.

Families should be given only as much information as they can constructively use. Too little information may prevent them from understanding the patient and caregiver and developing an appropriate care plan. Too much information can be overwhelming and frightening and can immobilize family members rather than enhancing their functioning. Many people are ambivalent about how much information they really want. The reasons for requests for information should be explored, because they can provide the counselor with insight into their underlying meaning as well as the family's understanding of the illness and the sensitivity with which the counselor should present the information. It is generally best not to tell families about the entire course of AD all at once, but rather to concentrate on information about the disease as it is currently affecting their relative and what they can expect in the near future.

The counselor may consider the following outline as a guide to the kinds of questions to ask family members in order to determine their knowledge about AD and its effects:

1. Diagnosis

    a. When, where, and from whom did your relative receive a diagnosis?

    b. What were you told about the disease?

    c. Do you have any questions that were unanswered?

2. Disease progression

    a. What do you know about the progression of the disease?

    b. How did you learn about the course of the disease?

    c. What are some of the impairments you've observed in your relative?

    d. Do you know what symptoms are due to AD and what might be due to some other cause?

3. Care options

    a. What options for care and support do you know about?

    b. Where do you get information about options for care?

    c. What types of resources have been most helpful to you?

4. Treatment options

    a. What do you know about available treatment?

    b. What do you know about experimental treatments?

By asking these questions, the counselor will learn the level of understanding the participants have about the illness and the areas in which further education is needed. This also provides an opportunity for the counselor to dispel common myths about AD and other misinformation family members may have.

## Summary

The impact of AD will vary and depends on many factors, including the role the ill person previously played in the family, the relationships among family members, other problems affecting individual members and the family as a whole, the coping skills of family members, and how much family members understand about the illness and availability of resources.

The desire to progress through normative life stages does not stop when a family member is diagnosed with AD. Caring for a person with AD can create conflicts for the adult children in a family between their roles in their new families and loyalty and obligation to their parents. It can also affect the parents, who did not anticipate having their children back in their lives as caregivers.

It is not unusual for negative interactions among family members to increase in response to the stress of caring for a person with AD. Family counseling can make family members aware of the extent to which their relative's illness and their caregiving responsibilities are the underlying reason for the deterioration in their relationships. By directly addressing these problems, they may find their relationships have improved. Those who are not contributing can be encouraged to become more active in caregiving. Counseling can also help ensure that others who are willing to help will not be excluded. A byproduct of successful collaboration in caregiving may be overall enhanced family functioning.

# Counselor Checklist

### Preparing for Family Involvement

☐ Address caregiver reluctance by explaining the benefits of family support.

☐ Use the assessment as a basis for discussion in identifying who should be included in family counseling.

☐ Determine if the person with AD will attend, meeting with the patient, if necessary, to evaluate the extent to which it is appropriate to include him or her.

### The Initial Family Meeting

☐ Introduce yourself and ask the family members to do the same.

☐ Explain the protocol, purpose of the meeting, scope of the services the agency provides, ground rules, and the counselor's role.

☐ Give each person an opportunity to express his or her perspective on the situation.

☐ Clarify the issues and get a consensus on which to address and in what order.

☐ Identify one or two objectives and help the family allocate tasks.

☐ Summarize your observations and make plans for the next session.

### Ongoing Counseling Sessions

☐ Review the previous session, asking the participants for their reactions.

☐ Review previous commitments, asking participants to discuss their progress and how they felt in carrying out tasks.

☐ Identify issues for current consideration.

☐ Summarize progress and review the goals still remaining.

### Final Session

☐ Acknowledge that it is the last session and summarize the progress made toward achieving goals.

☐ Repeat the pattern of previous sessions. When new issues are identified, relate them to previously solved issues.

## Understanding the Family

☐ Recognize that families have differing degrees of openness and tailor counseling to accommodate the differences in style.

☐ Help family members take on new roles while respecting the patient's place in the family.

☐ Be aware of individual coping styles as you guide family members to help the primary caregiver cope with the demands of caregiving.

☐ Be aware of the family style of communication in order to facilitate the expression of feelings.

☐ Recognize a family's cultural uniqueness and refer them to a specialized service if that would be beneficial to the family.

☐ Assess the family's knowledge of AD by asking them questions about the diagnosis, disease progression, care, and treatment options.

# 5

# AD HOC COUNSELING

The symptoms of Alzheimer's disease (AD), the functional and cognitive capacity of the patient, and the caregiver's need for support, information, and resources change over time. The NYU intervention strategy responds to these needs by supplementing individual and family counseling with telephone counseling when needed. We call this *ad hoc* counseling.

The concept of ad hoc counseling as a formal part of the intervention evolved from the experience of counselors at NYU, who observed that even knowledgeable caregivers who had received in-person counseling were calling their counselors with questions about care and resources, as well as for emotional support. The objective of ad hoc counseling is to respond to changing needs by providing caregivers with continual professional support throughout the duration of the illness. This system provides families with a safety net, a comfortable and secure place to which they can turn for relief, support, resources, information, and assistance when they need it.

This chapter describes the components of ad hoc counseling, guides counselors through the process of counseling over the telephone, and discusses how to set up an ad hoc system of counseling.

## The Benefits of Ad Hoc Counseling

Ad hoc counseling was designed to provide a quick response to family members in an expedient and cost-effective manner. A short consultation can potentially prevent a situation from escalating into a major problem that could then only be solved by more extensive professional help. The immediacy of the response by someone familiar to the caregiver can diffuse an emotionally charged situation. A caregiver may also derive enormous benefit from several 15-minute telephone conversations with a professional while solving a problem or dealing with a crisis, and then need no further help for several months. The availability of the resource is, in itself, reassuring.

## Ad Hoc Call

Gladys had been taking care of Nat for many years and very rarely complained. One day, she called the counselor, saying, "Last night I actually hit Nat! He knocked a full glass of milk over and it spilled on my clean tablecloth. This kind of thing has happened a hundred times before, but last night I just couldn't bear it. Afterward, I felt so bad about myself. What kind of person hits someone who can't help himself?" The counselor said, "Gladys, I've known you a long time, and I think the kind of person who hits a man who can't help himself is overtired and never takes a rest, no matter how many times people tell her she's doing too much. You don't need to feel bad. Just think about the fact that if you don't take care of yourself, you can't take care of Nat." Gladys said, "You know, my kids keep telling me I look exhausted and say they will take care of their father so I can take a break. Maybe I should go visit my sister in Florida for a few days and let them take care of Nat."

Ad hoc counseling provides continuity of care in two ways: the duration of the service and the continuity of the service provider. At NYU, families were made aware from the beginning that the intervention included help for all participating members and that all family members would be invited to contact the counselor as needed regarding issues of Alzheimer's care for the duration of the patient's illness. Although ad hoc counseling does not preclude the use of other resources by caregivers, it offers families the comfort of knowing that they do not have to search for a new source of counseling and support each time a difficult situation occurs.

Whenever possible, services are provided by the counselor who worked with the family in individual and family sessions. Caregivers may feel most comfortable calling a counselor who worked with them previously and with whom they have an established relationship. The counselor is already familiar with the caregiver's situation, the caregiver and counselor have an established rapport, and the counselor may be able to provide insight into the issue at hand that a new counselor will not.

When services cannot be provided by the counselor who helped the family in individual and family sessions, for instance, in the case of emergencies or when the original counselor is no longer at the agency, continuity is maintained by means of thorough written documentation of counseling sessions and telephone consultations that can be accessed by another counselor at any time.

## Introducing Ad Hoc Counseling Services to the Caregiver

For caregivers to use the system appropriately and to feel comfortable calling, the nature of the service should be clear. It is a support and counseling service to answer questions about caregiving for a family member with AD. The service can be made easy to use by supplying caregivers with an explanatory brochure or card with the telephone number on it.

The following parameters should be explained to potential callers:

■ Who can use the service (the client only or anyone in the family)

■ The hours during which the telephone service is available

■ What issues they can call about

■ How often they can call

■ The circumstances under which additional counseling can be made available

■ Whether calls will be answered by their regular counselor or any counselor on the staff

■ Whether the service is equipped to handle medical or psychiatric emergencies

■ If applicable, how much the service costs and whether these costs are covered by insurance

## The Ad Hoc Counseling Process

Ad hoc telephone counseling consists of short, episodic contacts in which the emphasis is mainly on solving specific problems and issues, providing information and resources, or helping and supporting the caregiver in a crisis or emergency. Through these telephone contacts, the counselor tries to identify the difficulties that are exacerbating a situation and guide the caregiver toward its resolution.

Many ad hoc calls may seem, on the surface, to be simply requests for information but may, in fact, be motivated by an unstated need for emotional support. Prior experience with the help-seeking style of caregivers during formal counseling will guide the counselor in understanding the probable underlying reason for the call.

The process of telephone counseling relies on many of the skills and techniques counselors use in individual and family counseling. However, there are two important differences. The first is that, in ad hoc counseling, the counselor helps the caregiver to use existing strengths and coping skills rather than to develop new ones. The second is that, unlike in-person counseling in which you can use many forms of communication, the counselor will have to rely entirely on nonvisual aspects of communication when engaging a caller over the telephone.

The following steps are suggestions to be used flexibly and modified as necessary, or possibly eliminated, in response to the needs of the caller, the apparent urgency of the call, and the familiarity of the counselor and the caller.

### Step One: Making a Connection With the Caller

Because they are not able to see body language and facial expression, counselors will have to listen carefully to verbal cues such as the exact words that a caller uses, the tone of the caregiver's voice, or the timing and frequency of hesitations or pauses to get a sense of the caregiver's emotional state during the call and to know how to respond.

Ted's illness had progressed to the point where he was at the moderate stage of dementia. One day Millie called her counselor, and it was obvious from her first words that she was very upset. "Gloria, you have to help me! Ted kicked me! I can't believe it. He never did anything like that in all our years of marriage!" Gloria said, "That must be horrible for you. Are you hurt?"

A counselor can build an alliance with the caller by asking questions that indicate interest and by listening carefully to the responses. The counselor should try to make an emotional connection with the caller that conveys reassurance that he or she is there to help. The counselor can create a safe, comfortable environment for a caregiver to share his or her thoughts by using verbal cues such as tone of voice and carefully chosen words. Often this will calm the caregiver, who can then start to share the reason for the call.

## Step Two: Assess the Severity of the Situation

A counselor will need to assess whether the situation warrants immediate attention, whether the caller is distraught but the situation is not dangerous, or whether the person is not unusually distressed but is asking for general support or information. This is very important when caregivers call in a heightened emotional state and may not be able to make these distinctions themselves.

On rare occasions, a caregiver will call about an acute medical or psychiatric emergency. It will be necessary for counselors to decide whether to suggest that the caregiver call 911 or to make that call themselves; counselors may also suggest that the caregiver inform other family members. Sometimes caregivers feel uncomfortable calling 911, because they want to avoid facing the fact that the situation is serious or they believe it is not serious enough to call for emergency assistance. The counselor can reassure the caregiver that, while the situation may not seem to need emergency care, calling 911 may, in fact, be the fastest way to assess its severity and obtain whatever care is needed.

After making sure that Millie was not physically hurt and that Ted had calmed down, Gloria realized that this was an emotional crisis and not a medical emergency and that she needed to understand more about the situation.

## Step Three: Gain an Understanding of the Reason for the Call

The next step is to understand the situation, the context, and its meaning to the caregiver. The questions a counselor asks will help him or her and the caregiver understand what may have precipitated the event that was the reason for the call. A counselor may be able to help the caregiver gain new perspective on the problem by encouraging him or her to acknowledge and express feelings and thoughts about the situation and understand the effect they have on their response to it.

> "Millie, I can understand that you are upset, but could you tell me a little bit about what was going on just before this happened?" Millie said, "Remember I told you that Ted has been going to day care?" and went on to describe their morning routine, getting him dressed, fixing breakfast, and so on. She said this usually took about an hour and a half. That morning her boss wanted her to come to the office half an hour earlier than usual, so she had to get Ted to the day care center earlier, too.

## Step Four: Explore the Caregiver's Attempts at Resolving the Problem or Issue

Most caregivers will try to solve a problem or issue themselves before reaching out for help. The counselor can get a sense of how the caregiver approached the situation by obtaining the following information. From the answers, the counselor can understand what caused the caregiver to respond in the way he or she did. Is it due to a misunderstanding of the effect of AD? How did the caregiver's emotional state influence the response to the situation? How did that response affect the situation? If this was not the first time the problem occurred, was the caregiver's response different this time and, if so, why? Are other family members, friends, or professionals working with him or her on this problem? If the counselor has previous experience with this caregiver and is familiar with his or her situation, it may be possible to suggest methods of handling the current situation that have been successfully used by this person in the past.

"I didn't want to change Ted's schedule, because I know that's bad for people with AD, so I woke him up at his usual time. I told him we had to hurry. I figured I could get him dressed faster, but when I tried to put his shoes on, he kicked me!" At this point, the counselor understood that Ted was probably reacting to Millie's tension about being late and attempts to get him to go through his usual morning routine more quickly. She also realized that Millie didn't understand that Ted was at a stage in his illness that made it impossible for him to understand why it was important to hurry or tolerate the stress of being rushed.

## Step Five: Develop New Alternatives to Solving the Problem

Based on his or her understanding of the situation and previous attempts at solutions, the counselor can discuss alternative approaches with the caregiver, assessing the feasibility of each option. It is generally a good idea to help caregivers understand the concepts behind the recommended strategies to strengthen their ability to find solutions on their own in the future.

Sometimes the counselor may encourage the caregiver to call several times. If a problem is complicated, a caregiver may need to make several calls, taking a few steps in between, to fully address the situation. The counselor may also encourage the caregiver to call again if the counselor feels that the underlying cause for the call is a need for emotional support.

The counselor told Millie she was right that people with AD have difficulty changing schedules, but that what she hadn't anticipated was how hard it would be for him to hurry. She explained to Millie that it was normal for people at this stage to move slowly, and that they may respond negatively to pressure. "Maybe he was also reacting to a feeling that you were under pressure." Ted couldn't tell her in words that he was upset at being rushed. The kick was his way of showing her he was frustrated. Millie said, "Oh, I get it. He didn't really want to hurt me, but I guess that means I can't ever plan to get to work early. What should I tell my boss the next time he asks me?" The counselor realized Millie understood that Ted's needs had changed but hadn't thought about how to meet her own needs, as well. She said, "Well, that's one way to look at it, Millie. Why don't we try to come up with a solution that works for both of you?" They talked about various alternatives, and Millie said it might have been better to wake Ted up a bit earlier and let him get ready at his own pace. She also realized she needed to think of a backup plan in case Ted couldn't go to day care, and she might want to consider having help at home when she knew she had to get out early. The counselor gave Millie the names of some home care agencies she could call if she needed an aide to come to their home for a day. Millie decided it might be a good idea to finally tell her boss that Ted had AD, even though she would have preferred to keep her personal problems out of the office. Then she could explain that she would need advance notice when he wanted her to change her schedule.

## Step Six: Conclude the Call

When the counselor feels that the caregiver's needs have been met to the extent possible within the confines of an ad hoc call, or that appropriate referrals for further assistance have been adequately made, the counselor can conclude the call. If additional resources have been suggested, the counselor should make sure that the caregiver understands why the suggestions are being made. The counselor should also reiterate that he or she is available for further consultation.

Millie said, "Am I glad I called you! It still hurts to think that Ted can't tell me how he feels anymore, but at least I understand what made him do it." The counselor said, "I'm glad I could be helpful. You know, Millie, you can always call me."

## Step Seven: Document the Call

Documentation about ad hoc telephone counseling should be similar to in-person counseling notes, providing a concise but complete picture of the interaction as well as the plan for future care. A form for recording telephone counseling notes can help counselors to document information in a uniform, consistent manner. This proves very helpful when notes need to be reviewed quickly while a client is on the telephone. A basic form includes the following, but it can be modified to suit the needs of each setting:

■ Time and date of call

■ Duration of call

■ Name of the counselor who took the call

■ Name of the client's regular counselor (if applicable)

■ Nature of the problem as presented by the caller

■ Counselor's assessment of the situation

■ Suggestions made to the caller

■ Follow-up plans (another counseling call, an in-person session, etc)

## What the Counselor Can Learn From Ad Hoc Calls

Just as clinical notes for in-person counseling are extremely important for providing continual, quality care to caregivers, so too are the notes that a counselor makes during ad hoc counseling calls. This is especially true when more than one counselor may answer calls from the same client. Counseling notes for telephone calls provide counselors with a picture of a caregiver's needs over time, recurring problems, frequency of problems, changes in a patient's condition, and the new challenges that these changes create for the caregiver.

Telephone counseling notes also reveal a caregiver's progress over time. As a caregiver calls with new issues and solutions are discussed, a counselor may observe that a client has made strides in meeting the challenges of caregiving—that, for instance, a caregiver has accepted the diagnosis and is now able to move forward with a care plan, has solved an issue that was particularly troublesome in the past, or has benefited by expanding his or her support system.

If there are many calls from the same caregiver within a short period of time, there is probably an underlying difficulty that needs to be identified and addressed. The caller may be feeling unusually stressed or anxious and not be aware of it. It is also possible that a situation the caregiver is not talking about may be motivating the calls. In a nonthreatening way, the counselor can make the caller aware of the fact that he or she is calling repeatedly and help the caller try to figure out the underlying reason for the calls. Helping the caregiver to identify and articulate his or her actual need can lead to finding an effective response.

Occasionally a caregiver may call several times and speak to different counselors about the same issue. If there are notes of previous calls available to all counselors, the counselor will know what other counselors have told the caregiver and know that the problem has not been solved to the caregiver's satisfaction. The caregiver may be seeking alternative opinions in order to make an informed decision or need additional support that has not been identified. Counselors may need to consult each other to develop a plan to respond effectively to these calls.

A flurry of calls from several family members may indicate that the family is unable to solve a particular problem or is in conflict. It suggests that family members are unable to talk to each other and are seeking either an ally or a mediator. A counselor will have to determine, on a case-by-case basis, whether a conference call, another family meeting, or some other resource is required.

A family member may call to ask a counselor to intervene with another family member. For example, an adult child may call if he or she thinks their caregiving parent needs additional help at home or the patient is not adequately supervised, and the parent refuses to accept advice from him or her. After exploring how the caller has attempted to solve the problem and why these attempts have not been effective, the counselor should try to help the caller to work out the situation directly with the parent. If this seems to be impossible, because of their history or because the patient or caregiver seems to be at risk, the counselor might agree to call the caregiver directly. It is essential that the caller understand that the counselor will disclose to the caregiver that the call is being made at the request of the family member.

There are some other circumstances under which a counselor may initiate a call to a caregiver or family member, rather than wait for a problem to occur or a difficulty to escalate. For example, a counselor who is aware that a patient is being discharged from the hospital or is going to be hospitalized may want to help them prepare. Another reason to call would be to provide the caregiver with information about a new service or resource. In addition, when the counselor knows that a caregiver is unable or unwilling to ask for help in spite of being encouraged to do so, it may be good practice to call the person periodically rather than wait for him or her to overcome the inhibition.

## Suggestions for Implementing Ad Hoc Counseling

Many settings have an established policy for responding to telephone calls from clients that may be well suited to the needs of families taking care of a person with Alzheimer's disease. Other agencies may decide to make adjustments to their system or may need to develop a new system to accommodate caregiver needs. The type of ad hoc counseling that can be offered will depend on the mandate of the setting to provide continual care, the availability of counseling staff to take calls, and how well trained and comfortable the staff is with providing counseling on an as-needed basis over the telephone.

For telephone counseling to be an effective method of providing assistance to caregivers, it must be accessible to the caregiver and not overwhelming or burdensome for the counselor to provide.

While the NYU intervention is open to all family members who participated in individual and family counseling, this may not be possible or appropriate in all settings. In each setting, guidelines have to be set regarding who can participate in ad hoc counseling and under what circumstances.

Some issues to consider when developing a system of ad hoc counseling for caregivers of people with Alzheimer's disease include who will respond to the calls, when the service will be available, what kind of training staff will receive, and what the limitations of the service are.

## Who Will Respond to Ad Hoc Calls?

Ideally, ad hoc counseling calls will be answered by the counselor who was assigned to the caregiver for in-person counseling. This counselor, knowing the history, will be able to respond efficiently to the caregiver's needs. If a counselor takes the call of another counselor's client, extra time will be required to assess the situation before focusing on the issue the caller presents.

In conducting the NYU intervention, we found that an average ad hoc counseling call generally lasts from 15 to 25 minutes. Since several calls may have to be answered in a day, a reasonable amount of time must be scheduled into the counselor's workday.

Calls may initially be screened by a volunteer or a receptionist or taken by an answering service. If a caller asks for resource information, the person who answers the call can offer to provide it. If the issue requires the attention of the counselor, the counselor can be notified and can call the caregiver back when he or she has the time.

## When Will the Service Be Available?

Counselors may want to set aside specific times during the day to receive or return calls. For instance, caregivers might be invited to call, if necessary, between certain hours on certain days when the counselor would be prepared to answer calls. In this system, both counselors and caregivers know when calls can be answered. When counselors set aside a specific time to return calls, they can prepare for them, perhaps by reviewing a client's file or gathering names of resources. A disadvantage of this system is that caregivers may find it difficult to call during specified times or may, when dealing with a painful issue, lose the courage to call if they have to wait for a specified time.

Caregivers may feel the need for support at any time of day or night. If ad hoc counseling after-hours is a viable option, there are several ways that such a system can be established. One option is to assign each counselor an evening when he or she would be on call or have each counselor respond only to calls from his or her own clients. Another option would be to have a 24-hour help line that would be answered by trained volunteers. Each counselor would have a beeper or answering service to notify him or her of calls that require the expertise of a counselor. If your setting is unable to handle calls after business hours, caregivers can be informed about services of the Alzheimer's Association 800 hotline number, which provides 24-hour, 7-day phone accessibility for caregivers and patients.

## What Kind of Training and Resources Are Needed?

Everyone who responds to ad hoc calls needs to know what kinds of questions they are authorized to answer, the types of questions that can be answered in an ad hoc call, what needs to be referred elsewhere, and how to identify an emergency. Nonprofessionals need to be cautioned not to offer counseling, advice, or personal opinions. In order to respond to these calls effectively, efficiently, and comfortably, counselors will have to be prepared by having a working knowledge of Alzheimer's disease and the issues that occur during its course, and also by having resource lists and other information on hand.

Counselors can also have checklists, information cards, or brochures and manuals that can be sent in the mail in response to questions that are consistently asked by caregivers. For instance, if a common question is what to look for when choosing a day care center, counselors can have a preprinted checklist to read while on the telephone with a caregiver or to send in the mail.

A complete resource list will include information about the following:

- National offices and local chapters of the Alzheimer's Association

- Support groups for people in the early stages of AD

- Support groups for caregivers

- Health care professionals who understand and specialize in Alzheimer's care

- Home care agencies

- Adult day care centers

- Residential institutions (assisted living facilities, nursing homes, etc)

- Community service agencies that provide services to the elderly or to people with AD

- Palliative care and hospice organizations

- Health insurance benefits for the elderly, such as Medicare and Medicaid

- Alzheimer's disease research centers

- Hospitals and outpatient clinics that provide specialized Alzheimer's care

- Books, videos, and Web sites that provide information about Alzheimer's disease

- Medical equipment and adaptive devices used in the care of Alzheimer's patients

## Ad Hoc Call

Harry, who had long been a client of the agency, called the counseling help line with what he said was a quick question. He said he had read everything he could about new discoveries in the treatment of Alzheimer's disease and regularly surfed the Internet. He wanted the counselor's opinion about enrolling his wife in a trial of a new drug he had read about on a Web site that he thought sounded very promising. "Do you think I should do it? My kids said I'd better be careful, because it could make her worse, but I'm willing to try anything at this point. She's getting worse anyway." The counselor said, "This is an important decision, and I can't tell you what to do. But you should find out as much as you can about the trial—the commitment that it will take to be part of the study, the risks and benefits of participating. I will send you a checklist of questions you might want to ask the people running the study before you decide." She went on to say, "It's great that you check the Internet, but don't forget, not all Internet sites are reliable. You might want to look on the government sites to see if there's any information about this new medication and talk to your wife's physician."

## What Are the Limitations of Ad Hoc Counseling?

Caregivers occasionally call with medical or psychiatric emergencies. They should always be instructed to call 911 immediately. Questions about new medical treatments or advances in research often require a response from a specialist, an AD research center, or an organization such as the National Institutes of Health. The telephone numbers and addresses of these resources should be available to those answering the telephone for ad hoc calls in a well-organized, up-to-date file.

When should a counselor offer additional in-person counseling to a caregiver? There are times when caregivers call with problems that are too complicated to respond to thoroughly over the telephone, for example, a family disagreement about whether to place a person with AD in a nursing home. Difficult emotional issues may require some in-person sessions or referral for therapy. Although telephone counseling is often the most efficient and cost-effective method of handling many of the issues caregivers present, there may be times when one additional session can produce better results with less stress on both caregiver and counselor.

### Ad Hoc Call

Over the course of several staff meetings, the counselors of a community center specializing in Alzheimer's care realized that they were getting an average of four phone calls per caregiver when the patient exhibited a new behavior that suggested the patient had become more severely demented. One counselor made the observation that four phone calls were the equivalent of one in-person session, but that she felt more confident of providing help in an in-person session for those dealing with a patient's significant decline. Several other counselors agreed. The counselors decided to ask the agency administrators whether it was possible to include one in-person session for situations like these and the option to provide additional sessions with a supervisor's approval.

This chapter has described ad hoc counseling, one form of continual support that can be made available to caregivers. Another form of ongoing support that can be very helpful to family members of people with AD is a caregiver support group, described in Chapter 6.

## COUNSELOR CHECKLIST

### Ad Hoc Counseling

☐ Maintain continuity of care through telephone consultations.

☐ Document counseling to maintain a history of contacts.

☐ Explain the parameters of the service in a brochure or card with a telephone number to call.

### The Ad Hoc Counseling Process

☐ Make a connection with the caller by initiating a dialogue and listening carefully to responses.

☐ Determine the reason for the call.

☐ Assess the severity of the situation and decide if the situation calls for immediate attention.

☐ Explore what the caregiver has done to solve the problem or issue prior to calling.

☐ Develop alternatives to solve the problem.

☐ Conclude the call, making appropriate referrals, if necessary.

☐ Document the call, including the nature of the problem, counselor's assessment, suggestions to the caller, and follow-up plans.

### Implementing Ad Hoc Counseling

☐ Determine who will answer the ad hoc calls.

☐ Establish ad hoc counseling hours.

☐ Train everyone who responds to ad hoc calls as to what kinds of questions can be answered and when to make referrals.

☐ Provide counselors with lists of resources.

# 6

# SUPPORT GROUPS FOR THE CAREGIVER

The well-being of family members is continually challenged by the demands of caring for a person with Alzheimer's disease (AD). In response to the ongoing need for support, the NYU intervention protocol requires that the primary caregiver join a support group at the conclusion of the individual and family counseling sessions. It has now become common practice, at NYU and elsewhere, to recommend that caregivers and other family members join support groups.

Family members and friends can provide valuable social support for caregivers. Support groups serve a complementary function, expanding the social support into a setting with peers. The experience of participating in a caregiver support group can provide unique benefits, including ongoing mutual support and sharing of information. A support group functions as a reservoir of experiences and knowledge, providing a vehicle for members to help each other grow and change.

This chapter will discuss the benefits of participating in a caregiver support group, how and when to refer caregivers to support groups, how to prepare them for the experience, how groups function, where to find them, and how to evaluate their effectiveness.

## Benefits of the Support Group Process

Social science research defines social support as a construct having many dimensions, including tangible assistance (physical and financial), information, emotional support, and socializing. Support groups provide members with several of these aspects of social support to enable them to cope with the distressing changes in the patient and their demands on the caregiver, and to help diminish feelings of hopelessness and isolation. They also provide education about the course of the illness and offer resources.

Caregivers benefit from talking to others who understand or have gone through similar experiences about the issues they are facing and the decisions they are making. Caregivers may be comfortable discussing issues with their caregiving peers that they feel are inappropriate or difficult to discuss among family and friends. Such issues include changes in their relationship with the person with AD, intimacy, disappointment with family and friends, financial or legal issues, and negative emotions. People who are isolated by caregiving and feel alone in their experience may benefit from sharing with others in the support group setting.

## Support Group Experiences

Marla and Jeff had always had an active social life. They had many friends with whom they went out regularly. They frequently gave parties and hosted many family gatherings. Jeff has had Alzheimer's disease for several years, and as it has become more severe, Marla has noticed that they have received fewer invitations. She no longer enjoys having people come to her house. It always seems so stressful. Marla decided to discuss what to do about her growing sense of isolation with her support group. Several group members said that they had had similar experiences. One member said that after she talked to her friends about her husband's illness and how it affected him, their friends realized they could still enjoy some activities together. Another member said she had found that she could still invite friends to her house if she had only a few at a time and didn't try to serve elaborate meals. Another caregiver said, "It hadn't ever occurred to me that I could go to a party and have fun without my husband. One day I got so lonely I decided to try it, and I was surprised that I actually enjoyed myself, even though I wished my husband could have enjoyed the party, too." Marla realized that there were possibilities she hadn't thought of. She said, "I guess my social life doesn't have to be over."

Through the experiences of other group members, caregivers can learn that it is possible to maintain their old social relationships, despite their relative's illness, and through the sharing of strategies, they can learn how to do so. They also can derive satisfaction from the group experience and relationships with individuals who are in the same boat.

## *Emotional Support*

A support group encourages, tolerates, and accepts the expression of painful emotions that can otherwise be overwhelming when experienced in isolation. Over the course of caring for a person with a chronic deteriorating illness such as AD, caregivers can feel angry and frustrated, guilty and sad, helpless and scared. Caregivers frequently are reluctant to express these feelings to family members and friends, both to avoid being a burden and for fear of being judged or misunderstood.

In sharing difficult feelings, the caregiver becomes aware that the emotions are normal and universal. This process helps release tension and allows expression and resolution of some of the frustration and grief created by the illness. The sharing of feelings and the subsequent sense of support and acceptance by others enhances the connection among group members and may be one of the most beneficial aspects of belonging to a group. One member's ability to come to terms with a particularly difficult issue may motivate others to deal with their own struggles.

Just as caregivers may have difficulty expressing their painful emotions, it may also feel awkward to describe to noncaregivers the satisfaction they experience in taking care of their ill family member. Some experiences may give a caregiver pleasure, such as taking the person with AD to a special event without any mishaps, that may seem trivial to those who are not involved. The positive aspects of caregiving can best be understood by other caregivers. For example, fellow support group members may understand a caregiver's pleasure in the fact that relationships that were previously difficult have improved during the patient's illness, because of a change in the patient's personality or the dynamics of the relationship.

## *Educational Resource*

An advantage of bringing caregivers together in a group is that it provides an opportunity to exchange knowledge about AD and resources, caregiving strategies, and personal experiences. Because the illness lasts for many years, the support group may include caregivers at different stages of the caregiving experience. Members who are new to caregiving can learn how to cope with symptoms and behaviors caused by the illness from those who are more experienced. Caregivers of patients in the more advanced stages can derive satisfaction and feelings of mastery from sharing information and strategies with those whose family members are in earlier stages of the illness. The presence of people who have been providing care for a long time makes a powerful statement about the enduring strength of caregivers.

Support group members can provide firsthand information about social and health services, legal and financial issues, entitlement programs, and community resources such as respite programs, home care, and nursing homes. The personal experiences of members add credibility to information, and sometimes caregivers will try a new strategy or resource if it is proposed by a peer rather than by a professional. Support group leaders monitor the veracity or reliability of information that caregivers provide to each other.

While each caregiver can provide information based on his or her own personal experience, the group leader can provide a different perspective, based on knowledge gained through professional experience. The leader may have access to more sources of information about resources. As a professional, the leader can also point out differences in caregiving situations and the limitations of information that is based on personal experiences.

## Who Should Be Referred to a Support Group?

Every family member of a person with AD can gain something from a support group experience. Emotional support may be the greatest benefit for some people, while education may be the greatest benefit for others.

Personality, culture, and value systems affect the caregiver's willingness to join and ability to participate in a support group. For some people, sharing feelings in a group is not customary, and the prospect of doing so may seem daunting or unacceptable. The question of joining should be explored with these caregivers to help them weigh their objections against the potential benefits. In some cases, it will become clear that the caregiver is not a suitable candidate, while in others the exploration may result in a willingness to try the group experience.

Millie realized that she needed to talk about Ted's illness almost all the time, but she thought her family and friends were getting sick of hearing about it. She called her counselor, who said, "Some time ago, I suggested that you might want to join a support group with other spouse caregivers of people with AD who are going through the same thing. Maybe this is a good time to try one." Millie said, "I like the idea of hearing about how other wives and husbands are dealing with AD, but I can't imagine talking about such private problems with strangers." The counselor said, "You don't have to talk about anything you don't want to." Millie said she would think about it.

People with many different personalities are suitable candidates for support groups. Diversity can enhance the richness of the exchange among members. Some people may be outgoing and contribute actively from the beginning. Others, who are initially silent and may seem to be unwilling to express their thoughts and opinions or to ask questions, may ultimately become active participants. It is important to remember that some people can gain just from listening.

In determining a caregiver's suitability for group participation, the strengths and weaknesses a caregiver may bring to the group and how these will fit into the group need to be considered. Caregivers who do not do well in groups are usually those who present extreme characteristics and personality traits—for example, those who are narcissistic, have difficulty listening to others, monopolize conversations, possess limited social skills, or are emotionally explosive or extremely shy. They might do better in a support group if they participate in individual counseling first.

A caregiver who presents a history of significant mental illness or evidence of any severe pathology might find a group too threatening or stimulating or may disrupt the group. There may also be some physical or medical conditions that preclude group participation.

There are caregivers who may eventually be suitable for a support group for whom a referral should be postponed. For example, people who are temporarily unable to commit themselves to the time required for regular participation in a support group, people who have just been told about their relative's diagnosis and have not yet really absorbed the implications of it, or people who are overwhelmed with difficulties and responsibilities and seem unable to focus on the objectives of a support group should not be in a group right away.

## What Should a Counselor Consider About a Support Group When Making a Referral?

A support group is characterized by its composition, structure, and leadership. Ideally, support groups are open-ended, meet every week, have a professionally trained leader, and have members whose age and familial relationship to the ill person are similar. The counselor's options for referral will be limited by the resources available in a given geographical area. The prospective group member and counselor should discuss the various types of support groups available and how they are organized to determine the kind of group that will meet the needs of the caregiver.

### *Group Composition*

A support group functions best if members can relate to each other comfortably and identify with each other. Some caregivers may feel strongly about being with others who resemble them, while others may appreciate more diversity. While all members of a support group share the common experience of being caregivers of people with AD, the following characteristics of group composition also should be discussed with a caregiver:

- *Age.* Caregivers may feel more comfortable discussing personal issues with people of a similar age.

■ *Ethnicity and culture.* Cultural values and norms may influence attitudes about caregiving, which some will find enlightening and others will find stressful.

■ *Religion.* Caregivers may find it comforting to be able to put their caregiving experience in the context of their religious beliefs.

■ *Socioeconomic status.* Since access to and utilization of resources are related to socioeconomic status, caregivers from vastly different financial and educational backgrounds may not be comfortable discussing these issues with each other.

■ *Relationship to the person with AD.* The impact of the illness on spouse caregivers is very different from its impact on adult children or other family members. While it is generally preferred to have separate groups based on relationship, it is not always possible. The benefit of a mixed group is exposure to the perspective of people in different relationships to the person who is ill; caregivers can gain insight into the attitudes of their own family members.

■ *Members of the same family.* It is generally not recommended that members of the same family attend the same group, because they might be inhibited about expressing their feelings in front of each other, and there might be a tendency to discuss family issues rather than focusing on caregiving.

■ *Stages of caregiving.* Hearing about the issues confronted by people caring for patients at different levels of severity may be distressing to some and informative to others.

The differences in composition do not have to keep anyone from participating in or gaining from the support group experience. A counselor can point out that beneath the apparent differences is the shared experience of caregiving.

## Support Group Experiences

Mike and Rick had been partners for 15 years when Rick was diagnosed with AD. During this period they had received their medical care in a center that was sensitive to the needs and feelings of the gay community. However, when Mike went to a caregiver support group meeting, he felt uncomfortable and not entirely welcome. At the end of the meeting he told the leader that he would not be coming back. He said he didn't think that the other members wanted him there because they weren't used to being with gay people. The leader acknowledged that this might be true of some members but not all, and asked if he would be willing to come back the following week and let the members know how he felt. She also asked if he had found the discussion of AD useful. He said that he had found it a little scary. Maybe he didn't want to hear all that stuff yet. The counselor told Mike that many caregivers feel upset when they hear others speak about the illness and that he should consider whether this was influencing his reaction to the meeting.

## Structure

When referring a caregiver to a support group, the following structural or organizational characteristics should be discussed:

***Time, Place, and Frequency of Sessions***   The group should be as accessible as possible and meet at a time that fits in with the caregiver's needs and lifestyle. Groups can meet weekly, biweekly, or once a month, during the day or in the evening. Typically, sessions last for about an hour and a half.

***Size***   Support groups generally range in size from six to eight members, in order that members have an opportunity for positive exchange with enough viewpoints to make participation a learning experience.

***Open vs Closed***   Open groups accept new members continually. A person considering an open group may be apprehensive about joining an existing group in which members have already established relationships. This is a realistic concern that can be addressed and overcome. Generally, open groups meet indefinitely, while closed groups are time limited, meeting for a specific number of sessions.

## Support Group Leaders

Support groups for caregivers may be led by mental health professionals or by laypeople (who are generally former caregivers). Some people may feel that a professionally led group will provide them with more reliable information and a secure emotional environment. Others may prefer to join a group led by a former caregiver, feeling that someone who has gone through the same experience may better empathize with their problems and understand their needs.

Whether the leader is lay or professional, he or she should be knowledgeable about Alzheimer's disease and the needs of caregivers and have experience with group process and interaction. Leaders may be similarly trained, yet have very different personalities and styles. The responsibility of leading a support group may be shared by two leaders. When possible, caregivers should be referred to a group whose leader's style appears to be most compatible with their own.

## How to Prepare a Caregiver for a Support Group

Once a counselor has determined that a caregiver is suitable for a support group, the next step is to introduce the idea to the caregiver, explaining the purpose of a caregiver support group, how the caregiver can benefit from joining, and what to expect. Some of the issues to discuss include whether the caregiver had ever been in a group, what this experience was like, the caregiver's expectations of how a support group would help, and any misunderstandings about how a support group for caregivers works. It is not uncommon for caregivers to be reluctant to agree to join a group or to be apprehensive, even if they are positively disposed toward the idea. Some may be concerned that they are being referred for psychological treatment. The counselor can explain the differences between a support group and a psychotherapy group. The purpose of a support group is to provide support, not to change personalities or interpret the behavior, defenses, or relationships among members.

Millie called her counselor and said, "I told my friend Julie that I was thinking about joining a support group, and she told me that I probably would hate it. She said she used to be in group therapy, and she had to talk about things that were very personal. I don't think I could do that." The counselor told Millie that support groups don't have the same goals as group therapy and explained the difference. She went on to say that she still thought Millie would get a lot out of a group, but that if she was concerned about having to reveal personal information, she should talk to the group leader about it before she joined. Millie said, "I'm I glad I called you. I liked the idea, but Julie scared me. Now, I think I might give it a try."

Some people will be eager to join a support group because of unrealistic expectations of what such an experience can offer. To avoid disappointment and to help the caregiver use the group appropriately, these expectations need to be discussed before the referral is made. For example, caregivers may expect a group to increase their opportunities to form new personal relationships. Caregivers should be made aware of the fact that this is encouraged in some groups and not in others.

If the caregiver agrees to the idea of participating in a support group, the counselor will help the caregiver locate a group that is convenient and seems appropriate. The counselor should explain that the process of joining a group usually includes an individual interview with its leader.

Agreeing to join a group does not immediately mean a permanent commitment. It is generally expected that the caregiver attend at least three meetings before deciding whether or not he or she wants to remain in the group.

## Reluctance and Apprehension of Caregivers About Participation

Caregivers give a variety of reasons for being reluctant or unwilling to join a group, including their own or other people's previous experience with groups, fear of the interactions that will occur in a group, and the content that will be discussed.

*Past Experience*  The counselor can explore with the caregiver what the previous experience had been like, the ways in which the recommended group may be different, and how the caregiver can handle the group experience differently to make it more satisfying.

## Support Group Experiences

Dan said, "I went to a support group once and it was awful. One person monopolized the conversation and only talked about her needs. I never went back. What was the point?" The counselor responded, "That does sound like a bad experience. I understand why you are reluctant to try again. But keep in mind that not all groups are the same, and in another group you may have a much better experience. Before you join another group, though, you may want to tell the leader what you told me and ask how the leader handles situations like this."

***Expectations Based on Other People's Opinion and Experience*** If a person whose opinion the caregiver values has had a negative group experience, the caregiver may be swayed by that person's reaction to the group. Counselors can point out that the other person's needs may have been different, and the assumption that the caregiver might feel the same way may or may not be accurate. The counselor can suggest that it might be worth having one's own experience before deciding on the potential value of a support group.

***Fear of the Interactions That Occur*** The caregiver may fear having personal issues exposed, feeling unwelcome or different, being caught in conflict, being put under pressure to contribute, and having to focus on other people's problems. The counselor might remind the caregiver that these are common fears of people who have not had a group experience, and these fears are generally relieved over time as the members get to know each other. The counselor can suggest that the caregiver make the leader aware of these concerns before joining and as they occur so that the leader can help the caregiver feel comfortable in the group.

***Fear of What Will Be Discussed*** A caregiver may fear hearing about sad, painful, or frightening experiences and emotions that other people have while caring for someone with AD or about the illness itself. For example, a caregiver whose relative is in the early stage of AD may fear hearing about behavior problems, while a caregiver of someone in the middle stage may fear hearing about the physical care needs of people in the end stages. The counselor can point out that the benefit of a group is that painful feelings become more tolerable when one is supported by peers in an environment made safe by an experienced leader.

## The Screening Interview

Before accepting a new member into a group, there is generally an opportunity for the group leader and the potential member to meet. The purpose of the interview is for the leader to assess whether the caregiver is appropriate for the group and for the caregiver to decide whether the group will suit his or her needs. The interview provides an opportunity for the leader to explain to the caregiver the purpose of the group, how the group functions, how the leader sees his or her role, and what is referred to as the group contract or group norms. The purpose of this contract is to ensure that members feel safe and secure and know what is expected of them. Group members and the leader(s) will generally agree to a "contract" that defines the agreement and will include expectations such as these:

- The meetings will begin and end on time.

- Everything discussed in the group is confidential.

- Each member is encouraged to participate.

- Communication should be respectful.

- Feelings will be expressed verbally, not physically.

- Members unable to attend a meeting will notify the group leader.

- Members will commit to coming three times before deciding the group is not suitable.

- Members will discuss plans to leave before doing so.

Among the norms that the leader will probably convey to a potential support group member is that the purpose of an ongoing group is to be available throughout the course of the illness. In most support groups, caregivers are expected to leave the group after the person with AD dies. The caregiver's needs will then have changed and can be more effectively met in a bereavement group.

Millie called her counselor and said she had definitely decided to join a support group and asked her to recommend one. The counselor told her there was a group for spouse caregivers that met in the evening near her job. Millie took the phone number of the leader, called the next day, and made an appointment to meet with him. At the interview, she talked about her fears of exposing her private life in public. The leader reassured her that many of the members had voiced similar concerns, and he always told them that they only had to talk about what they wanted to. He said, "It's okay to respond to a question you think is too personal by letting people know that you prefer not to answer. It's part of my job to make sure that every group member feels safe." Millie said, "Well, that makes me feel better. Maybe I'm worrying too much and I should just give it a try."

## *Where to Locate Support Groups*

In the NYU intervention study, caregivers were referred to existing groups at NYU and groups that ran under the auspices of the Alzheimer's Association. Other community agencies and organizations that run support groups for caregivers include nursing homes, senior centers, and adult day care programs. There are also support groups led by private practitioners. If a support group for Alzheimer's caregivers is not available or feasible for the caregiver to attend, a general caregiver support group might be recommended.

## COUNSELOR CHECKLIST

### Who Should Be Referred to a Support Group?

☐ Stress that most caregivers can benefit from and contribute to a support group.

☐ Postpone referring those candidates who are not yet prepared to make the commitment required by a support group.

☐ Do not refer caregivers who have a mental or physical condition that would prevent them from participating appropriately.

### What to Consider About the Group Before the Referral

☐ Discuss the group composition with the caregiver before referring.

☐ Discuss the organizational characteristics (time, place, frequency, size, open vs closed) with the caregiver.

☐ Refer a caregiver to a group where the leader's style will be compatible with his or her own.

### How to Prepare a Caregiver for a Support Group

☐ When introducing the idea of a support group, explain the purpose of such groups, the benefits and limitations, and what to expect.

☐ Help the caregiver locate an appropriate and conveniently located group.

☐ Explain that the process of joining a group usually includes an individual interview with the group leader to discuss what is expected of members.

### Where to Locate Support Groups

☐ Investigate the location of groups through the Alzheimer's Association, other health agencies, and organizations such as nursing homes, senior centers, and adult day care centers.

# 7

# HELPING CAREGIVERS ADAPT TO CHANGE

Each caregiver has a unique personality, life circumstances, and history that shape his or her reaction to Alzheimer's disease (AD) and responsibilities of caregiving. Nevertheless, some common themes underlie individual caregiving experiences. By understanding these themes, the counselor will have a context within which to view the individual and shape an effective intervention. This chapter describes some of the emotional responses of caregivers to the illness of their relative and their approaches to the caregiving role, and gives suggestions of ways that counselors can be helpful to them.

## Adapting to the Caregiving Role

Caregiving may feel natural and comfortable to people who have nurturing personalities, are easygoing, or derive satisfaction from helping others. Such caregivers may only need information about the illness, resources, and care planning, and with encouragement or a supportive environment will be able to make decisions and solve problems. Other people find caregiving antithetical to their personalities or so emotionally or physically draining that it overwhelms their ability to cope. The illness may reawaken emotions associated with previous painful experiences, such as the illness of another relative or even their own, and intensify their response to the current situation. These caregivers may require additional support from family, friends, or professionals.

Caregivers also differ in the timing of their use of services. Some may benefit from counseling soon after their relative is diagnosed. Others will need time to absorb the implications of the diagnosis or will wait until the symptoms of the illness become more severe before they seek or are willing to accept counseling. In settings in which counseling is routinely offered in conjunction with other services, a counselor may encounter caregivers who would not ordinarily apply for this kind of help but may still benefit from getting information and knowing that help is available.

## How Counseling Can Help Caregivers

Caregiving creates powerful stressors that can be ameliorated through interventions such as counseling. While most caregivers may not need therapy, they may benefit from the supportive interventions described in this book. There are times when caregivers need consultation with a knowledgeable and sensitive professional. In a supportive and safe emotional environment, a caregiver can pose the issues he or she confronts, get feedback from the counselor, and formulate solutions or plans to address them. In addition, the counselor can help a caregiver to develop new strengths and skills, as well as to resolve past issues related to caregiving.

In order to provide a counseling plan that is responsive to the caregiver's individual experience, it is important not to make assumptions about whether any particular caregiving task is easy or onerous or about appropriate emotional responses on the part of a relative of a person with AD. One has to work from the caregiver's perspective on which aspects of caregiving are tolerable and respond to the feelings he or she presents.

Within the diversity of the caregiving experience, some common themes emerge. Almost all caregivers will suffer emotionally when they are confronted with evidence of the illness progressing and may temporarily lose their sense of equilibrium. The process of establishing and losing inner balance may be repeated many times in the course of caring for a person with Alzheimer's disease and to some degree follows the course of the illness. Although AD is characterized by gradual, progressive decline, certain symptoms are viewed by many caregivers as turning points when they emerge because they have special symbolic meaning ("I don't mean anything to my father now that he doesn't recognize me") or practical implications ("Now that my husband is up most of the night, I can't sleep either"). These changes may require major readjustments to lifestyle or care plan and may at least temporarily overwhelm the caregiver. Counselors can help caregivers to face these new challenges by being available to them for consultation, by providing information and support, and by being realistically optimistic that this challenge, like those before it, can be met.

It is important to keep in mind that most caregivers are motivated by feelings of love and attachment, feel that they have grown as human beings, find value in the experience, and take pride in providing care and comfort to their ill relative.

## Caregiver Experiences

One caregiver, whose husband suffered from AD for more than 10 years, looked back on these years and made the following observation. "I used to be the kind of person who would try to cram so much into a day that I was always late and in a rush. But now that my husband George has AD, I know he can't be rushed. I prided myself on my good memory and talked with pleasure about a meal I had eaten years ago, but George immediately forgets what has just happened. I was always planning the next vacation but George can't contemplate the future. Taking care of George has taught me the value of slowing down and living in the present. I try to take the time to focus on what I am doing and what is going on around me—in short, to appreciate the moment. I guess you could say I learned the hard way, but Alzheimer's taught me an important lesson."

## Emotional Reactions Over the Course of the Illness

### When a Caregiver Learns the Person Has AD

Caregivers can have any number of emotional reactions when they learn that their family member has AD. The immediate reactions are generally shock, fear, grief, and anger. Some people openly express these feelings: "I can't believe it! What am I going to do now?" Other people may appear to be calm or indifferent, although this may only reflect their way of behaving in public and they may be masking very strong feelings. A counselor, by being a sympathetic and understanding listener, can make it possible for the caregiver to express these feelings.

Caregivers will speak about the unfairness of the illness. "Why did this have to happen to us?" "We don't deserve this after all we have been through." "We were just about to take the cruise we'd been putting off for years." They will anticipate the many losses the illness may cause. Some of these issues, while having emotional consequences, also have practical implications such as causing changes in retirement plans and threatening financial security. The caregiver's hopes for the future may now never be fulfilled. Instead, the caregiver will have to adapt to these unanticipated circumstances. The new view of the future may seem very bleak.

A person who is new to the caregiving role may not be able to conceive of still being able to have a satisfying life. Some of the intensity of a caregiver's reaction may be a function of lack of information or belief in some of the myths about the disease. When this is the case, dispelling such ideas as "All people with AD become aggressive or have to go to a nursing home" can begin an educational process that will start the caregiver on the road to realistic appraisal and planning.

Caregivers who have difficulty accepting that their relatives are ill may be trying to protect themselves from feelings of sadness and grief that would stem from recognizing the losses to themselves and to the patients and from having to make the changes that would result from this recognition. The counselor can help caregivers understand that their own survival and well-being depend on a new view of the person as ill, which is constantly jeopardized by the fact that the person can also seem very much like his old self some of the time.

Fear and worry are common and pervasive feelings. Caregivers often express fear of what the future holds for the person with AD. Will he suffer? Will she be embarrassed? Will people reject him? Spouse caregivers, who are generally elderly themselves, may worry about who will care for the person with AD if they should also become ill. Sometimes the person with AD was taking care of his or her ill spouse; in that case, other family members may be afraid of the responsibilities that they will now have to assume. Family members may also worry that they are at risk for developing AD themselves. People frequently worry that they will not be capable of adequately caring for the patient. The emotions caregivers experience when finding out about the diagnosis may be exacerbated by the fact that they are afraid they will not know how to go about handling their new responsibilities. This may make them feel overwhelmed and helpless.

The counselor can be supportive by normalizing these feelings—letting the caregiver know that it is both common and acceptable to have them. It is important to give caregivers time to talk about their feelings and not to rush them into getting over the painful emotions. The counselor should wait until he or she feels caregivers are able to hear new information rather than imposing it before they are ready.

Often the diagnosis is not entirely a surprise. Occasionally caregivers even express relief that the cause of their relative's problems has been identified and they can finally take action and talk openly about the issues that have been troubling the ill person and other family members. At times the diagnosis is made when the person is no longer in the early stage of the illness. Family members may have been trying to accommodate their behavior to the changes in their relative without asking anyone for help and without understanding why the person has changed. They can now be provided with information about treatment and care strategies that can ease their caregiving tasks.

We have found that some common concerns generally cause caregivers distress when they are told that their relative has AD.

***Can I Be Sure the Diagnosis Is Correct?***    This question may reflect genuine concern about the accuracy of the diagnosis. In that case, it may be advisable to suggest that the caregiver seek a second medical opinion. Or it may be an expression of hope that their family member really does not have the disease. "I don't believe it. He's not that different from the way he's always been." "What can you expect of a man his age?" A counselor can be helpful to caregivers who seem to be having trouble accepting the diagnosis by gently asking them to consider what their feelings would be if they admitted to themselves that their relative really did have AD. A counselor may discover that the caregiver is feeling overwhelmed, not so much by the reality of the relative's current situation as by fears of the future fueled by misinformation. In this case, it can be helpful to provide an accurate picture of the course of the illness and of the resources that are available, without minimizing the fact that the situation is serious.

### Do I Have to Tell Family and Friends About the Diagnosis?

Caregivers may be unsure about how and when to tell other people that their relatives have AD. People in the early stage of AD can frequently continue to function quite well in familiar social situations. At this stage, caregivers may decide it is only important to tell people to whom the information will be significant, such as close family members who need to be involved in planning for the future. It will not be possible to conceal the diagnosis indefinitely, because the patient's symptoms will eventually become obvious.

Exploring the caregivers' perception of the potential impact of disclosing the illness to others will help them come to a decision about whom and when to tell. There are several commonly expressed reasons for not revealing the diagnosis. If caregivers want their lives to appear "normal" or to believe that nothing has changed, it may be difficult for them to tell anyone about the diagnosis. Some caregivers may be ashamed that their relative has AD; perhaps they equate it with being "crazy." They may also fear that people will stop including them in plans and activities or that their relative will be ostracized. The counselor can help the caregiver evaluate the degree to which his or her concerns are likely to materialize.

The experience of telling a few people may increase the caregiver's confidence in the support of his or her social network. Are there some people with whom the caregiver feels comfortable enough to tell them about the relative's condition? Who has the caregiver counted on to be supportive in the past? The counselor can also help the caregiver to accept that some people are not comfortable being with a person who is sick. Rather than focusing on those who cannot tolerate the patient and on feeling rejected, it will be more productive to seek out those who can. Of course, some caregivers feel close and secure enough with family members and friends to freely disclose the fact that their relative is ill.

*I Don't Think I Can Handle This*   New caregivers often express fears about their ability to handle changes in their relatives and the new responsibilities brought about by the illness. Caregivers may find comfort in being told that there will be time to adjust to the illness and that it is unlikely to cause drastic changes all at once. In fact, a person in the early stage of AD may continue with many usual activities. While the responsibilities formerly handled by the patient will ultimately have to be taken on by others, this can also generally be done in stages. Helping the caregiver to identify the tasks that the ill relative can no longer be expected to handle properly is the first step the counselor can take to help the caregiver assume some of these tasks and roles or identify others in the family or appropriate professionals to help with these responsibilities.

*Will I Get AD Too? Are the Children at Risk?*   When a family member is diagnosed with AD, others in the family often ask whether they are also at risk. If the affected person is a close relative or many people in the family have had the illness, the concern is likely to be greater. A counselor can explain that the likelihood of any individual getting the disease cannot be predicted with certainty. The younger the age at which the person became ill with AD, the greater the risk of a genetic abnormality for other family members. Family members who want to get information about their individual risk should be referred for genetic counseling and, if they choose, for testing. There is much research currently in progress to discover possible environmental, hormonal, and dietary risk factors for AD. Currently, advanced age is the most significant known risk factor for AD.

## Caregiver Experiences

Paul, who was 47 years old, was having significant memory problems and went to an Alzheimer's Disease Center for an evaluation. The physician at the center told the family the tests indicated that Paul had AD. Then a social worker met with the family to answer any questions about what steps they should take and recommend resources. Recognizing that they seemed to be stunned by the diagnosis and needed time to absorb the information, she suggested they come back to talk to her another time. Paul's wife, Joan, and daughter Susan returned to see the social worker a few days later. They were still feeling pretty shaky. Joan said she was worrying about Susan getting AD, since she had heard that it could be inherited. And then she said, "Maybe Paul doesn't really have it. He was great this week. Really, just like he used to be." The social worker said that people with AD often have their ups and downs in the early stages and can appear as though nothing is wrong. She also said that the familial form of AD is extremely rare and suggested that if they were worried about it they might want to get genetic counseling to learn more.

## When the Illness Becomes More Severe

*Emotional Reactions to Changes in the Patient*  The functional level of a person with AD may remain relatively stable for a period of time, allowing the caregiver to accommodate to it. When a new symptom emerges, the established pattern is broken and the caregiver is forced to make new adjustments. Frequently the new symptom or behavior will occur intermittently at first and only become established gradually. Until the caregiver realizes that the change is not temporary, it is possible to minimize it. A caregiver may try to ignore the importance of the first incident or not understand its implication and therefore neither take any action nor make any changes to address the new situation. On the other hand, a caregiver may, on some level, be aware of the new symptom and be trying to protect himself or herself from accepting that the disease is progressing—a state that can be described as "knowing and not knowing." The counselor will need to assess the degree of danger posed by ignoring the situation and focus counseling accordingly.

The counselor will also have to assess whether the caregiver's perception of the symptom is realistic; how often the symptom occurred; whether it could have some cause other than dementia, such as a physical illness or temporary stress; or if the symptom is in fact consistent with the stage of the illness. It is always important to explore the meaning of the symptom to the caregiver. Does it make the caregiver feel tremendous sadness and grief over the losses the patient is suffering? Does it mean the patient can no longer appreciate the caregiver or being in his or her own home? Does it mean that the caregiver can no longer feel enough affection to be willing to continue to provide care? Is the symptom itself intolerable, or is it just "the last straw"?

A counselor should remember that the emotional reaction to a new symptom is likely to subside with time. Since the caregiver will not generally be able to accept that this is so if he or she is very upset, initially it may be most helpful to acknowledge awareness of the intensity of the caregiver's feelings. Generally, the counselor's empathy will enable people to calm down enough to begin to explore ways of coping with the problem.

The counselor can try to rectify any misconceptions the caregiver has about the seriousness of the symptom and then help the caregiver to deal with its emotional and practical implications. Reframing the meaning of the symptom may help the caregiver view it in such a way that it can be tolerated. It may be possible for the caregiver to feel that the patient's condition is manageable with more social and practical support. If, based on knowledge of the caregiver or the intensity of the reaction, the counselor concludes that the caregiver cannot cope with the symptom, then together they can discuss alternative care plans. These may range from having someone else handle the problem (another relative or paid help), if that is possible, to placement in a different living situation.

## Caregiver Experiences

Rhonda's friend Josie looked at her serious face and downcast eyes and asked if she was feeling depressed. "No, I wouldn't say I'm depressed; I'm just really sad." Rhonda hadn't realized how sad she was feeling until then. Rhonda decided she would make an appointment to see her counselor. When she met with her counselor, she told her that she was feeling very sad and her friend was worried that she was depressed. The counselor asked her what she thought was making her feel that way. "I guess it's that I feel so bad for my mom. Now she really forgets so much. When I went to see her last night, she told me that she was feeling very lonely and wished that I would come to see her more often. I had spent an hour with her that very morning, but she had completely forgotten about it by evening. I guess what really got to me is that no matter how much I do, I can never make her happy except by being there, and I can't be there all the time." The counselor said, "That is true, Rhonda, you can't. You still have to have time and energy for your own life. Rhonda, I understand your sadness. You have created an excellent care plan and your mother has the best life possible under the circumstances." The counselor understood that Rhonda needed time to accept the harsh truth that she could not fill the gaps in her mother's life that were caused by the disease.

It is important to remember that the inevitable changes in the patient will have a different meaning to each caregiver and to the same caregiver at different times. The counselor has to consider the context in which the symptom is occurring. The caregiver's reaction is influenced not only by the patient's behavior but also by the other stresses and events in the caregiver's life. Helping the caregiver respond appropriately to the symptom may not resolve the caregiver's emotional reaction if other factors, such as poor physical health or the quality of the present or prior relationship between the caregiver and the patient, are fueling the reaction.

Sometimes caregivers have reactions to changes in the patients that seem to the onlooker to be completely out of proportion to the severity of the problem. This reaction can take various forms, ranging from depressive to explosive. The change in the relative may feel to the caregiver like a major turning point; the caregiver may fear that the emergence of a particular symptom means there is now no choice but to place the ill person in a nursing home. The symptom may also make the caregiver aware that there has been a shift in the patient's capacity to have a meaningful relationship. This may leave the caregiver feeling lonely and abandoned.

The counselor can help the caregiver to gain a realistic appraisal of the ill person's capacity and of the meaning of the new symptom or behavior. A caregiver who initially says, "Our family is destroyed" may, with the counselor's guidance, be able to shift to, "This really marks a significant change, but our family can make the necessary adjustments." The counselor can then help the caregiver to find the practical and emotional supports needed to manage the new situation.

*Grief and Depression*  Some caregivers experience the illness as a series of losses for which they cannot stop grieving. Many say that they almost always feel sad, both for themselves and for the patient. This feeling may persist throughout the course of the illness but is not always in the forefront. Caregivers who are able to maintain their interests and connections or to develop new ones may feel relatively satisfied for large stretches of time but slip back into sadness or even depression when the pressures become too great.

While many caregivers experience symptoms of depression, these do not necessarily indicate a clinical illness but may be an indication that the caregiver is becoming emotionally more fragile and in need of additional support or respite. When a counselor observes a major shift in a caregiver's mood and ability to function that persists for more than a few days, the caregiver should be referred for psychiatric assessment and, possibly, additional treatment. The caregiver may not be able to care for the patient, and other arrangements may need to be made, at least temporarily. The counselor may have to get the caregiver's permission to contact other family members. In a case in which the patient or caregiver appears to be in danger, or the patient seems to be neglected and there is no other potential family caregiver, it may be necessary to contact adult protective services. It is possible that additional support, such as respite services in a residential facility, increased help from other family members, or hiring additional help may make it possible to maintain the patient in the current environment until the caregiver recovers.

***Stress and Burnout***   Stress and burnout can be caused by the everyday tasks of caregiving and the burden of constant responsibility for the well-being of the person with AD, whose needs change and increase over the course of the illness. The person's changing needs create a situation that is always unstable and can be especially stressful to those who are more comfortable with predictability. The effort required to find and manage resources and to fill the gap between what the resources can provide and the needs of the patient and the caregiver is also a constant cause of stress. For example, some day care programs have limited hours (such as 3 hours each morning every other day); this leaves the caregiver worrying about where to get help or care for the patient for the remainder of the day and on other days of the week. To maintain entitlements like Medicaid, the caregiver is required to submit paperwork and documentation periodically for review; this creates a nagging concern that the benefits or services may be decreased.

Not all caregivers find the same circumstances stressful. Counselors should approach each individual's situation with an awareness of the stresses that are generally associated with caregiving, but not assume that these are the ones troubling him or her. Only by gaining a detailed picture of the client's specific strengths, problems, and needs can the counselor identify the remediable stressors for the caregiver. The counselor can then help the caregiver think about changes in the care plan, including possible use of more resources in the community that would reduce the stress as well. The caregiver also should be encouraged to take care of himself or herself by exercising, eating a good diet, socializing, or having time alone.

Caregivers can underestimate the toll caregiving is having on them and then discover that they have allowed themselves to become burned out. They may find themselves saying things like, "I can't face this anymore" or "I'm exhausted." Although it is not regarded as a "classical" stress disorder, burnout often is preceded or accompanied by periods of acute or prolonged stress. The continuing emotional burdens linked to caregiving play a pivotal role in causing caregiver burnout. Burnout can be experienced as physical symptoms including exhaustion, fatigue, headaches, and trouble sleeping. When caregivers complain of nonspecific pain, reduced attention span, feelings of meaninglessness, apathy, or detachment from work, counselors should suspect that they may be suffering from burnout. These caregivers may report that they have become less tolerant of the patient's behavior and that they no longer have the inclination or energy to withstand the daily demands of caring for the patient. They may express the wish that the caregiving responsibility would be over or say they want to quit. Some caregivers may not recognize the meaning of these feelings and wonder about what has happened to them that they can no longer find the strength to continue.

By naming these feelings "burnout," the counselor can help the caregiver to make sense of them and develop a plan for responding. Together, the counselor and caregiver can determine whether this feeling might be temporary and could be relieved by increased support or respite or whether the caregiver has come to a turning point and cannot continue to care for the patient. If there is any doubt that the caregiver has made an irrevocable decision, the counselor may suggest that the caregiver try to get some distance from the situation by either taking a vacation, putting the patient in temporary care, or getting more help before making a final determination of a permanent change in care plan.

***The Tedium of Routine Care*** Caregivers who live with the patient and even those who visit may express feeling bored and unmotivated to interact with the patient. Being with a person who is cognitively impaired is often tedious and boring. Spending many hours with a person who has very poor short-term memory, asks repetitive questions, is unable to participate in a discussion with the caregiver, and needs to be directed to activities to keep him or her occupied or repeats the same activities over and over can feel extremely tedious. The consistent routine that the caregiver must provide to accommodate the patient's needs is devoid of the spontaneity that many people enjoy. When the routine is broken, it is not a welcome change, as it usually comes as a result of an emergency or decline in the patient's condition.

Some caregivers may enjoy being creative or even whimsical in finding activities to share with the patient to relieve the routine. Caregivers sometimes lose sight of the opportunity that day-to-day activities such as cooking and cleaning, which have to be done anyway, can offer for sharing a positive experience with the patient (taking the ends off the string beans or folding the laundry, dusting the books, singing out loud).

The counselor can encourage caregivers to find ways to spend more time away from the patient if that is possible. Caregivers who prefer to stay at home may try to meditate, exercise with a videotape, or listen to music or books on tape with earphones to create a personal emotional space for themselves, even if they still need to be physically present.

Sometimes when the patient declines to a more severe stage, caregivers look back with regret on opportunities they missed with the patient when he or she was more functional. The counselor's intervention can minimize the likelihood of this happening as well as help the caregiver to find ways of staying connected to the patient in each stage of the illness while engaging in activities that also provide some satisfaction to the caregiver.

## Caregiver Experiences

Roberta confided to her counselor that she was beginning to hate going to see her mother because the visits were so tedious. She found herself postponing visits until just before she needed to refill the pillbox that contained a week's worth of medication for her mother (she kept the rest of the medicine in a locked box for safety). Since the home health aide was not permitted to do this task, she had no choice but to go. At her mother's house, while she was arranging the pills, her mother kept trying to get her attention by bringing her things to look at. Roberta didn't even look at her mother's trinkets, which she had seen dozens of times before, but just said, "Those are lovely, Ma," every now and then. She could feel her stomach tighten, and she found herself wondering what to do with her mother until she could reasonably escape. Roberta felt ashamed of her feelings and hopeless about how to deal with them.

Her counselor smiled and said, "I just attended a workshop on how to make visits to a relative with AD more pleasant, and I was just waiting to give the information to someone who could use it." She explained that the distress Roberta experienced is shared by many adult children when they are with their parents with AD. The counselor suggested ways in which Roberta could include her mother in the tasks she had to do rather than ignore her and then try to invent things to do with her. Roberta and the counselor planned that on the next visit Roberta would ask her mother to sit with her at the table and let her help by returning the medicine bottles to the lockbox after Roberta had taken out the required number of pills.

In her next session Roberta reported how happy her mother had been to sit next to her and watch her put the pills in the little spaces in the pillbox. Her mother lined up the medicine bottles in a row and contentedly rearranged them until Roberta finished the job. It wasn't a big deal, but Roberta said that she had felt less tense and bored during this visit and thought she might bring some photos the next time. Maybe her mother would recognize the pictures of the old neighborhood. And if she didn't, she could put them in piles. Her mother seemed to enjoy putting things in order, and Roberta said that she hadn't felt as painfully bored and tense as she often did when she was with her mother.

*Disgust*  As a result of the illness, some people with AD begin to behave in socially inappropriate ways. Their table manners may deteriorate, they may not flush the toilet, shower, and change their clothes frequently enough, and may have bowel and bladder accidents. Caregivers vary in their capacity to accept these symptoms. Some are not able to deal with maintaining the hygiene of an incontinent adult. They may regret their feelings and become self-critical even though they continue to provide those aspects of care that do not upset them. Others get over their initial reaction to incontinence and find themselves put off by other behaviors.

## Caregiver Experiences

Sam's eating habits embarrassed his daughter Miriam. At her son's wedding Sam had gone from table to table collecting food, piling it on his plate, and then stuffing it into his mouth. No amount of gentle persuasion could get him to sit down at his table and stop bothering the other guests. She remembered that the counselor had suggested that she not leave her Dad alone in social situations and asked her aunt to go with him into another room for awhile.

Counselors can help caregivers anticipate situations in which their relative is likely to behave inappropriately and, if the situation cannot be avoided, learn how to provide the additional supervision necessary to minimize the impact of the behavior. Perhaps when caregivers accept that the behavior is a symptom of Alzheimer's disease, they may find it more tolerable. The behavior may be less embarrassing to the caregiver if the other people present know that the person is ill.

## Caregiver Experiences

Harold said he felt like this was the last straw. He was disgusted with himself, with his wife Marjorie, who was in the severe stage of AD, and with his home. Even though he and a wonderful aide did their best to keep Marjorie clean, she had become fecally incontinent and, if no one was present to clean her immediately, would pull on her clothes until the bowel movement wound up on the floor. He said the house often had a bad smell, and there was no way he would ever invite friends to visit again. He knew Marjorie couldn't help herself, but sometimes he just didn't even want to go home. The counselor said this is one of the most unpleasant symptoms of AD, but reminded him of how well he had dealt with other difficult symptoms. The counselor said he could stop it from happening so frequently by becoming aware of her schedule and reading her cues (such as fidgeting). Since Marjorie couldn't walk as far as the toilet any more, seating her on a commode at the time when she usually had a bowel movement might prevent accidents. There are also household sprays that can be very effective against unpleasant odors.

***Loss of Hope*** The caregiver has to cope with the knowledge that currently there is no treatment that will substantially alter the course of the illness, and that the patient's condition will only get worse. Caregivers may feel that the illness has robbed them and the patient of a normal life. They may not be able to envision how to lead a meaningful life now, nor feel hopeful about their own future. Older caregivers may fear that they themselves may become ill or impoverished, and find it difficult to think of anything to look forward to. The counselor should acknowledge the force of these feelings and say something like, "I know that it is hard for you to imagine the future now, while you are so consumed with caregiving." The counselor can ask the caregiver to describe what he or she does during a typical day and remind the caregiver of the value of his or her efforts on the patient's behalf, even though they cannot alter the course of the illness. The counselor can also say, "I will be available to help you get through this." If the caregiver hasn't already done so, the counselor can suggest that it may also be helpful to join a support group and meet other people who are coping with the same situation. Finally, the counselor should rule out the possibility that the caregiver is suffering from depression.

## Lifestyle Changes

### Role Changes

***Assuming New Roles*** Caregivers will have to progressively take over tasks that were previously performed by the patient or delegate them to someone else. Because of the variability in patient functioning, caregivers find it difficult to strike a balance between maintaining patient autonomy and stepping in to avoid problems.

On occasion caregivers may allow a person with AD to perform a task for which he or she is no longer qualified.

One stumbling block to taking over responsibilities from the patient is reluctance to confront the reality of the patient's decreased level of functioning. This problem is often exacerbated by the fact that many patients insist on continuing to perform activities that are beyond their abilities. Many caregivers are unaccustomed to asserting themselves with their ill relatives or making decisions alone. Counselors can help them to understand the reasons for their behavior as a first step to change. Are they afraid to admit that the patient has changed? Are they afraid to insult the patient? Are they afraid of a conflict with the patient? Are they afraid of assuming the task themselves or of making a mistake?

On the other hand, some caregivers take over responsibilities too soon, underestimating the abilities of the patient or perhaps taking the opportunity of the relative's illness to assert control. There is a danger in taking over too much responsibility. Patients who are prematurely deprived of opportunities to be active participants in the family and in their community can feel incompetent and suffer from a loss of self-esteem.

Counselors can help caregivers to assess the tasks the patient can currently continue to perform, as well as those they can no longer fulfill, and help them master their fears. Counselors can point out the potential consequences of both inaction and overprotectiveness. Counselors should make caregivers aware of situations in which their inaction can put the patient and others at risk (driving a car or preparing tax returns). If the caregiver cannot act, he or she may be able to have a family member intervene.

When people are inhibited by fears of taking action, it may be helpful to find out if they had a bad experience trying to be assertive in the past. If so, the counselor can use imagery and role-play to visualize or enact a different outcome that may enable the caregiver to practice and become more comfortable behaving in a new way. The counselor can then work with the caregiver to develop a concrete plan for taking over or delegating responsibilities to someone else. Some caregivers are constrained by cultural values and traditions from taking over roles of people of the opposite sex or of their elders. The counselor or these caregivers can consult with a knowledgeable leader from their own community about how best to handle the situation.

***Giving up Roles***   Caregivers may reduce or discontinue activities that were previously the source of satisfaction, financial gain, or service to others. They may leave full-time jobs, work fewer hours or fewer days, and reduce travel and overtime, which may interfere with their opportunities for career advancement. Volunteer jobs are often relinquished, and grandparents whose adult children relied on them to babysit so that they could work are forced to find arrangements that are less satisfactory for all concerned. Because AD is a progressive disease, these lifestyle changes are usually made over time and not all at once. There are often ways to mitigate their impact or find acceptable alternatives.

Counselors can advise caregivers about resources such as home and day care and encourage them to utilize them. Though caregivers may initially be reluctant to pay for services even if they can afford them, counselors can provide the support to encourage them to put value on their own well-being. Caregivers may also have access to unpaid help, such as friends, family, and church members, that may be willing to provide some of the patient care, which they should be encouraged to call upon. Counseling the caregiver to continue valued activities is humane as well as practical advice, reducing the emotional cost of providing care for the patient.

## Caregiver Experiences

Sally enjoyed babysitting for her new granddaughter, but her husband Joe could not tolerate sharing Sally's attention. She told the counselor she felt torn between her desire to care for the baby and help her daughter and her sense of responsibility for Joe. She said she found herself getting angry at Joe, even though she knew he couldn't help himself. "Do you think I should tell my daughter to find another babysitter?" The counselor asked her how she would feel if she did that. "The house would seem desolate without the baby. She lights the place up. I wonder if I could get a babysitter for Joe instead," she said wistfully. The counselor picked up on this idea and reminded Sally that Joe could go to day care all day if she wanted. "Would that be fair to him?" Sally asked. "From everything you've said, Joe is happy in day care, so this might be better for him, too." "But it's going to cost more money," objected Sally. The counselor remained silent. "Well, I guess it's worth it to be able to take care of the baby. Maybe my daughter will help pay for the extra day care if she realizes it's the only way I can continue to babysit for her," concluded Sally.

***Balancing Roles***    Caregiving almost always entails added roles to be juggled along with other ongoing responsibilities. Some people thrive on performing many roles and enjoy the challenge of balancing them. Caregiving may also add meaning to some people's lives. However, some caregivers feel overwhelmed by the number of tasks and upset by feeling that they cannot possibly carry them all out. If they are unable to give up any roles, lower the standards they hold for themselves, or delegate tasks to others, caregiving may have negative consequences in other aspects of their lives. Caregivers may displace feelings of frustration or anger onto other family members because they feel they should not criticize the patient. Adult children who are raising families or building their careers may find caregiving particularly difficult to balance with other responsibilities. Spouse caregivers who are employed or very involved in community activities may resent the additional demands made on them by the illness of their husbands or wives.

Counselors can help caregivers assess whether they are managing their time and energy effectively. Perhaps reviewing a typical week with the caregiver can clarify whether the caregiver is trying to do too much and identify tasks that can be eliminated or shared with others. While it is possible that nothing can be changed in the daily routine, and the caregiver is doing the best under the circumstances, perhaps the stress of caregiving can be reduced by taking periodic breaks or going on vacation or away for the weekend.

The counselor can help the caregiver consolidate certain tasks, change the frequency with which they are done (buying items in bulk and having them delivered, so as to shop less frequently), or perform tasks in an order that is more efficient and interferes less with other responsibilities (visiting the ill parent before work rather than on the way home when the caregiver is more tired, the babysitter needs to leave, and the children are waiting for dinner and help with their homework).

Caregivers who insist on performing tasks themselves because they feel they are the most qualified may be able to give up some of their responsibilities if they can accept that, while the person to whom they delegate them may not do them the same way or even as well, the substitute is good enough.

## Caregiver Experiences

Several years ago Brad's father had a stroke that left him partially paralyzed and unable to speak. When his mother, who had been taking care of his father, developed Alzheimer's disease, Brad, who was an only child, became responsible for both of them. He spent most of his free time with them, visiting before and after work. Brad was the manager of a furniture store and a volunteer for Big Brothers. He frequently felt exhausted and even bitter about his situation. His best friend, Sam, who worked in the same store, noticed that Brad was becoming increasingly irritable, neglecting his job, and losing weight. Sam felt he had to confront him, "You can't continue like this indefinitely. You'd better do something before your life falls apart. My sister got help from a counselor. Do you want me to find out her name?" To Sam's surprise, Brad agreed.

Brad told the counselor that even though he wished for relief from his caregiving tasks, he took pride in the expertise he had developed and his ability to do so many things. There was no one else he could really trust. There was a home health aide who had been hired to take care of his father, but she didn't understand Alzheimer's disease. Since his father was unable to speak, only Brad could respond to his mother's confused conversations. It was not hard for the counselor to appreciate the poignancy of Brad's dilemma, but she pointed out that he was jeopardizing his job and could make himself ill. Brad said, "A part of me knows you are right, but I feel I need to be there for them." She suggested that he consider cutting back his visits to once a day. She also recommended enrolling his mother in a day care program where staff would know how to talk to her. Even though his friends had made many of the same suggestions, when they came from a professional, Brad was able to follow them.

*Daily Life* Eventually, almost every aspect of the daily life of the person who lives with a relative with AD is affected by the illness. Schedules and plans need to be made with the limitations of the person with AD in mind. Everything needs to happen at a slower pace. The caregiver may no longer be able to make or change plans spontaneously, but will have to consider whether the person with AD will be adequately cared for.

It is almost always eventually necessary to hire help to care for the patient. This means that caregivers will have to supervise and maintain a congenial relationship with the people on whom they depend but with whom they may not feel comfortable. Having hired help in the home changes the atmosphere. The space must be shared with more people. Most caregivers feel uncomfortable relaxing when the aide is working and resent the loss of privacy in their homes. Of course, not all caregivers experience hired help as an intrusion. In some cases family caregivers, patients, and hired help form strong bonds of affection and even begin to think of themselves as extended family and enjoy their relationship.

Caregivers frequently become depressed and angry at the demands and impositions the illness of their relatives makes on daily life. These feelings may prevent them from taking any pleasure in whatever time they do have available to themselves. When they do get an opportunity to be alone at home, they say they are either too tired to enjoy it or need to make phone calls to take care of paperwork or other postponed chores.

A counselor can commiserate with caregivers' feelings and then help them to carve out pockets of respite for themselves. If the caregiver is uncomfortable when there is paid help in the house, the counselor can discuss potential activities for the caregiver outside the home. Perhaps the caregiver can take a course or make dates with friends to go to a restaurant or a movie. The counselor can help caregivers review the care plan to see if it is the most suitable for them and, if so, to accept that some of the intrusions into their lives are inevitable. Counselors can help caregivers to make changes in their attitudes and behaviors and to think about how to use their free time and resources more effectively. If the caregiver is too depressed to make the necessary changes, a referral for further treatment may be warranted.

## Caregiver Experiences

Mrs Jones complained bitterly that she no longer could enjoy her home. When the home health aide arrived early in the morning and wanted to chat, Mrs Jones felt that she needed to respond even though she would have preferred to have her coffee and read her newspaper undisturbed. She wanted the aide to tend to her husband and to leave her alone, but she was afraid to offend the aide, whom she really valued, by not engaging in conversation. With the counselor's encouragement, Mrs Jones decided that she would explain to the aide how much she appreciated her promptness and reliability, but that she desperately needed to have some private time in the morning. This small change restored a part of her life to Mrs Jones that meant peace and tranquility to her.

***The Effect on the Caregiver of Impairments in Communication***  The multiple levels of functioning that characterize AD patients create a constant state of ambiguity. How does the caregiver interpret what the patient says and does? If the patient is irritable, is it just an ordinary bad mood or a sign that the illness is progressing and causing a personality change? Will the patient remember what the caregiver has said? Can you base your plans on what appears to have been an agreed upon plan, or will he or she deny having said it? When the patient says, "You never told me that," how does the caregiver interpret it? An elderly caregiver, confronted with such a denial, may wonder whether his or her own memory is at fault. The person's word is no longer her bond, which leads to unpredictability at all times. Caregivers may be afraid that, in trying to simplify or adapt to the patient's abilities, they may antagonize or insult the patient. When people have been in long-term marriages, much of the relationship is based on habits and assumptions, none of which can be relied on anymore when one of the partners has AD.

Counselors can help caregivers to acknowledge that one of the effects of the illness is that there will be times when they will not share a common reality with the patient. Either they will have forgotten what was said, misinterpreted what was said, or be suffering from delusions that are real to them. Because the patient may look exactly as he always has, it is even harder for the caregiver to accept that the behavior is not under his or her control, but is a function of the illness. The inability to communicate may make caregivers feel sad, lonely, or angry.

Nevertheless, most caregivers manage to maintain an affectionate emotional connection with the person and are not continually disappointed when the symptoms prevent him or her from rational verbal communication. Some caregivers are more able to accept the way the patient is than others. Individual caregivers may be more or less tolerant at different times. They have to learn not only to accept the patient's limitations but also to forgive themselves for their own lapses. Some spouse caregivers may fare best by developing new relationships and interests they can pursue without their partner. Others, who would prefer to be alone or with the spouse despite his impediments, should not feel pressured to behave otherwise. Until very late in the illness, a caregiver can spend some time sharing enjoyable activities with the patient, such as listening to music or taking a walk together. Sometimes just sitting with the patient in companionable silence can be a source of comfort. The caregiver is more likely to enjoy the time with the patient if there are also opportunities for socializing and pursuing separate interests.

## Caregiver Experiences

Pearl was sitting in her support group one winter day and silently fuming. Finally she said, "You know sometimes I get so mad at you all. Everyone keeps telling me that I have to get out more. Well, frankly, I hate the cold, and I actually enjoy sitting in my living room with Al and watching TV together. I know Al doesn't really understand what he's watching, but it feels comfortable. That's what we always did after dinner and it suits me fine to keep doing it. Maybe the rest of you always need to be running around, but right now, I don't want any more advice about meeting new people and going new places." The support group leader said, "I'm sorry if you have felt pushed and criticized for doing what's right for you. I'm glad you spoke up. Does anybody else feel the same way?"

## *Social Consequences of Alzheimer's Disease*

*Isolation From Friends and Social Life*  Caregivers often feel anger at friends for what they perceive as inadequate support or for excluding the patient from social activities. Because of the anger, they cut themselves off from social relationships, which leaves them more isolated. A spouse caregiver may say, "I don't go anywhere without him," or "I did a lot for her and now she isn't willing to do anything for me." The counselor can help them to have realistic expectations of people. Friends may be worried about saying the wrong thing and not knowing how to interact with the patient. The presence of the patient can sometimes interfere with the pleasure of other people. The counselor can suggest that the spouse caregiver go with the patient to certain events, where he seems to be comfortable, appropriate, and welcome. They can also think about what it would be like to go to some events alone. If they are uncomfortable being without their spouse in a group of couples, they should be encouraged to spend more time with single people, or try being with couples and see if it is as bad as they expected. Some couples are more accepting of a single person than others, and the caregiver can only know with whom he or she will feel comfortable by trying. Explore the interests of the caregivers and help them think about activities that would bring them into contact with other people with the same interests. The counselor can reassure the caregiver that going out without the patient does not mean that they are abandoning the patient, but rather is a recognition that their needs are different at this time.

It can be difficult for the caregiver to determine whether the patient can continue to participate in social activities or not. Since the patient's level of functioning is inconsistent, he or she sometimes may be appropriate and other times not, so that the caregiver cannot predict what the outcome of taking the patient will be. After a few situations in which the patient is clearly overwhelmed by a conversation and seems uncomfortable, and in which the other people present are also uncomfortable, it becomes clear that it is not fair to anybody to include the patient. The caregiver may worry that the patient is being deprived of social contact. The counselor should encourage the caregiver to think about alternative situations for the patient in which he will be welcome and be able to function appropriately.

The decline in the patient's ability to socialize as the illness progresses has an impact on the social life of others. The social life of the spouse caregiver, more than other relatives, is eventually profoundly affected. As the impairments in the patient are usually subtle at first, a couple can generally continue their regular social activities, as the well spouse will cue and cover for the patient when necessary. When the patient's symptoms begin to interfere more with socializing, the caregiver may turn down invitations and restrict entertaining at home. If the caregiver is embarrassed by the patient's behavior, or if friends are not tolerant, the caregiver may feel that he or she has no options. Some spouses who have always socialized as a couple are too uncomfortable to go out on their own, even when they are invited, or feel too guilty about no longer including their partner. For many caregivers this is the beginning of social isolation. Adult children and other relatives generally do not have the same issues because they probably have not socialized regularly with the patient. They may, however, cut back on their socializing to spend time with the patient or to relieve the primary caregiver. This may result in increased isolation for them as well. They begin to turn down invitations, take longer to respond to calls from friends, drop a class, and contract their social life.

The process of becoming isolated evolves over time, as can the process of reengaging and renewing or developing new social contacts. Caregivers may not even be aware of how much they are limiting their contacts, or feel they have no alternatives and not address the issue until they become depressed or the problem is pointed out to them. The counselor who is aware of the possible danger of isolation should be alert to changes in the caregiver's social activities and can intervene before the caregiver has cut himself or herself off from friends and family. Sometimes a caregiver will only come for counseling when feeling the impact of the choices they have been making.

Counselors need to help caregivers identify the reasons for their withdrawal and to address them. When the counselor makes the caregiver aware of his or her shrinking life apart from caregiving, the reasons for the behavior may emerge. Sometimes the problem is concrete, like finding someone to stay with the patient. Some caregivers are unable or unwilling to trust others to care for the patient. While this caregiver may know the patient better than anyone else, it is fair to neither the caregiver nor the patient to rely totally on one person. The counselor can help the caregiver to prepare the kind of information and instructions that another person would need to care for the patient and start to plan for the caregiver to take breaks. In other cases the reasons are more emotional, for example, feeling sorry that the patient cannot be present, reluctance to go without the patient to a previously shared activity or event, or fear of being on their own. Whatever the reasons, counselors should not ignore caregiver isolation. There is almost always something that can be done and some activity a caregiver can take part in that will bring him or her back into the social world. A counselor can help more traditional older people who may never be comfortable socializing without a partner to find activities such as joining a chorus or pursuing some other interests that do not threaten their values or traditions. It may be useful to share with the caregiver the fact that research has shown the value of social support in maintaining well-being.

***Loss of Freedom***    Even caregivers who try to carry on with their normal activities find that their caregiving responsibilities are never entirely out of their thoughts. There is always the lurking anxiety that a problem may develop and that the caregiver will have to cut short whatever he or she is doing. This feeling has been labeled, "Always on call." Some caregivers stop making plans rather than risk having to cancel or cut them short. Caregivers may not be fully aware that this is what they are doing but rather are caught in an insidious process. When caregivers complain of being tied down, counselors can assess whether they just need to express the feeling or are open to taking steps to remedy the situation.

Counselors can help caregivers to take steps toward planning time away and to deal with the ambivalent and anxious feelings that are evoked when respite is being considered. In some cases, caregivers express concern that if they let themselves go, they will not want to return. The counselor can reassure the caregiver that a wish to stay away will not prevent him or her from returning. These are common and understandable feelings, and having the feeling is not the same as acting on it. At times when the caregiver feels confident of the quality of care the patient is receiving in his or her absence, the weight of the responsibility may recede.

***Embarrassment by the Patient***    The symptoms of AD can lead patients to behave in socially inappropriate ways. They may, for example, press all the buttons in the elevator, causing it to stop on every floor, or speak too loudly, or address strangers in an overly friendly way, or accuse their caregiver of hurting or even trying to kidnap them. Caregivers have described feeling ashamed of the patient's behavior and angry at the public display of such dysfunction. They may also feel embarrassed for their relatives, who may not realize that others are reacting negatively to them. Counselors can help caregivers accept their emotional reactions to the patient and find ways to avoid situations in which the patient is most likely to behave in peculiar ways (see Chapter 9). In public places it may be necessary to explain to others that the patient has an illness and cannot help himself or herself. Patients in the early stage of AD may behave in ways that a person who knows them well recognizes as symptoms of the illness but that others may respond to with annoyance or embarrassment. However, strangers or those who are less emotionally involved with the patient may either not notice the behavior or not be put off by it. When the person with AD lacks the awareness of the impact of his or her behavior on others, and his presence interferes with others' enjoyment of an event, and that of the caregiver, it may be appropriate for him or her not to attend or for additional supervision to be provided.

***Accepting Help From Family and Friends***  Caregivers who say they need more help either to care for the patient or to give them free time, nevertheless may turn it down when it is offered. This reaction may seem incomprehensible or frustrating to those who would like to help and may be concerned about both the patient's and caregiver's well-being. When this issue is raised by counselors or fellow support group members, caregivers give several kinds of reasons for providing all the care themselves. One reason is a sense of duty: "He's my husband, for better and for worse, and it's my job to take care of him" or "A good daughter should take care of her father." Another reason is the feeling that no one else can do the job as well or the patient won't be comfortable with somebody else. Caregivers also complain that often the kind of help that family and friends offer is not exactly what they or the patient need. For example, a daughter can offer to come by in the evening after work so her mother can go out. The mother might not want to go out by herself in the evening and prefer to stay home. Another problem for caregivers is that they are afraid they are imposing and will never be able to reciprocate. Caregivers also worry that someone who does not have experience taking care of a person with AD may not know what to do if the person becomes agitated or ill. "It takes so long to tell my sister how to take care of Jay that I don't have the energy to go out. And besides, there's no way I can ever repay her," said one long-term caregiver. It should be noted that male caregivers generally are offered help more frequently from family members and find it easier to ask for help than female caregivers.

The counselor should respect caregivers' decisions not to ask for help from family and friends if they are determined to care for their relatives on their own and neither they nor the patients seem to be at risk. When the caregiver continues to express dissatisfaction with lack of help and seems unable to accept the help that is offered, the counselor can assist the caregiver in resolving this issue by understanding what thoughts or feelings are getting in the way and trying to help him or her to accept some help. Caregivers who cannot utilize supports that are not completely satisfactory are putting themselves at risk of becoming exhausted.

## Caregiver Experiences

Paula's husband Frank was in the moderate stage of AD, and it was difficult to take him anywhere anymore. Frank's younger sister, Antonia, had always had a special relationship with him. She was a widow and retired from her job. Antonia made repeated offers to stay with Frank so Paula could go out and could not understand Paula's repeated refusals. Paula called her counselor. "Antonia is being so nice. She can't understand why I won't let her help. She must think she has offended me or I'm crazy. She'll probably stop calling me soon. I would really like to go out without Frank, but how can I tell her my real reason for not accepting her help? I don't want her to know that the brother she has always looked up to is now incontinent." The counselor told Paula that she respected the fact that she was trying to protect Frank and preserve his image in his sister's mind. "What this also means is that Antonia is being deprived of a chance to help her brother. Do you think you may be underestimating how much Antonia cares about him? Why don't you leave the decision to Antonia?"

*Loss of Status in Community* The ability of all people with AD to function in their regular roles will decline over time and will affect their place in the family and the larger community. In some cases this change may result in the family's or caregiver's loss of the status that derived from the patient's position. The wife, husband, or child of the person who is now a patient may have been accorded particular respect or afforded certain privileges that are no longer available. In addition, the financial costs of caregiving may have led the caregiver to alter his or her lifestyle to a more modest one. These changes can feel like enormous blows when superimposed on the loss of the relationship with the patient, especially when the caregiver has relied on the connection to the relative to enhance his or her own feelings of self-esteem and to define his or her place in the community.

Counselors can help such caregivers adjust to this significant loss either by exploring possible sources of meaning within themselves (such as developing interests or relationships they have not pursued and reassessing their personal qualities) or by developing new personal connections that can fulfill this need. Recognizing self-worth is likely to be a slow process but can ultimately result in developing new strengths and areas of competence. For some spouse caregivers, what starts out as a devastating loss of the identity derived from their husband or wife becomes an opportunity to discover their individuality and potential.

## Financial Issues

Reactions to the financial implications of caring for a person with AD are frequently very intense. No matter how much or how little money a family has, AD has financial implications: the loss of the patient's income if that person is still employed, possible loss of the caregiver's salary as well, additional medical expenses, and additional costs of caregiving. By planning in advance, families can protect their financial assets and ensure appropriate access to entitlements.

### Creating a Long-Term Financial Plan

Caregivers may not be aware of the financial issues that will arise as a result of the care needs of their relative during the long course of the disease. People with AD may need custodial care (supervision and help with the activities of daily living) for many years. While this care can be provided at home or in a nursing home, in either case it is costly, and it is important to make financial provisions to cover it.

The counselor can educate caregivers and their families about the need for financial planning; refer them to the appropriate professionals such as lawyers, accountants, and estate planners; and help them work collaboratively in making the necessary arrangements. The Alzheimer's Association or a local community agency that provides services to seniors may be able to provide suitable referrals. In some states, Medicaid provides for some of these services for those who are eligible. Medicare also provides for home care for short periods of time, usually after an acute hospitalization.

## Finances and the Family

Since money is generally a taboo subject, often even more so than sexual issues, there is frequently no precedent for discussing financial concerns among family members. In many families the children have never been privy to information about their parents' finances, and parents who prefer to maintain this boundary may find it difficult to involve the children and to share information with them. Family members may differ not only in their comfort level in discussing finances but also in their understanding of the financial ramifications of the illness. Counselors need to help family members deal with the emotional aspects of financial planning as well as practical matters.

To varying degrees, the family as a whole and each person will be dealing with financial arrangements as well as with the feelings of loss of the future they expected and the resulting changes in roles and responsibilities. Family counseling may provide a forum for educating family members about the need for financial planning, for facilitating discussion about allocation of financial responsibilities, and for sharing feelings evoked by the financial arrangements that need to be made.

The kinds of financial concerns that confront a family member are largely determined by his or her relationship to the patient. Spouses of the patient often have these concerns:

- Previously made plans for retirement may no longer be suitable.

- All the resources will be depleted caring for the ill spouse.

- Money intended for the children will be spent on health care.

- Financial information will have to be shared with adult children or other family members.

- Control of assets may have to be given over to others.

- Family members may disagree about the most appropriate financial arrangements.

Adult children may have the following concerns:

- Family members may have to assume responsibility for their parent's financial well-being.

- Anticipated funds may not become available.

- Siblings may not agree on the use and control of resources.

- Spending money on the ill parent may cause conflict with the adult child caregiver's spouse.

When an adult child or a spouse feels unable or afraid to undertake a new financial role, such as paying bills or working in the family business, the counselor can assess with them whether they want to make the effort to overcome their reluctance or find someone else to assume the task.

The counselor can try to help family members find a way of addressing these issues that is consonant with their values, loyalties, abilities, and history. On the practical level, they can be informed about resources and helped to access and use them effectively. Counselors can teach problem-solving and negotiating skills to enhance the family's ability to work out their differences.

## Caregiver Experiences

Dorothy lived in South Carolina with full-time home care. Each of her three children, Mark, Melanie, and Adrienne, periodically went down to visit and check on her status. Then they realized they were running out of money and could no longer afford this plan. Mark and Adrienne wanted to have their mother transferred to a nursing home in New York where they lived. Melanie was sure that the change would kill her. Melanie threatened that she would never forgive her brother and sister if anything happened to their mother, and they were afraid to act without her consent. The three children met with their counselor to try to work out a plan they could live with. Based on what they told her, the counselor identified the following issues: They had to deal with the fact that the money was running out and some change would have to take place. She said that the choice seemed to be between a nursing home in South Carolina and one in New York. She pointed out that it would be preferable for family to be close by to supervise, because their mother had been hospitalized several times for medical problems and they couldn't keep running down to South Carolina. While moving had some risks, which she would tell them how to minimize, it might be better if their mother were in a place where she would be well taken care of and they could visit more frequently and easily. They decided that the move to New York was the best choice. They got a special private aide for a few weeks after the move to help their mother adjust to her new surroundings, and she seemed to be thriving in her new setting and enjoying the frequent visits of her children.

## COUNSELOR CHECKLIST

### How Counseling Can Help the Caregiver

☐ Help the caregiver face new challenges by being available for consultation, providing information and support, and being realistically optimistic that these challenges can be met.

### Learning About the Diagnosis

☐ Educate the caregiver about the symptoms and progression of Alzheimer's disease.

☐ Help the caregiver accept that the patient's behavior is a result of the illness.

☐ Help the caregiver make realistic care plans.

☐ Acknowledge the caregiver's feelings and let him or her know it is common and acceptable to have them.

☐ Address reluctance to accept the diagnosis and tell friends and family.

☐ Reassure family that the familial form of AD is extremely rare.

### When the Illness Becomes More Severe

☐ Explore the emotional meaning of a new symptom with the caregiver.

☐ Help to correct any misperceptions about the severity of the symptoms.

☐ Help the caregiver deal with the emotional and practical implications of changes in the patient.

☐ Refer the caregiver for a psychiatric assessment if there is a major shift in mood and ability to function.

☐ Identify the specific stressors that affect each individual client and help him or her adjust the care plan to address those points of stress.

☐ If caregivers seem extremely stressed, help them determine if they are able to continue to care for the patient.

☐ Encourage the caregiver to find new ways to add variety and interest to life to relieve feelings of tedium and boredom.

☐ Help the caregiver anticipate situations in which the patient may behave inappropriately in order to avoid them or to provide enough supervision to minimize their impact.

☐ Help the caregiver overcome feelings of hopelessness. Assess for possible depression.

### Lifestyle Changes

☐ Help the caregiver assess what responsibilities the patient can no longer perform and address any fears about taking over certain tasks.

☐ Counsel the caregiver to continue valued activities.

☐ Help caregivers assess whether they are managing their time and energy effectively, and identify tasks that can be eliminated or shared with others.

☐ Help the caregiver accept that caregiving will cause intrusions into daily life and identify sources of respite.

☐ Help the caregiver understand the limitations of the patient's ability to communicate and find new ways to interact with the patient.

☐ Help the spouse caregiver build a social life without the patient.

☐ Assist the caregiver in resolving issues that may be getting in the way of accepting help.

### Financial Issues

☐ Educate the caregiver and his or her family about the need to develop a long-term financial plan, referring them to professionals to make necessary arrangements.

☐ Help families address the emotional, as well as the practical, aspects of financial planning.

# 8

# RELATIONSHIP-RELATED ISSUES

The previous chapter discussed common emotional reactions to the illness of a relative with Alzheimer's disease (AD). This chapter discusses the impact AD has on the relationship between caregiver and AD patient, whether the relationship is spousal, parent-child, or friend-friend.

## Meaning of Loss of the Relationship With the Patient

If the patient is a family member with whom the caregiver has a strong emotional relationship, new symptoms may be experienced as an assault on their connection with each other. The cognitive and functional declines that characterize AD alter the nature of the experiences that can be shared. As the illness progresses, the person's personality and reactions generally become less and less like those that could be expected before he or she became ill, while the person may still appear physically unchanged. Caregivers will express feelings of loneliness; of missing the companionship and camaraderie and the exchanging of ideas and jokes; and of loss of a partner, parent, or sibling with whom to solve problems and by whom one can be comforted.

While the old relationship is gradually eroding, a new one is emerging in which the focus is increasingly on providing care directly or ensuring that it is provided by others. Some find satisfaction in this new role. Occasionally caregivers report that previously unsatisfactory relationships have improved because the patients have become more affectionate or amiable. In most cases, however, as the disease progresses, caregivers suffer the loss of the connection with the patient and need to find support and intellectual rapport with other people.

Counselors can be supportive by giving caregivers the opportunity to talk about their feelings and guiding them in thinking about how they can sustain themselves in the face of their losses. In time, the counselor can help them recognize untapped internal resources and find external supports from their family, friends, and the community that will enable them to rebuild a life that has satisfaction and new meaning. Joining a caregiver support group can provide companionship and a place to share feelings with others who are going through a similar experience and to gain the encouragement to seek additional opportunities for social interaction.

## Spouse Caregivers

### *Issues of Loss*

Changes in the person with AD alter the nature of any relationship that can be maintained with him or her. In this section we explore the various losses a spouse experiences as caregiver: the loss of companionship, sexual partner, and support.

Millie said to her counselor, "I know that I have come a long way since the time we started working together. I accept that Ted has AD, I understand the symptoms it causes, and I have even begun to do new things I've never done before. But inside, I sometimes feel so sad and alone. I miss the old conversations, even the dumb jokes we used to tell each other, and taking long walks and just talking to each other. I know that by now I shouldn't expect him to remember that tomorrow is our anniversary. He always used to plan a surprise for me. We went to Bermuda once. Another time he had a fancy dinner delivered to the house. I'm going to make a little party for just the two of us, but it certainly doesn't feel like the old days. I have to admit it has gotten me down." The counselor said, "I understand how much you have lost. The feelings are probably especially strong on a day that is meant to celebrate the relationship you shared." "They are," Millie said, "And I guess I'll have to deal with this loss as I have with the others. You just have to go on."

*Loss of Companionship*  Dealing with the emotional pain of acknowledging that the patient can no longer enjoy experiences that would previously have been meaningful is a regrettable and inevitable part of caregiving. Spouses may have relied on each other for emotional support and companionship. Before one member of the couple became ill with AD, they probably shared common interests; their involvement with their children, grandchildren, and other family members; making decisions together; and discussing the experiences each of them had when they were apart. The mutual nature of the relationship shifts with the progression of AD, leaving a major void in the life of the spouse-caregiver. In family counseling, spouse-caregivers can share with other family members their feelings about the losses they are experiencing. When other family members understand the nature of their well parent's losses, they may increase their own involvement with the caregiver.

When the caregiver has been accustomed to sharing an activity with the patient, he or she may feel that there will be no joy in having the experience without the spouse. However, counselors can help caregivers to identify activities they enjoyed together with their spouses in the past in which they can continue to find pleasure for many years if they can adjust to the changes the patient's decline requires. In addition, counseling can help caregivers differentiate between activities that are still appropriate for the patient and those that they might enjoy more on their own.

## Changing Relationships

Mrs Green came to her first session with a counselor. She said, "My husband and I have always been a team. We do almost everything together. We have a concert subscription, and we go to all the baseball games when the team is in town." And then she started to cry. "But now he stands up in the middle of the concert, saying he's hungry and wants to go home. I know he doesn't really get what's going on, although sometimes he seems to enjoy the music. When we're at the game, he keeps asking me which team is up and who is on base. The truth is, we really don't share these things anymore. I feel like I am dragging him around from place to place when he would really be better off at home. At least there I'm not telling him to sit down or be quiet every minute. When my friends tell me how handsome he still is, instead of making me feel better, I feel even worse. What difference does it make how handsome he is when he really isn't with me anymore?" The counselor said, "It sounds like the old ways of doing things aren't working." "You're right. I know I'm going to have to start doing things differently, but I just haven't felt ready. I really don't want to go alone, so I'm going to give the tickets away." "Maybe you could do that some of the time, but maybe you could invite a friend to join you occasionally, too. I know this is easier to say than to do, but I think you understand the illness well enough to know that your husband really can't continue to go everywhere with you. It's not fair to either of you. Since many caregivers have to face this problem, maybe you want to bring it up in your support group and see how others have dealt with it."

*Changes in Sexual Relationship* Many couples enjoy the warmth of physical closeness and continue to share a bed and take pleasure in sexual relations despite the fact that one of them has Alzheimer's disease. However, as the illness progresses, the sexual life of the couple often undergoes a major change. Some patients behave inappropriately; others lose the ability to be adequate sexual partners. The well partner may find the idea of sexual relations with the ill partner to be unattractive.

## Changing Relationships

Connie, who used to be a buyer in a department store, was married to John, who had been a very successful automobile salesman. For 45 years they had a wonderful marriage. Now Connie's husband was in the middle stage of AD, although he had been diagnosed only 3 years earlier. She said, "One of the things I miss the most is that we can't have decent sex. John no longer knows what he's doing but he keeps trying. His awkward attempts just remind me of my loss even more. This has begun to upset me a great deal." The counselor, who had been working with Connie since John was first diagnosed, responded, "You know, I can't restore the old John, but I have an idea that might work. Since he doesn't remember, you might try saying to him, "We just had wonderful sex. I enjoyed it so much. But now I'm tired. Let's go to sleep. Although there's no perfect response, this may be the kindest solution." Connie said, "I'm willing to try it, because anything is better than these painful feelings." She called the counselor on the phone a few days later to tell her that while it broke her heart to lie to him, her suggestion had been helpful.

***Loss of Assistance From the Patient*** "Is it too much to expect
that Jerry will continue to help me with the chores?" Caregivers of
patients in the early stage of AD may be irritated that their relatives
sometimes cannot perform some of the tasks they had in the past,
while at other times they function quite well. Their best efforts to
be helpful sometimes result in more work for their caregivers. Even
those who recognize that these changes are related to the illness
sometimes find themselves wondering whether the person is intentionally not doing what is asked. Counselors can help caregivers to
accept their feelings of confusion and frustration as a natural reaction to a person whose level of functioning is erratic. Underlying
the distress about tasks with which the patient is no longer able to
be of assistance may be anxiety about having no one to rely on in
situations that were previously the patient's responsibility. Having
him or her perform these tasks provided a sense of comfort and
security. The counselor can encourage the caregiver to try and learn
how to perform some of these tasks without the patient's assistance, which may ultimately give the caregiver a sense of pride and
independence. The caregiver may also have to learn to ask others
for help with, or hire people to perform, tasks that are beyond his
or her ability.

## New Opportunities

While experiencing numerous losses in the spousal relationship,
the caregiver may also struggle to balance them with opportunities
to socialize separately from the AD patient and to form new
relationships.

***Building a Life Apart From Caregiving*** Caregivers who are still
working or have meaningful hobbies generally have built a life for
themselves that they may be able to continue in spite of caregiving
responsibilities. These activities may provide respite as well as satisfaction. Some even say that they go to work to escape or that working saves their lives. However, many spouse caregivers do not work
outside the home and have become so consumed by caregiving that
they have given up other relationships and activities. When they
take time away from their ill spouse, they may feel guilty or worry
they are depriving their husband or wife of their care and companionship. When these caregivers finally become aware of a need
to be with other people, they may find that they have lost

contact with friends and say they have nowhere to go and no one to go with.

Counselors have to recognize that for some caregivers going out alone may be upsetting for symbolic and emotional reasons. It may be an open acknowledgment that their spouse can no longer be a suitable companion. For those who are accustomed to going out as part of a couple, it may feel awkward or embarrassing to go out without their spouse. Some caregivers are hesitant to reconnect with friends for fear of rejection. The counselor can encourage such caregivers to discuss their fears, imagine how they will feel if their worst fears come to pass, and picture successfully dealing with the anticipated situation. It can be helpful to role-play a conversation with someone the caregiver would like to contact so that he or she can develop a comfortable approach before making the actual call.

It is essential to the well-being of most caregivers that they find a balance between caring for a loved one and exploring independent activities. The counselor has to be very careful not to push such caregivers too hard. The counselor can encourage these caregivers to weave new elements into the patterns of their lives. They can suggest that the caregivers begin by choosing an activity that is not too threatening in order to slowly build confidence. For example, a caregiver may not be able to imagine leaving the patient for a whole day but may be willing to get tickets with an old friend for a show and ask an adult child to stay with the patient for the evening. Caregivers who say they have lost all their friends may meet new people if they take a class or join a senior group.

## Changing Relationships

Barry had been caring for his wife Sarah, who had been ill with AD for 10 years and was now in the severe stage of AD. They had had a wonderful marriage. Sarah was the one who had run their very active social life. Barry had made no effort to contact their friends since Sarah had become ill, and when they called, he told them he was busy caring for Sarah and had no time to talk. Gradually they all stopped calling. Barry was feeling very lonely and really wanted to reconnect with the outside world. He called his counselor and said, "I don't know where to go. I don't know what to do." They had a brainstorming session and wrote down all the things he had wanted to do and never got around to. His face brightened. "When I was younger, I dreamed of being a sculptor, but I was always busy building my business. If I take a class at the Y, maybe I'll meet other people interested in art there." He enrolled in a class at the Y the following week. A year later he phoned the counselor to invite her to an exhibit of student work. "A gallery owner is thinking of taking some of my work on consignment. That class opened a whole new world to me."

***Obstacles to Forming New Relationships***  Some caregivers, though suffering from great loneliness and sadness, will abstain from new romantic relationships for a variety of reasons, including feelings of loyalty to the ill spouse. Others are interested in forming new relationships but feel ambivalent because of their ethical, moral, and religious concerns. Sometimes friends or acquaintances suggest that a new relationship may be the solution to caregiving problems. These recommendations are not always welcome or suitable.

### Changing Relationships

Elizabeth complained to her support group that she was fed up with taking care of her husband, Bert. One of the group members said, "You're young and good looking. Why don't you find another guy?" Elizabeth said, "I don't believe in doing that sort of thing." Another group member said, "We need to be more sensitive. We have to respect how she feels. Actually, I'm jealous that she has the support of her beliefs." The group leader then turned to Elizabeth and asked her why she was feeling so upset that day. It turned out it was because she had applied for day care for Bert and she was told there was no room. The discussion shifted to problems of day care. Later, the counselor raised the subject about members' thoughts about new romantic relationships.

Many spouse-caregivers have fears about how their family members and friends will react to a new relationship. These concerns are realistic: adult children and friends are often critical of people who form new relationships. This can make the caregiver feel guilty and unsupported and disrupt family relationships. To the adult child, the parent's new relationship may be evidence that the patient has been written off as a real member of the family. While adult children may have difficulty accepting a parent's divorce and remarriage, in this case there is no death or formal agreement of separation, and the new relationship may be viewed as especially disloyal or as a desertion.

In such situations, it is often useful to have one or more family counseling sessions where all family members can openly communicate their feelings. With the counselor present, the parent may be able to reveal the depth of his or her loneliness and feelings of loss and need for companionship. The counselor can ask the adult child about his or her own fears and feelings of loss. The son or daughter may be able to talk about feeling that the other parent has been betrayed or abandoned. In addition, some adult children, who have been playing an important role in supporting the well parent in caregiving, may feel rejected and unneeded. They may feel that they have lost two parents—one to illness and the other to the new relationship. Some adult children may worry that the caregiving parent will neglect the patient. They may also worry about the financial consequences of a new relationship. Knowing how other family members feel may make it possible to have a dialogue and begin to talk about the realities of the future. By listening to each other's fears, concerns, and needs, they may be able to reassure each other and reduce the number of misunderstandings between them.

In many situations a well spouse forms a new relationship, has the full support of family and friends, and continues to provide care to the patient. A counselor is less likely to hear about situations like these, in which there is no problem.

## Family Relations

*Asking the Children for Help*  Throughout most of a child's life, a parent has been there to support and guide him or her. Children take comfort in the presence of their parents, and parents take pleasure in providing for their children. It may be extremely difficult for a parent to change the traditional pattern and ask a child for help.

Adult children accustomed to the self-sufficiency of their parents may not recognize when a parent's needs have changed or may be reluctant to offer to help out of concern for the parent's pride.

When this conspiracy of silence persists, spouse-caregivers often tell members of their support group or their counselor that they wish that the children would be more helpful. "I shouldn't have to ask. Don't they see what's going on? They know their father has Alzheimer's disease, and they act as if nothing has changed. They still come on Sunday afternoon and expect that lunch will be on the table when they arrive. Don't they see I'm falling off my feet?" It may seem obvious that the parent should ask the child for the help he or she needs. Yet many parents say, "I shouldn't have to ask. They should know." When nothing is said, the parent may suffer in angry silence, and the children can continue to behave as if their parent is not ill.

There are several observations a counselor can make to families struggling with these issues. It is common for people to hope that others will understand their needs without their having to express them, although this is an unrealistic expectation and usually leads to disappointment and anger. Another common fear is that expressing a need will mean that they are needy, a highly devalued condition. The counselor can point out that having needs is part of the human condition. Children, family, and friends often value the opportunity to be helpful, do not know how to offer, but may welcome a request from a parent. If the counselor is working individually with the caregiver, it may be possible to encourage him or her to initiate a conversation with the children about the new circumstances in the family. It may also be useful to have a family session either to open the dialogue or to augment it.

*Second Marriages*   Several characteristics of second marriages may have an impact on caregiving. There may be a great age difference between the partners, or there may be children from previous marriages who are loyal to only one spouse. The marriage may have been of short duration, in which case the well spouse may feel that he or she has finally found happiness, only to have it taken away by the diagnosis of AD shortly thereafter. Three major issues confront such families: the willingness of the spouse to provide care, the involvement of the children of the well spouse in caring for the ill spouse, and the use of financial resources for the care of the patient. When stepfamilies truly become blended, they may be able to bring more resources to support the caregiver and each other.

## Changing Relationships

Shirley had been divorced for many years, and her children were grown and married when she met Larry, a widower with three grown children himself. He was everything to her that her first husband was not: kind, considerate, generous, and a great companion. They had been married for only 3 years when Larry began to have memory problems, and they discovered he had AD. For awhile, they were able to continue to live very much as they had before. But now, Shirley told the counselor that all the children were critical of what she was doing and that she was at her wits' end about how to get them to cooperate. The counselor suggested a family session with all the children present.

In the family session, it became clear that Shirley was very close to her children, who had always included Larry in family functions. Now, however, her children resented having Larry around since he could no longer behave appropriately. They were also furious that she was spending her time caring for him, but they didn't offer to help her. When she asked, they said Larry wasn't their father, and his own children should help. His children said Shirley should take care of him, because she had benefited from his money. Shirley said angrily, "I'm getting exhausted, but it is clear that somehow everyone has a reason why they won't help." The counselor said, "I see there are really deep gulfs between you. Perhaps each of you can think about whether there is anything at all that you are willing to do to help your mother or father."

The next time she saw the counselor individually, Shirley said nothing had changed. The counselor told Shirley that she could understand why she was looking for support from the children, and maybe, in time, they would be more helpful. Right now, she needed to take charge of the planning for Larry's care, and if she couldn't do it all alone, she should hire help. Perhaps once she had help in place and the children didn't feel like so much was being demanded of them, they might be more willing to become involved.

***Families Reunited Because of AD*** Spouses who have separated sometimes return to care for the partner who has developed AD. In some cases the children who have maintained relationships with both parents are instrumental in encouraging this arrangement. Other times, the couple may have remained on good terms, and in the absence of another caregiver, a former spouse agrees to provide care. In such a situation a counselor can help the caregiver, patient, and children to redefine their relationship in light of the new situation and to address the legal, financial, and medical issues and decisions that have to be made. A series of family sessions may provide a forum in which to offer education about AD, develop plans for the future, and address old grievances if they intrude.

---

### Changing Relationships

Mrs Liddle, who had been divorced for many years and had retired a few years before, had been seeing a counselor because she was feeling depressed about getting old. She felt marginalized, unproductive, and very lonely. She had thought it would be a good idea to go back to work, but she was unable to find a job and was not satisfied with just volunteer work. She told the counselor that one of her children had called that week and told her that her former husband, Sal, had just been diagnosed with Alzheimer's disease. Her son said Dad told him he really needed her now and was sorry they had ever split up. Mrs Liddle was really torn. She had never forgiven Sal for the affair that precipitated the divorce, but she had never stopped loving him, and the affair was a long time ago. She didn't want the children, who had lives of their own, to have to take care of him. She told the counselor that she felt good that Sal wanted to be with her, but she was afraid she might be jumping into something that was more than she could handle. The counselor asked what her worries were. Mrs Liddle said, "I don't always feel that well myself. What if I get sick? Besides, I have gotten used to living alone and I love my little apartment. But Sal still has the big house we raised our kids in, and my old friends live around there, too." The counselor said that it was a big decision and she should give herself time to think about it. "Next time I see you, if you're still interested, let's talk more about what it would mean to be a caregiver of a person with AD."

---

## Adult Child Caregivers

Adult children of a parent with AD experience a variety of emotional reactions to assuming the role of caregiver to their parent. When the parent becomes ill, it may be the first time that the children experience the vulnerability of the parent, who had previously been perceived as powerful and protective. Being the source of comfort to a parent who has become so dependent can evoke feelings of profound sadness. Adult children may find new feelings of compassion for the parent with whom they may have had a difficult relationship prior to the illness. These tender feelings may be expressed in the generosity with which they provide care for their parents.

Caring for a parent can evoke negative as well as positive feelings and, in most cases, a mixture of both. Caregiving can feel like a threatening and unwelcome burden for the individual adult child and can create conflict among siblings and other family members. Siblings who may not have been in close touch with each other may find that they need to work together, though in many cases, one person seems to carry most of the responsibility. Some child caregivers may be sharing the caregiving role with their well parent, with whom they may disagree about how to care for the parent with AD.

The tasks of caregiving do not generally have to be assumed all at once. Individuals and families usually have the opportunity to grow into the caregiving role, taking on responsibilities gradually as the patient's condition declines. Though stressed by the tasks, most adult children take pride in their ability to care for their parents. Many are very competent and use the Internet and other resources to get information and become effective caregivers. Nevertheless, they still suffer from the sadness of the loss of the previous relationship and of watching their parent decline.

Many adult children will have other roles that they play such as a job, family of their own, or taking care of another ill parent or relative and will have to rearrange their lifestyles to accommodate the caregiving role. (We discuss this issue in detail in Chapter 7.)

## *Change in Parent-Child Relationship*

Gaining an intimate knowledge of a parent's resources, medical condition, and sometimes, literally, his or her physical body can feel like a violation of the boundaries that had previously defined family relationships. Asserting authority and determining what tasks a parent can and cannot fulfill signals a shift in the relationship. The parent who protected you now needs your protection.

## Changing Relationships

Laurie said to her counselor, "I used to talk to my dad about investments. I really relied on his judgment. Now he still gives me advice, and I listen, but I don't trust what he says anymore. The problem is, he writes down the names of the stocks he tells me to buy and looks them up in the paper. He is so happy when he thinks I made money. That's fine. But he gets really upset and angry with himself when he finds out a stock has gone down. When that happens, I'm so tempted to console him by saying I didn't buy it. I hate lying to my dad. I never have." The counselor says, "I'm sure it feels disrespectful. But in this case, the issue isn't really about lying. It's about how you can preserve your father's sense that he still has something valuable to offer, and that's more important now. Maybe you can reassure him by reminding him about the stocks you bought that went up and tell him that, thanks to his advice, you've made some money. This way you can continue to share a common interest."

## *Ways Adult Children Provide Care*

*Managing Care of the Patient Who Lives Alone*   If the patient is in an early stage of dementia and lives alone, the caregiver may worry about whether the patient is safe and is taking care of himself or herself appropriately. Many caregivers find themselves constantly checking up on the patient or receiving calls from the patient while at work. This may jeopardize the caregiver's ability to function or jeopardize the job itself. A counselor may suggest that the caregiver have a social worker go to the patient's home to assess whether the patient can still live alone. If the current situation is deemed safe, then the counselor can help the caregiver tolerate the anxiety and minimize the day-to-day uncertainty by enrolling the patient in community programs such as a senior center and using services that will go to the patient's home. For example, the caregiver can arrange for food delivery services such as Meals on Wheels to bring meals to the patient's home, or the caregiver can ask a neighbor to look in on the patient.

## Changing Relationships

Bob, who was an only child and whose mother had AD, visited her every few weeks and called her regularly. His mother, who lived alone in an apartment, said she was fine whenever he called. One day, after Bob had been away on a long business trip, he visited his Mom, bringing her ice cream as a special treat. He went to put the ice cream away and discovered that there was nothing in the refrigerator. He got worried and checked the kitchen cabinets and discovered only chocolate bars, on which she had apparently been subsisting. It was immediately clear she could no longer care for herself. He couldn't believe that he had been there so often and hadn't realized how bad things had gotten. After stocking the house with food, he realized he needed advice. He called the Alzheimer's Association help line.

***The Long Distance Caregiver*** Siblings or other family members who live far away may feel left out, powerless, and angry with the family member who lives nearby and has day-to-day responsibility for the patient and who expresses constant dissatisfaction with their efforts to contribute to the care of the patient. They may feel that they are doing their best to be helpful, visiting when they can, offering to make telephone calls for the primary caregiver, and communicating with the patient by telephone or letter. The long distance caregiver may feel that his or her concern for the patient is not appreciated and that the primary caregiver is being too controlling and not allowing the more distant caregiver to have enough input regarding the patient's care.

## Changing Relationships

Rebecca said to her counselor, "My sister Jennifer thinks that because I am far away I am getting a free ride. She doesn't realize that when I give her advice, I'm trying to help. She always takes it as a criticism. Mom is my mother, too. It's not my fault that I live far away and that Jennifer lives near Mom. I'm tired of Jennifer always treating me like a second class citizen."

The counselor told Rebecca she understood her perspective. She said she could also easily imagine what her sister Jennifer would be thinking. She asked Rebecca to do the same. Rebecca did, in fact, have some ideas about what it was like for her sister to be "always on call," and she knew that she benefited from this in many ways. Rebecca was able to pursue her career with few interruptions because her sister was taking care of their mother. "Maybe it would be better if I asked her how she was doing, instead of always offering advice. Maybe then she'd be more willing to listen to what I have to say."

This kind of conflict among siblings is very common. It may be helpful, in the absence of long-standing animosity that is being played out in a new situation, for siblings to express to each other how they are feeling. Each may be able to better appreciate the pain that the other is feeling and perhaps to renegotiate some aspects of the care plan to make the situation more tolerable for both. The counselor may offer to host a conference call to facilitate the discussion. Even with a legacy of a poor relationship in the past, the counselor can recommend putting the past aside in order to deal with the present. Sometimes the issues evoked by the current caregiving situation may provide an opportunity to look at the past from a new perspective.

***The "Young" Adult Child Caregiver***  Most commonly, a person gets diagnosed with AD at an advanced age, and his or her children are middle aged or older themselves. However, sometimes this is not the case, and an adult child caregiver may be dealing with a child in nursery school and play dates at the same time he or she is trying to find an adult day care center for his or her mother. One such caregiver who had enjoyed a very close relationship with her grandmother tearfully shared with her counselor how sad it made her to realize that her daughter would not have the kind of relationship with her grandmother that she had hoped she would. In addition to the emotional impact of caregiving, the concrete tasks themselves may be difficult and require the person to learn about issues pertaining to the elderly that would not have been relevant to them in terms of their own place in the life cycle. A young person may find the process of becoming responsible for a parent's well-being very daunting.

***Changing Living Arrangements to Accommodate the Illness***
Many adult child caregivers choose or feel compelled to have their

ill parent move in with them, especially if their other parent is not alive. They may build an addition to their home, have children give up a bedroom to the parent, give up their own bedroom and sleep on the sofa in the living room, or make other accommodations. These changes may cause disruptions in family life, resentment, anger, and lack of privacy. Children may be embarrassed to bring friends home and may have difficulty adapting to the grandparent's behavior. The behavior of the patient may cause conflict between the spouses about how their lives have changed. These problems may be anticipated to some degree, but what is more difficult to anticipate is how the constant changes and symptoms caused by the illness will affect their lives and their feelings about the patient as time goes on. The caregivers may have overestimated their ability to provide the kind of care that is required. This may evoke feelings of guilt and helplessness. Many families feel that their homes have been irrevocably changed. Grandma may get into fights with the small children, let the dog out of the yard, and burn the food. Families may not anticipate the emotional impact of having the ill person in the home.

Family or couples counseling may be very helpful in such cases, giving each person an opportunity to express his or her point of view. This may make it possible to shift the discourse from a blaming mode to a problem-solving mode. Perhaps agreement can be reached about allocating and sharing tasks and resources. The family may be helped to see the necessity for respite. Perhaps day care for the patient will allow the rest of the family members to be alone together. Some caregivers may choose to find or increase their own employment in order to hire someone to stay with the patient. Others may cut back on paid work to reduce the number of tasks they have to fulfill. These suggestions may solve some of the practical problems. However, some families may still continue to have conflict and emotional stress. This may be relieved by joining support groups or developing a mechanism within the family for regular discussion about their needs and the patient's care.

## Conflict Among Siblings

The illness of a parent may precipitate conflict among siblings. They may have different ideas about how responsibilities for care should be allocated and the value each sibling places on the time, energy, and life roles of the other. Each sibling has had a different relationship with the parent that may influence his or her ability or willingness to provide care. The illness of their parent may have a different impact on each of their lifestyles. Issues and dissatisfactions that may have been buried may resurface under the stress of caregiving.

## Changing Relationships

Carmela and Nina's parents had grown up in a small village in Sicily, got married as teenagers 65 years ago, and emigrated to the United States. They had started with a small vegetable stand that had grown into three successful grocery stores. Their father had a heart attack and died when he was in his early 50s. Both Carmela and Nina had also married young, and each had several grown children. Carmela was a homemaker and Girl Scout leader and was very active in the church. Nina had stayed at home while the children were growing up, but then she had gone to college and become a successful stockbroker. She was so proud of her corner office. Then their mother was diagnosed with Alzheimer's disease. When her dementia became more severe and she couldn't take care of herself, Carmela spent the weekdays with her and Nina took care of her on weekends. Carmela was getting more and more resentful. She said, "I do all the work and you get to go to that glamorous job." Meanwhile Nina was becoming exhausted, she couldn't do her work the way she used to, and her husband was complaining that they weren't spending any time together anymore.

When Nina got demoted and lost her corner office, she went to a counselor for help. The counselor suggested that Nina might consider paying someone to come in and take care of Mom. Nina protested, "But I can't hire someone to take my place. Daughters are supposed to do that." The counselor reminded Nina that she was already a kind of pioneer, going to school and building a career after she was 50 years old. "Maybe we should have a family meeting to see what can be worked out." At the family meeting Nina's husband insisted that he needed his wife back. Either she gave up her job or she gave up spending weekends with her mother. The counselor tried to suggest alternatives, which the family rejected. Nina finally said, "I really can't tolerate this stress. I'm giving up my job. My family comes first."

## Other Caregivers

An AD patient may be cared for by a person to whom he or she is neither biologically nor legally connected. Whether this person is a friend, neighbor, or partner, he or she may not have "official standing" unless named in legal documents such as advance directives or powers of attorney, may not be allowed to make decisions for the patient, and may encounter barriers to providing help in spite of a strong caring relationship. Counselors can help these people decide whether they want to pursue legal guardianship for the patient to overcome these barriers and help them with the caregiving difficulties that any caregiver confronts. On the other hand, friends or neighbors may be expected to take more responsibility for the patient than they are prepared to assume and feel burdened with the demands on them and not know how to step back without jeopardizing the care of the patient. The counselor can help those who have become more involved than they would like to be to find supplementary services or, when necessary for the safety of the patient, to arrange for a suitable placement.

### Changing Relationships

Anna was an administrator in an accounting firm in which Rose was a bookkeeper. Over the years they became good friends, and Anna and Rose often went to the movies together. When an apartment became available in Anna's building, Rose moved in. Rose noticed that Anna was having problems doing her work and was not surprised when she was encouraged to retire early. However, Anna declined rapidly and Rose, who had really become like a sister, brought her to a neurologist to be evaluated. She was diagnosed with Alzheimer's disease. The doctor asked whether Anna had any family member who would look in on her and help her to make arrangements for her future. There was no one. Even though she really cared about her, Rose was a little overwhelmed to realize that she might have to be entirely responsible for Anna. The doctor referred them to the case management agency in their neighborhood, where they were helped to develop a care plan that didn't depend entirely on Rose.

## COUNSELOR CHECKLIST

### Spouse Caregivers

☐ Help caregivers identify which activities they can still enjoy with their spouses, adjusting to the declining capabilities of the patient, and which they might enjoy more on their own or with others.

☐ Support caregivers in taking on new roles and using resources effectively.

☐ If a caregiver is hesitant to try new activities, encourage a step-by-step process to build confidence.

☐ Consider family counseling when a caregiver's new relationship creates a problem for family members.

☐ Encourage caregivers to discuss their changing needs with their children and have a family session, if necessary, to facilitate a dialogue.

### Adult Child Caregivers

☐ Counsel caregivers who do not live near the parent to have a professional assessment to determine whether the parent can still live alone.

☐ Suggest that caregivers make use of community services that will go to the patient's home as needed.

☐ Facilitate discussions among siblings by conference calls if on-site family counseling is not possible.

☐ Educate younger adult child caregivers about resources for the elderly of which they may not be aware.

☐ Counsel families who are considering moving their ill relative into their home of the implications of their choice.

### Other Caregivers

☐ Assist caregivers who are not family members to overcome the barriers to providing help.

☐ Help those who feel more involved than they want to be to create care plans using supplementary services or to arrange for placement in a care facility.

<br>

# 9

# MANAGING BEHAVIORAL AND PSYCHOLOGICAL SYMPTOMS OF ALZHEIMER'S DISEASE

Over the long course of Alzheimer's disease (AD), characteristic behavioral symptoms emerge and become problematic, then fade and are replaced by other symptoms. Each stage is typified by categories of symptoms. In the early stage, symptoms generally relate to short-term memory loss. In the middle stage, symptoms of agitation become more prominent. In the late stage, the cognitive losses are so severe that, ultimately, people with AD require someone else to perform the most basic activities of daily living for them. (See Chapter 1 for a complete overview of each of the stages of AD.)

This chapter provides a conceptual framework for understanding the patient's behavior, recommendations on how to help caregivers alter the patient's environment and lifestyle to fit the needs and functional limitations of their ill relative, as well as strategies for working with specific psychological and behavioral symptoms of AD.

## Understanding and Responding to Symptoms of Alzheimer's Disease

### The Caregiver's Interpretation of the Patient's Symptoms

The way a caregiver interprets the patient's behavior influences his or her response and ability or willingness to make necessary adjustments to accommodate the patient's needs. Some caregivers misinterpret a patient's symptoms because of lack of knowledge about Alzheimer's disease. Others ignore, minimize, or deny the symptoms of the patient's illness so as to avoid taking action or acknowledging the impact of the illness.

In the early stage of AD, it is especially hard for family members to know when to attribute their relative's behavior to the illness. Many caregivers mistakenly believe the patient is intentionally doing something that is, in fact, out of his or her control. This misunderstanding is reinforced by the variability in the patient's level of functioning from day to day. For example, one day the patient may be able to answer the telephone and take a message, while a day later, he or she may answer the phone, not take a message, and forget there was a call at all. The caregiver may become angry and accuse the patient of deliberately not telling him or her about the call.

Some caregivers believe their relative's lack of initiative stems from laziness. "He likes to be served. He just sits there and waits for me to do everything," or, "She could help herself if she wanted to." "She could do better if she tried. Whenever she goes to the store she forgets half of the things we need." Caregivers sometimes convince themselves that the patient is less impaired than he actually is. "Why should I lay out his medication for him? He's perfectly capable of following the doctor's instructions. He knows when to take his medication."

Misinterpretation of behavior can lead to exaggeration of its meaning. For example, caregivers may have heard that people with AD become violent and interpret the least bit of resistance or a small assertive act, such as pushing a plate away forcefully or throwing a coat on the floor, as an act of aggression. This behavior would not necessarily have the same meaning to the caregiver if the person had not been diagnosed with AD.

When a person with AD begins having symptoms such as delusions and hallucinations, some caregivers think the patient is "going crazy." The fact that the word *demented* means crazy to many laypeople reinforces this misconception and the stigma associated with AD.

Often the caregiver's appraisal of the patient's behavior results in unconstructive responses, increases caregiver and patient distress, or puts the caregiver or patient at risk. If this is the case, the counselor should seek to shift the caregiver's perspective to a more realistic appraisal so that he or she can consider a more appropriate response.

## Helping Caregivers Understand the Symptoms of AD

Caregivers may find it easier to make adjustments to accommodate the illness if they have a basis for understanding the cause of the patient's symptoms and behavior. The following concepts may be useful in helping caregivers interpret the changes they see in their relatives and learning or devising appropriate responses.

***The Direct Impact of Neurological Changes in the Brain***  The mechanism by which behavioral and psychological symptoms of dementia (BPSD) occur in Alzheimer's disease is not completely understood. However, it is clear that the primary cause of the behavioral symptoms is the increasing loss of brain function that also affects cognition, emotions, and functional capacity. For example, because of frontal lobe damage, a person with AD may not be able to appropriately channel emotional responses and may be more reactive to any emotions he or she is feeling. Neurologic changes in the brain of a person suffering from AD cause behavioral disinhibition. It has been shown that there is a correlation between the degree of neuronal loss, changes in cells and tissues, and behaviors such as aggression.

***The Progressively Lowered Stress Threshold***  The concept of the progressively lowered stress threshold (PLST) is one useful way of explaining the patient's behavior. It is based on the theory that a person with impaired cognition is particularly susceptible to influence from the environment. According to the PLST model, the diminished capacity of people with AD to remember, make judgments and choices, solve problems, adjust to new situations, and understand complex ones increases the stress they experience in trying to deal with situations that appear challenging. Stressors can be physical, including fatigue or illness; changes in environment, caregiver, or routine; internal or external demands that go beyond the cognitive abilities; or multiple competing stimuli. People with AD are often unable to articulate what is disturbing them and may respond with irritability, agitation, aggression, withdrawal, and depression when they are faced with demands they cannot meet.

The concept of a reduced tolerance for stress (PLST) can provide a useful explanation of a patient's reactions throughout the course of the disease. For example, in the mild stage of the illness, a slightly forgetful and mildly anxious person may burst into tears and become completely overwrought when she cannot find her hand-bag. In the moderate stage of dementia, a person who cannot answer a question may become angry at what feels like a test he cannot pass.

One of the jobs of the counselor is to help caregivers understand this concept and think about how to alter their expectations of their relative. This framework can also provide a guide to the changes that can be made to the environment to make it less stress-ful. A problem with the PLST model, however, is that it does not indicate when to increase activity or how to provide a balance between high and low environmental press. Too little stimulation can result in what appear to be behavior disturbances, as can too much.

Millie called her counselor and said, "You won't believe this. Ted burst into tears yesterday. He never cries. Yesterday evening after we spent most of the day gardening, I asked him whether he wanted to visit our daughter Carol. He screamed, 'Leave me alone.' I said, 'But you know you love Carol.' He said, 'Who is Carol?' How can he not remember his own daughter?"

The counselor said to Millie, "It must be really hard for you to deal with the fact that his illness has advanced to the point where he might not associate the name Carol with his daughter. When a per-son with AD is tired and a demand is made on him, he gets over-whelmed. Perhaps that's why he cried." Millie said, "Maybe I just tried to pack too much into one day. Ted seems so strong. I didn't realize the gardening would be so exhausting for him."

***The Unmet Needs Model***  Too little stimulation is associated with a decline in both cognition and function and an increase in behav-ioral symptoms. A behavior such as agitation may be an indication of unmet needs rather than overstimulation. Sensory deprivation caused by poor vision and poor hearing can create unmet needs and promote visual hallucinations and paranoid beliefs.

A person with dementia becomes less and less able to meet his or her own needs without help. Moreover, unlike cognitively intact people, who will generally find ways to stimulate and entertain themselves, people with dementia need someone else to motivate them. The unmet needs may be lack of social contacts, lack of exercise, or an unstimulating physical environment. Patients with unmet needs may sit apathetically or, on the other hand, may become agitated and start to pace, wander, or fidget. Sometimes the behavior may be an attempt to communicate the unmet need.

The benefits of stimulation with music, arts and crafts, rummaging boxes (ie, boxes containing stimulating manual activity items), pets, and reminiscence include increased socialization, alertness, and emotional expression, as well as improved mood and functioning and heightened self-esteem.

## Implications for Care

It is important for caregivers to understand that the underlying disease process cannot currently be controlled or altered. Nevertheless, the environment can contribute to or exacerbate symptoms, and caregivers can make changes that have a positive impact. Counselors can guide caregivers through the practical changes they will have to make, as well as the emotional struggle involved in making these adjustments to their lives.

Caregivers will have to learn to adjust the amount of stimulation to the needs of the patient—neither so much as to cause the patient to become overexcited and agitated, nor so little as to cause the patient to become more functionally impaired than necessary for this stage of the underlying dementia process. Caregivers will have to be ready to adapt the environment and level of stimulation as patients' abilities, tolerance, and needs change over time.

Millie realized she needed to make some serious changes in how she treated Ted. She made an appointment to see her counselor to talk about what to do. The counselor said, "It seems that Ted gets tired more quickly than he used to and his memory is more of a problem. Let's think what you can do to make things easier for both of you." Millie said, "From now on I'll have to give him a chance to rest if I want him to go out with me." The counselor said, "It may help Ted if you give him a cue by saying, 'Let's visit our daughter Carol,' rather than 'Let's visit Carol.'"

## Helping the Caregiver Appreciate the Patient's Experience

When caregivers appreciate the patients' experience of the illness, they will be more likely to implement the necessary alterations in environment and routines in a sensitive and respectful manner. Patients are experiencing changes in the most basic ways in which they have formed their identities and are continually being forced to give up ways in which they have come to value themselves. Long into the illness, people with AD remain aware of their failing memories and limitations, of their increasing need to ask for help, of their awkward fumbling with words and objects, and of the humiliation of being frustrated by a formerly simple activity of daily life that now has become a formidable challenge. They need a compassionate response from a caregiver to maintain a sense of dignity and self-worth.

Particularly in the early stages of the illness, patients are likely to resist a change that they perceive as threatening to their identity, dignity, or independence, even if the change is meant to make their lives easier or safer. For instance, many patients have difficulty giving up activities such as driving or going out alone, as well as responsibilities that they may no longer be able to handle, such as working or taking care of children or ill family members. Their resistance may become a source of stress to their caregivers.

### Lifestyle Adjustments

Nora's grandmother, Catherine, who had recently been diagnosed with AD, had been watching Nora's children while Nora was at work. This had been a convenient arrangement since Catherine lived with them, but now Nora was worried about her grandmother's ability to take care of the children. "After Grandma was diagnosed, I approached her with the idea of getting someone else to watch the kids. She said that she knew she would eventually be unable to care for them, but right now she is fine and can do it perfectly well. Lately, however, when I get home, the children are running around wildly, their toys are all over the floor, and Grandma is staring at the TV in the family room. Yesterday I got really scared. A pot of stew had boiled over and burned on the stove. She still claims she's okay and I don't want to make her feel bad, but I'm worried about the kids. What can I do?" The counselor suggested that Nora might have to explore options that would get the children out of the house, rather than have someone come in to care for them. "Maybe you can look into day care centers for the children or set up play dates at other children's homes for when you need to be out of the house. Your grandmother would probably agree that it would be good for your children to be with kids their age, and it will give you a way to change the situation without focusing on your grandmother's illness as the reason.

Caregivers will continually have to make changes in their *own* lifestyles, activities, and way of responding to the patient. Many caregivers will find the idea of making changes to their and the patient's lifestyle and surroundings easy to accept, and they themselves will ask counselors for help in determining the best arrangement of the furniture or the most appropriate tasks and activities for the person with AD at a given stage.

Some caregivers will need help to understand the necessity for change or to come to terms with the effects of these changes on themselves. They may express feelings of loss and resentment and may try to hold on to the old ways as long as possible. These feelings need not stop caregivers from ultimately making the necessary changes. A counselor can help these caregivers by reinforcing the idea that creating an environment that helps the person with AD function better may reduce the chances of negative behaviors commonly associated with AD, such as aggression or withdrawal, and will ultimately lead to a more stress-free life for both patient and caregiver. However, unless a situation is clearly dangerous, the counselor should accept caregivers' pace in making changes. Adjusting to the role of caregiver is a process that takes time.

It is not unusual for a caregiver to underestimate or overestimate the patient's abilities and needs, being either overprotective or not responsive enough. A realistic understanding of the person's symptoms, strengths, and limitations will help such a caregiver to start the process of change.

## Lifestyle Adjustments

Angela's husband Tony was just beginning to experience symptoms of the moderate stage of AD. Angela called her counselor in despair and said, "He can't do anything anymore. I feel terrible just watching him get worse, but what can he do?" When the counselor asked Angela to describe how Tony spent his day, he realized that, in an effort to make life easier for him, Angela had taken over almost all of Tony's former responsibilities. Now Tony sat around with almost nothing to do all day. The counselor said to Angela, "You are right, Tony can't do everything he did before he became ill, but you and I may be able to come up with ways to include Tony in some of the activities he used to do." The counselor and Angela discussed what Tony used to do around the house and reviewed the information they had from the doctor about Tony's symptoms and his functional limitations to see what he still might be able to do. Angela said, "You know, Tony always liked to cook. Maybe I should ask him to make dinner with me. That might be something we could enjoy doing together. I can assign him the simple tasks and help him when he needs it."

## Creating an AD-Friendly Environment

The symptoms of AD make it increasingly harder for people to maintain their former lifestyle and to function in their surroundings the way they used to. Counselors can help caregivers think about how to accommodate to the illness and to respond to specific symptom-related issues. For example, if a person with AD picks things up and puts them down somewhere else, the counselor can help the caregiver to understand that the patient may no longer understand the reason why an object belongs in a specific place. If the caregiver becomes especially distressed by not being able to find important items, the counselor can suggest putting them in a place the patient cannot get to.

## An AD-Friendly Environment

An environment that is suitable to the needs and limitations of the person with AD will minimize difficulties for both patient and caregiver. We define environment very broadly to include the neighborhood a person lives in, the layout of the home, the people that make up his or her social network, and the interactions they share. Counselors can help caregivers think about the impact of all aspects of the environment on the patient's functioning and behavior. An environment that is well suited to a person with Alzheimer's disease:

■ Does not tax the person's cognitive and physical abilities

■ Does not provoke or exacerbate symptoms

■ Is accommodating to the symptoms

■ Enhances a person's functioning to the extent possible

■ Provides enough stimulation to keep the person as active as possible given the functional limitations caused by AD

■ Provides a balance of support, safety, and independence

■ Helps a person maintain his or her dignity.

Changes will inevitably have to be made to the environment to accommodate symptoms. However, the dilemma is to keep the environment as familiar as possible so that the person with dementia can still benefit from his or her familiarity with it, while making the changes that will enhance safety and maximize functioning.

## Changes to the Physical Environment

Since Alzheimer's disease causes decline in such abilities as judgment, coordination, balance, and visual and spatial perception, it is very important for caregivers to make changes to the patient's home to create a safe, disaster-free environment. Counselors can provide caregivers with guidelines on the types of changes to make to maximize safety and help caregivers accept the need for change. If home visits are possible, a counselor may find it easiest to schedule a session in the patient's home and make suggestions based on his or her observations.

Safety is the first issue that a counselor will want to address with caregivers—prevention of fires, accidents, and falls. Caregivers should try to remove or secure any flammable liquids or materials and matches in order to minimize the risk of fire. The memory loss associated with AD may cause a person to forget that a stove has been left on. Some caregivers find it helpful to take the knobs off the stove. Toxic substances such as cleaning products and medications should be locked up or kept out of the patient's reach.

People with AD experience a gradual loss of coordination. Relatively early in the disease, they may hurt themselves using electrically powered equipment. Power tools, electric kitchen equipment with sharp cutting edges, or other objects that may cause injury can be secured in a locked cabinet until needed. Poor coordination and changes in visual and spatial perception may put a person in the later stages of AD at risk for falls if there are no clear paths or if the home is poorly lit, causing shadows and other distortions.

Counselors can help caregivers determine whether furniture can be rearranged or removed to provide more free walking space or whether items can be removed from shelves or countertops to create a more clutter-free environment.

Other changes may include the addition of safety and assistive devices to various parts of the home. For instance, grab bars should be installed in the bathroom, along staircases with only one banister, or other areas where the person with AD may not have something to hold to secure their balance. Sharp edges of furniture may need to be covered with stick-on attachments that create a soft, rounded edge. Extra lighting may have to be installed in dim or dark areas.

Counselors may refer caregivers to written information about how to make a home more Alzheimer's friendly and to catalogues that provide information about medical supplies and assistive devices that may be adapted for a patient's particular needs.

Caregivers may find it emotionally difficult to make some changes to their home. This is especially true when the caregiver attaches sentimental value to a particular object, such as a crystal vase given as a wedding present; or when the layout of a room has particular meaning to the caregiver, for instance, an adult child not wanting to destroy the look of a room that brings back warm, happy memories of childhood.

When a caregiver is resistant to making a particular change, the counselor may seek more acceptable solutions. If this is not possible, it may be helpful to clarify the reasons for the resistance by asking questions such as, What is the special significance of the item or layout? What would it mean to see them change? Would it signify a loss? A threat to the caregiver's identity? Giving in to the illness? What would make the change tolerable? Preserving certain aspects of the old environment? The counselor can help the caregiver understand the benefit of the change to the patient's functioning or to the caregiver's supervisory role. It is important to emphasize that a simple and calm physical environment will reduce stress on the patient and that this will make life easier for the caregiver as well.

## Lifestyle Adjustments

For many years after the kids had grown up and left home, Mr Wilson insisted on keeping their home exactly as it always had been. Finally, several years ago, he gave in and let Mrs Wilson completely redecorate their home and make a sewing room out of one of the kids' bedrooms. Eventually he became comfortable with the changes she made. When Mrs Wilson got AD and began to have trouble keeping her balance, his children insisted that it was time to install grab bars in the bathroom. "I'm not an old man and I am always there to help Mom when she uses the bathroom," he said. The children couldn't convince him. It was only after Mrs Wilson slipped while getting out of the tub, and Mr Wilson threw his back out catching her before she fell, that he relented. "Don't say I told you so," he roared. "I know I should have done it sooner, but I like to keep things just the way they are. I wish Mom would stay the same, too."

## Changing Lifestyles

Caregivers should establish and maintain consistent routines and rituals for the person with AD, enabling him or her to know what to expect every day. In addition, daily activities, social interactions, and tasks should be kept fairly short and uncomplicated in order to accommodate decreasing cognitive and functional capacity.

It is difficult for people with AD to adapt to change, which is generally experienced by them as stressful. Therefore, caregivers will have to make many accommodations and changes in lifestyle to create an environment that is suitable for the patient.

## Changes in Social Interactions

A person with Alzheimer's disease may continue to enjoy socializing at any stage of the illness. In the early stage he or she is usually able to participate relatively normally in social interactions but may nevertheless not feel comfortable because of difficulty finding the right words and forgetting names or new information that may come up in conversation. As a result, people in the early stage of the illness may withdraw from social activities. In general, it is more comfortable for a person with Alzheimer's disease to attend small gatherings of familiar people for short periods of time.

Counselors can suggest that people with AD who have difficulty with communication are more likely to be comfortable in gatherings with relatives or close friends who can be patient and supportive. The caregiver can help the patient enjoy social activities if he or she accompanies the patient and helps with any problems that arise, filling in words that the patient forgets, for example.

### Lifestyle Adjustments

Harry had been talking to his counselor about how to help his wife, Martha, through a family wedding they had to attend. Martha, who was in the early stage of AD, was very self-conscious about the fact that she often forgot words and names and had difficulty following long stories. She was afraid that she would look foolish at the wedding. Only a few members of the family knew about her illness, and although she didn't have a problem discussing it, she didn't want to start telling everyone at the wedding. The counselor suggested that perhaps Harry could help his wife participate in conversations by reminding her of what he thinks she might be wanting to say. He could also help her remember names by inserting them into the conversation. He could say, for example, "So Maryanne, are you enjoying yourself?" He could whisk his wife away to the dance floor if a conversation were getting too complex for her to follow. After the wedding, Harry came to see his counselor extremely satisfied. "I tried every strategy we talked about and came up with a few more

> on the spot. Some people may have caught on that Martha wasn't herself, but we made it through the evening. I'm glad I was able to bring her; she seemed to have a really good time."

A person with AD may become overstimulated or fatigued from the effort of interacting with others and need some quiet after a limited amount of time at a social function. The symptoms of moderate stage AD make social interactions difficult since the person has decreased vocabulary, may not understand what is being said to him or her, and may not be able to respond coherently. The patient may also exhibit behaviors that others may view as strange, such as wandering or seeing and hearing things that are not there. Counselors may suggest that patients in this stage attend social engagements for a short time and that the engagements themselves be relatively calm and quiet affairs.

Patients at the severe stage can still enjoy having visitors, although they may have very limited ability to communicate verbally. Counselors can suggest ways for family and friends to interact with a person who can no longer speak. Caregivers will have to monitor patients' reactions to see whether what they are doing is appropriate.

## Lifestyle Adjustments

Gary wanted his mother, Agatha, who was in the moderately severe stage of AD, to be able to still see her family and friends, but he realized that this would be difficult since most people felt uncomfortable, not knowing how to act around her. He asked his counselor for help. The counselor suggested that Gary could approach the situation in one of two ways. He could plan a quiet gathering for several people and have Agatha attend only for as long as she seemed comfortable. That way, the focus would not be on Agatha, but she could enjoy having people around. Or Gary could plan very short visits, inviting only one or two people, and be sure there was some activity, such as listening to a new CD or looking at family pictures. This would take the pressure of talking to Agatha off the visitor.

## *Changes in Recreational Activities*

A person with AD may have enjoyed some form of recreational activity, such as playing baseball, going to the theater, or gardening, before becoming ill and may be able to continue these interests for a long time with guidance and help from the caregiver. At each stage, however, the caregiver will have to make changes to the way the person with AD can participate in these activities and may have to find new activities in order to accommodate symptoms. For instance, someone who liked to play tennis may be able to participate in the sport in the early stage of AD. In the moderate stage, this same person may no longer be able to play the game but may still enjoy watching a game on TV or may find it interesting to collect tennis paraphernalia. In the late stage of the illness, this person may also enjoy having the TV tuned to a game, even though he no longer understands it, or may enjoy handling a tennis ball and feeling its soft, fuzzy texture.

The counselor can help the caregiver think about suitable activities by asking about the patient's past and current interests. He or she can then help the caregiver decide whether the patient can participate in the activity on his own, whether someone will have to lead the patient through the activity, or whether variations on the patient's interest will be the focus. For example, someone who had a lifelong interest in tennis may no longer be able to keep score in a tennis game in the mild stage of AD, but still enjoy playing.

In order to understand the skills required to complete a task and to plan an activity accordingly, caregivers may find it useful to visualize an activity and mentally walk themselves through each of the steps required to do the task. The counselor can guide caregivers through this process, keeping the following questions in mind:

- What are the individual steps required for a particular task?

- How long will each part of the task take the patient to complete?

- What materials or tools does the patient have to handle in order to do the task?

- Is the environment conducive to the patient's carrying out the activity with ease?

Counselors can help caregivers determine which parts of an activity may have be to prepared in advance in order to help the patient complete a task. For instance, when planning an arts and crafts project such as making a pillow, the caregiver may need to stitch together three sides of the pillow, leaving only the fourth for the patient to sew.

Counselors can help caregivers develop a sense of the type of help a patient needs: verbal encouragement or cueing, tactile encouragement such as hugs or caresses, visual cues, or physical assistance. Counselors may want share the following guidelines with caregivers when planning activities:

■ Patients should never be forced into activities.

■ Activities should highlight a patient's strengths, not disabilities.

■ Activities should be simple.

■ Complex tasks should be broken down into simple steps.

This approach, used here for recreational activities, can also be useful when planning a person's participation in activities of daily life or social interactions.

## Communicating With a Person With AD

At all stages of the illness, patients may experience difficulties in either expressing their thoughts or comprehending and responding to what other people say. In the early stage, a person may have difficulty finding the right words to use but may understand what is being said to him or her. In the moderate stage, a person may lose the ability to speak in complete sentences or communicate whole thoughts and may not understand what is being said to him or her, particularly if the idea is abstract. In the severe stage, a person may no longer be able to speak at all or to understand what is being said to him or her.

From the early stage of AD, a person may require more time than a caregiver expects to process a thought and respond accordingly or may forget words or use them inappropriately. The caregiver may not realize that these are symptoms of AD and become annoyed or impatient. Patients at this stage may feel frustrated at not being able to get their thoughts across. Counselors can help caregivers understand that their relatives need more time to collect and verbalize their thoughts than they did before.

In the moderate stage, a person's ability to communicate slows down even more, and the ability to comprehend or hold a thought is decreased. The person may get stuck on a word or phrase and repeat it continually, speak in incomplete sentences, make up words, and have difficulty understanding complicated sentences. Counselors can help caregivers develop strategies to make communication at this stage easier for patients and themselves. Distracting the patient may help him or her move past the word or phrase they are repeating.

Listening carefully for clues or key words within a person's seemingly unintelligible verbalizations may help the caregiver make sense of the communication. Counselors may also need to help caregivers become aware of the fact that patients may be using non-verbal communications in the absence of verbal skills. By fidgeting in a chair, the patient may be indicating boredom or a need to go to the toilet or to exercise.

It is generally best to speak to moderate stage patients in simple sentences, look directly at them, and speak slowly, clearly, and in a calm, natural tone. Caregivers may also be cautioned to speak in concrete terms: "Do you want eggs?" rather than, "What would you like to eat?" They should make suggestions rather than give choices. Statements like, "Let's go for a walk now," are better than, "Would you like to go for a walk?"

As people progressively decline through the late stage of AD, they are perhaps able to say a few words or repeat words that are spoken to them, but they probably do not comprehend the meaning of these words and are unable to respond, either by verbally answering or by physically acting on a thought. People at this stage may make sounds such as a moan or clicking (from the throat) that might be a communication. Counseling for caregivers at this stage includes helping them to decode nonverbal communications and to understand and accept that, although they may never know whether their attempts at making the patient comfortable are suitable, they are doing their best in an extremely difficult situation.

**Lifestyle Adjustments**

Morton's mother was in the severe stage of AD, and her speech now consisted of repeating the last two words of what was said to her. He phoned the counselor and said, "How can I tell if she is hungry? I am not sure how I can make her feel comfortable and protected." The counselor encouraged Morton to work out a schedule for meals, hygiene, and passive exercise. "But will she understand if I tell her I love her? I feel so sad and helpless." The counselor told Morton that there are ways of communicating without words. He could still hug her, hold her hands, or just sit quietly by her side. Several days later Morton phoned the counselor and said, "I think Mom still knows I'm here for her. I brought her some of her favorite ice cream and fed it to her. She smiled at me and I feel like I made a connection. I guess she knows I love her."

Counselors may need to help caregivers develop communication skills that are conducive to a dialogue with a person with AD. Caregivers may have to adjust their usual patterns of speech, tone, and body language in order to communicate effectively with their relatives. If a caregiver is used to speaking quickly or slurring words, he or she will most likely confuse the person with AD or not be able to get an appropriate response. If the caregiver has a booming voice or uses quick hand gestures while speaking, he or she may appear angry to a person with AD and frighten them. If this is the person's natural way of communicating, it may take time and practice to develop a style that will be more comfortable for a person with AD.

If the counselor needs to get a better idea of the kinds of problems a caregiver is having with communication, he or she may want to try a role-play with the caregiver. This may help counselors to get a clearer picture of the interactions and the types of changes that would fit in with the caregiver's personality and personal style. Caregivers may also find role-play helpful in practicing new communication skills.

## Lifestyle Adjustments

Candy called her counselor and said, "I really need your help. I'm so frustrated. A conversation with my mother is like going on a hike without a map; you never know where the trail is leading and what to do when you hit a dead-end. She gets angry when I don't understand her, and I feel lost a lot of the time." The counselor said, "When a person with AD tells a story, you need to listen in a different way, trying to figure out what they are getting at. A good strategy is to act like it's your fault if you don't understand. If your Mom can't remember someone's name and you don't know who she's talking about, you could say something like, 'Sorry, Mom, I'm not so good with names anymore, either. I guess we're both getting old,' so she doesn't look bad. Or, 'Could you be talking about . . .' and make a guess. If she's told you the story before, you may be able to help her with the parts she forgets. Do you want to pretend you are your mother and I'll be you and see what kind of conversation we can have?"

## *The Need for Supervision*

The symptoms and behaviors associated with AD, even in the early stages, require that a family member or other responsible individual begin to monitor the patient. At first, it may only be necessary to check periodically to be sure the person is taking care of his own welfare and responsibilities—keeping appointments, taking medication, and paying bills. Eventually, the patient requires continuous supervision, both for his own safety and that of others and to prevent damage to property. For example, patients may still know how to toilet themselves but then throw inappropriate items in the toilet and cause it to back up.

## Lifestyle Adjustments

Ruth came to her counseling appointment frustrated. "You won't believe the week I had! On Monday night, my husband Peter told me he was going to take a bath. I said okay and kept watching my movie. About an hour later, when I turned off the television, I heard the water running and went upstairs to the bathroom. It was flooded! The water was flowing out into the hall! I turned the water off and went to find Peter—he was sleeping! I always thought the early stage of the illness was going to be the easiest. I never thought something like this could happen—he always does fine taking a bath on his own. What am I supposed to do to prevent this from happening again?" The counselor suggested that Ruth look into safety devices such as a flood alarm or a water control device to prevent another accident. "You may want to get these devices for the sink as well, to prevent this from happening anywhere in the house. This way Peter can continue to do what he needs to without either of you worrying about accidents." She went on to suggest that Ruth look into other safety devices for the kitchen area and other rooms of the house.

## *Managing Instrumental Activities of Daily Living (IADLs)*

Instrumental activities of daily living (IADLs) include shopping, driving, managing finances and legal matters, and organizing and planning events. Patients' abilities to carry out these activities gradually decline as the disease progresses. A dilemma for caregivers is to be sensitive to the person's dignity while not allowing him or her to put anyone at risk. Caregivers will have to monitor the patient's performance of these activities and transfer the responsibility for these tasks when the patient can no longer carry them out.

A patient may not agree with the caregiver's assessment. Some patients will want to continue a task beyond the time when they can perform it adequately. Others recognize that they are not performing as well as they used to and strategically withdraw from difficult tasks. This withdrawal should be graciously facilitated.

***Managing Finances and Legal Matters***   Important tasks such as preparing income taxes and keeping up with mortgage payments, rent, or other bills can have serious financial and legal consequences if neglected or not done properly, so counseling a caregiver about these issues has the weight of urgency about it. They are also some of the hardest tasks to transfer, especially when patients have held the responsibility of managing finances or legal matters throughout their lives. People with AD may find it difficult to give up these tasks, because it feels like giving up part of their identity or because they believe they are capable of the tasks when, in reality, they are not. Counseling in this case focuses on strategies to help the caregiver transfer responsibilities from the patient and find ways to support the patient through the process.

Caregivers, in an effort not to assault the person's self-esteem or because they themselves are afraid of taking over the tasks, may deny or ignore the need to make a change. In these situations counselors should try to understand why the transfer of tasks is difficult and find ways to support and guide caregivers through the process. For instance, in the example below, the counselor helps with practical approaches to the situation that also address Midge's fears.

## Lifestyle Adjustments

Patrick, a retired accountant who was diagnosed with early stage AD, had always taken care of the family finances. His wife, Midge, never took any interest in these matters because, "Patrick, of course, knew what he was doing as an accountant," and now was reluctant to take the task away from her husband despite several bounced checks and other problems. "I read somewhere that people with AD retain abilities for tasks for a long time if they have a skill or talent in a particular field. That's Patrick with finances." After several conversations with Midge about taking over the finances, the counselor realized that Midge had never seen herself as good with numbers and was terrified of taking control of the finances. "I know this isn't right, but I would rather put up with the consequences of having Patrick take care of financial matters than have to go through the anxiety of doing them myself." The counselor acknowledged that taking on a task that Midge never felt competent in might be very scary for her, but that she didn't have to feel that she had to take on the whole task. The counselor suggested that she hire an accountant to help with some of the more complex financial matters, and that she enlist the help of her daughter in some of the everyday financial and legal matters if this was comfortable for her. Also, the counselor suggested that Midge look into some books on home finance or courses that might help her understand the subject more, so that it was not so frightening.

*Driving* Driving is an important issue that often comes up in counseling, especially in areas where driving is the only practical way of getting around. Caregivers often ask whether the person with AD should stop driving and, if so, how to get him or her to stop. There is no definitive answer to whether people who have been diagnosed with AD should or should not be driving. The decision needs to be made on an individual basis and periodically reevaluated since AD is a progressive illness. Counselors can use their knowledge about the early stage of AD to alert caregivers to potential problems if the patient continues to drive. For instance, very early in the illness a person may have difficulty reacting quickly and not be able to swerve out of the way to avoid a pothole. As the illness progresses, a person, though still in the early stage, may have problems with coordination, and tasks such as signaling a turn while stepping on the brake may become difficult. Poor judgment and visuo-spatial deficits may cause such a person to miscalculate the time that he or she has to pass a car on a two-lane highway with oncoming traffic.

The counselor can suggest a driving evaluation to determine whether the person with AD can continue to drive. In some areas there are professionals with certification from the Association for Driver Educators for the Disabled who can perform a driving evaluation. The name of a specialist may be available through rehabilitation centers and driving schools.

---

### Lifestyle Adjustments

Linda was worried about how to stop her husband, Herbert, from driving. She had just learned that the elderly neighbor next door, who did not know her husband had Alzheimer's disease, was asking him to drive her to the supermarket occasionally when Linda was not home. She mentioned this to her support group. Another member of the support group suggested that she tell her husband that the insurance would not cover anyone with his particular diagnosis. This worked like a charm; instead of becoming angry and defensive, Herbert accepted her explanation that if anything happened, any accident, they would be financially wiped out. "That's terrible," he said, and stopped driving.

---

*Courtesy of Lois M, EdD.*

While driving is generally an issue that comes up in the early stage of the illness, some caregivers who rely on the patient to drive may continue to do so in spite of the fact that it may no longer be safe. In these situations, a counselor should recommend that the patient stop driving and help the caregiver to arrange alternative means of transportation.

## Managing Activities of Daily Living

Patients can generally perform activities of daily living (ADLs), such as dressing, grooming, bathing, and using the bathroom, independently until the moderate stage of AD, unless they have some other disease that has an impact on functioning.

In the moderate stages of AD, patients will begin to need help with ADLs. Cueing, providing a physical hint of what the person has to do, such as putting a jacket on the handle of the front door on a cold day, may enable a moderate stage patient to continue to conduct activities of daily life relatively independently. Eventually, in the late stage of AD, caregivers will have to perform most personal care tasks for their relatives.

***Difficulty Getting Dressed***  In the moderate stage of AD, cognitive deficits such as difficulty making choices, poor judgment, and loss of concentration become intensified and cause a variety of difficulties with getting dressed. Patients may choose inappropriate clothing. For instance, a woman may think she is dressed and go out wearing only a slip. In instances like this, rather than criticize what they are wearing, caregivers might say, "That's very nice. How about putting this on top of it?" and hand her a dress.

Some patients may want to wear the same clothes every day, sometimes even sleeping in them. Counselors may suggest that the caregiver be flexible in his or her standards of dress code. It may not be worth the struggle to get the patient to put on pajamas rather than sleep in day clothes or to require the patient to wear different clothes every day.

If the clothes need to be changed because they are unclean or ragged, the counselor may suggest that the caregiver try to determine why the patient wants to wear the item of clothing all the time. Is it because the patient believes he or she has just changed and doesn't need fresh clothing? Does the patient like the feel of the fabric, the color, or the comfort the item provides? Is it too much trouble to change into something else? Understanding why the patient wants to wear the clothes may give the caregiver some clues about how to solve the problem. Maybe the patient will wear a different piece of clothing made of a soft material or a similar color. Maybe the caregiver can purchase an identical or similar article of clothing so that the patient can wear one while the other is in the laundry. Sometimes it is possible to take the clothes away and exchange them with others when the patient is being bathed or has changed into nightclothes.

---

### Lifestyle Adjustments

John had called his counselor over the telephone several times over the past week about the fact that his wife, Susan, would not stop wearing a black knit sweater long enough for him to wash it. "It has stains all over it. She's been wearing it nonstop for 3 weeks." After John failed several times to get Susan to take off the sweater, the counselor suggested he try to think of an approach that might appeal to her. John remembered that when his wife was well, she would always do the laundry on Tuesdays, so on the next Tuesday, he took a deep breath, approached his wife, and simply said, "It's Tuesday—time to do the laundry. Please give me that sweater." He was surprised and relieved when she took it off and put it in the washing machine.

---

In this example, John was able to solve the problem by tapping into his knowledge about Susan's former routine. Susan probably responded automatically when a familiar behavior pattern was evoked by his request.

Patients may not tolerate the process of getting dressed if they feel rushed or they no longer understand what is expected of them. Counselors can help caregivers find strategies to make the process easier and faster. For example, caregivers can lay the clothing out ahead of time, choose clothing that is easy to put on (does not have a lot of buttons, clasps, etc), and give themselves enough time to help the patient get dressed.

***Bathing***   Patients in the moderate stage of AD are frequently resistant to being bathed. They may say they did it already or they will do it later. If the caregiver tries to force the issue, they sometimes react by refusing to take off their clothes, trying to leave the room, or screaming.

## Lifestyle Adjustments

Betty was having great difficulty getting Edward to take a bath. She even tried to use force, since he hadn't bathed in over a week. She called the counselor and said, "I finally got desperate and dragged Ed into the shower. I was able to wash him, but then he started to scream and seemed terrified. I saw that he was staring in horror at the water going down the drain and pointing at it. I realized he might have thought he was going to go down the drain with the water. I don't think he'll ever get into the shower again." The counselor suggested that Betty have Ed get into the shower facing away from the drain and that she put a picture on the shower wall of something he liked, laminated with plastic so it was waterproof. She also suggested offering Ed a massage with a lotion he liked to get him to take his clothes off and divert him from anxiety over taking a shower.

Counselors should be careful to help the caregiver understand the emotional aspect of a person's resistance to taking a bath. The patient may be embarrassed about being exposed and having someone else help with what is normally a private act, especially when the caregiver is an adult child or sibling. Sometimes the patient may be more comfortable with someone else, such as another family member or an aide. Counselors may also suggest alternative ways of bathing, such as sponge baths, during which the person does not have to be fully exposed.

When a patient experiences problems with balance and coordination, he or she may feel unsteady and anxious in a slippery bathtub. Counselors can suggest to caregivers that they can make the person feel more secure while taking a bath by installing grab bars in the bathroom, placing nonslippery mats on the base of the tub or shower stall, and using assistive devices such as a shower chair.

## The Most Common Difficult Behaviors Associated With Alzheimer's Disease

Almost all people with AD will exhibit mental or behavioral disturbances at some point in their illness. Behavioral syndromes including agitation, aggression, and psychosis occur in more than 80% of patients with Alzheimer's disease. These symptoms are very distressing to caregivers and can precipitate institutionalization of patients.

Nonpharmacological management of behavioral symptoms depends on trying to understand the context in which they occur and if they may reflect overstimulation or an unmet need. This includes looking at what happened before the behavior occurred and what the person's reaction was in order to identify what can be called behavioral triggers and reinforcers. Once the action or activity that precipitated the behavior is identified, it may be possible to find alternative approaches. Frequently the cause of the problem is insisting the patient do something that is too difficult, rushing him or her, or speaking in an impatient or angry tone. People with AD need more time than they formerly did to understand what is being asked of them and to respond. Often, modifying one's behavior toward the patient by speaking slowly and calmly, giving simple instructions, and choosing tasks that are easy for the patient to manage will result in a positive response. Sometimes changes to the environment, such as reducing clutter and altering the daily routine, can reduce the confusion that may be causing the difficult behaviors.

Medication can be helpful in controlling some symptoms. Anxiety, depression, hallucinations, delusions, agitation, and aggression can be alleviated with medication when psychosocial approaches are inadequate on their own. Caregivers should be reminded to ask the doctor about the possible side effects of medications that are prescribed and how to best administer them to reduce their risk. When a person takes medication, it is essential to monitor the reactions, be alert to side effects, and assess whether the medications are still needed, since some problems remit when the patient moves to another stage. A geriatrician or geriatric psychiatrist can prescribe the medications and monitor their effects.

## Behaviors Typical of the Early to Moderate Stages of AD

***Repetitive Questioning***   Repetitive questioning, one of the symptoms of early to moderate stage AD, is usually extremely irritating to caregivers, who feel obligated to respond in order to avoid frustrating or upsetting the patient, although the answer is immediately forgotten and the question is asked again. Anxiety about an upcoming event is often the motivation for these repeated questions. Sometimes just knowing it is not being done maliciously to annoy the caregiver, but that the patient cannot help himself, may decrease the caregiver's irritation. If the caregiver can distract the patient, he or she may forget the question and stop asking it.

---

## Lifestyle Adjustments

Jerry kept repeating over and over, "When are we going home?" His wife Alice said, "I am going crazy; I tell him over and over we are home. He doesn't listen and keeps on asking the same question. What can I do?" The counselor acknowledged this is very difficult and seems to be very upsetting to most caregivers. She said, "Let's think about what he might mean and what feeling he is attempting to express." Alice said, "I keep telling myself it's the disease, but it still drives me crazy." The counselor praised Alice for understanding Jerry is ill and not trying to deliberately annoy her and asked her if she would like to speculate on what Jerry is trying to express by wanting to go home. Alice said, "I know Jerry is going back in time; maybe he is thinking of his childhood home, or maybe he feels lost." The counselor and Alice discussed ways of diverting Jerry so he would stop asking the same question repetitively, at the same time allowing him to express his feelings. Alice thought he might like to talk about himself as a child since he seemed to remember things from way back. The counselor said, "Alice, that is a wonderful idea; let me know what happens."

---

***Wandering and Getting Lost*** Wandering takes many forms. If it consists of pacing around the house or a secure place, it may be annoying to the caregiver but is not dangerous. It may indicate that the person is bored or needs exercise.

When a person with Alzheimer's disease leaves home unaccompanied, he or she may get lost. Most patients who wander away from home cannot find their way back unaided and are in danger of exposure to the elements if not found for a long period of time. Many of them are found standing in the middle of a street or road where they are in danger of being injured by a car.

People with AD sometimes give reasons for wanting to leave the house, such as needing to go to work or wanting to go home, not understanding that they are at home.

The caregiver can use the reason the person gives for wanting to leave as a basis for conversation and try to distract him from actually leaving. If the patient insists, the caregiver may have to go along with him. Perhaps the caregiver can then distract the patient by talking about something else until he forgets his original plan and is willing to return home.

It is difficult for a caregiver of a person in the early stage of AD to know when to restrict his or her freedom for safety's sake. One does not want to prematurely limit independence, nor does one want to put the person at risk. As a safeguard, all caregivers should be urged to register their relatives with AD in a Safe Return Program. Every chapter of the Alzheimer's Association nationwide has such a program, coordinated with local law enforcement agencies. It is suggested that patients wear a bracelet, tag, or other form of identification and caregivers carry a card identifying them as responsible for the patient.

## Lifestyle Adjustments

Mr Sims, who had AD, still walked into town every morning to buy a newspaper at the general store. One day, when he hadn't returned by lunchtime, his wife became worried and called her counselor in a panic. "He always comes back in an hour or so. I thought maybe he ran into a friend and stopped to have coffee, but 3 hours have gone by. I drove to the store, and the manager told me he had left a long time ago. What should I do now?" The counselor told her to call the local police precinct. Mrs Sims told the detective who answered the phone that her husband had Alzheimer's disease. He asked her if she had a recent photograph to give to the police officer he was sending to her house. He advised her to stay home and call him if her husband returned. Fortunately, a neighbor recognized Mr Sims walking along the highway a little while later. He stopped the car and offered Mr Sims a lift. Mr Sims said, "Thanks. I want to go home. Do you know where I live?" The neighbor said he did and drove Mr Sims home. Fortunately, outside of being hungry and tired, he was okay. He had no idea why anyone was worried and kept repeating, "What's the problem? I knew where I was." Mrs Sims called the police to say that her husband had been found and then called the counselor. She told her that she felt really guilty that she had allowed this to happen. "What would my children say if they knew their Dad had gotten lost?" The counselor pointed out that there was no way of knowing when Mr Sims would no longer be able to follow his regular routine, and that the pleasure he had gotten had been worth the risk. "Up to now he never got lost." Mrs Sims said, "I guess I'll have to go with him to buy the paper from now on." The counselor agreed and added, "I know you've been hesitating, but it is clear that the time has come to enroll him in the Safe Return Program in case he wanders out when you aren't looking; you might also consider putting special locks on the doors."

*Shadowing*  Patients in the moderate stage of AD often will try to stay close to their caregivers, whose presence is reassuring to them. This behavior is called *shadowing*. Caregivers complain that they cannot get a moment alone, sometimes even in the bathroom.

### Lifestyle Adjustments

Mr Bing followed Mrs Bing all over the house. She told the counselor, "I can't prepare a meal without him being under my feet." The counselor reminded Mrs Bing that the reason for this "shadowing" was that AD caused people to feel insecure and afraid. He followed her around since she was, in a way, his security blanket. The counselor suggested that when she was in the kitchen preparing a meal, she should give him a chore, such as helping make the salad by washing the lettuce and tearing up the leaves. She cautioned Mrs Bing not to let him use sharp knives or leave them around. Keeping Mr Bing busy relieved this frustrating situation and actually made it possible for him to be helpful.

*Hiding Things and Difficulty Finding Things*  Patients who hide things are trying to keep them in a safe place to protect them. There is often no apparent logic to the place, but there is a certain logic to the act. Since they cannot remember anything about putting the item away, they cannot find it and may assume someone else may have taken it. The caregiver may be advised to suggest that the item is lost and help the patient look for it. If the patient has a typical hiding place, such as the refrigerator, the caregiver can look there first. If the item cannot be found, eventually the patient will forget what he or she is looking for and become interested in something else.

---

### Lifestyle Adjustments

Pamela's brother was her caregiver. He had begun to manage her finances, since she had trouble keeping track of bills, either paying them over and over or not at all. Once a month, he would go to her house, pay the bills, take her pension check to the bank, and withdraw housekeeping money for her. One day he called the counselor and said, "I can't find my sister's bankbook. She said she put it where she always has, but I checked all the drawers and it's nowhere to be found. She also told me she's been looking for her good watch for days. She wondered if someone had taken it." The counselor suggested that perhaps he might try looking in some unconventional hiding spots, like the refrigerator, the bathroom cabinet, or a pocket of a coat. He called the counselor and said, "You were right; her bankbook and watch were both in the refrigerator. My sister was always concerned about food spoiling, so maybe that's why she put important things there."

---

***Depression, Apathy, and Withdrawal***   There are several possible reasons for the symptoms of depression that frequently occur in the mild and moderate stages of Alzheimer's disease. Experts disagree about whether these symptoms are due to the neurological changes caused by Alzheimer's disease itself or are psychologically based.

People with dementia may be apathetic and passive or withdrawn. They may move slowly and speak less often. They may also become tearful and even say they want to die. If a patient is becoming withdrawn and spending most of his or her time in isolation, it may be helpful to provide more stimulating activities that are appropriate to the patient's current abilities and former interests.

If these symptoms last for more than a few weeks, the caregiver should seek advice from a physician. Whatever the cause, depression in AD can be effectively treated. There are medications for depression that are suitable for an elderly person with dementia.

A caregiver may also suggest that the patient join a support group for people in the early stage of AD. These groups provide companionship and help people cope with their illness. By reducing

isolation and increasing self-esteem, these groups can also help
relieve depression. If the caregiver thinks the person is withdrawing
from regular social activities because he or she is embarrassed by
his or her disabilities, less challenging social situations or activities
geared toward people with memory impairment or dementia may
be helpful.

## Behaviors Typical of the Moderate and Moderately Severe Stages of AD

*Agitation*  Agitation is vocal or motor behavior (screaming, shouting, complaining, moaning, cursing, pacing, fidgeting, wandering,
etc). These behaviors are often disruptive, unsafe, or interfere with
providing care. Agitation is the most troubling symptom to families
and caregivers and is the single most frequent reason for institutionalization in long-term care facilities and for referral to specialists.
Unlike other behavioral symptoms, agitation is common and persists
for a relatively long time. *Sundowning* is the name that has been
given to the occurrence or exacerbation of symptoms of agitation
in people with Alzheimer's disease in the afternoon and evening.

Agitation may be the first sign of a medical problem. Before other
measures are considered, there should be a thorough medical evaluation to search for a treatable cause, such as urinary tract infection,
fracture, decubiti, constipation, or reaction to a medication or drug
interaction. Once a physical illness has been ruled out, the underlying psychopathology should be determined and treated
appropriately.

Agitation may simply be the attempt of a person with AD to express
feelings and needs he or she cannot verbalize, such as hunger, fear,
or pain. The caregiver can learn to read the signs and know whether
a certain kind of agitated behavior is likely to indicate a need to go
to the toilet, boredom, or pain from sitting in one spot for too long.

Sometimes agitation can be ameliorated by taking the person into a
different room or outside for a walk. It is also often possible to distract the person by involving him or her in a pleasant activity, such
as looking through a magazine or listening to music, folding napkins, or arranging objects. The physical environment may be contributing to the agitation; it may be helpful to change the amount
of light in the room, as glare and shadows may be disturbing to a

person with AD. Sometimes, even if there is no intervention, the person will calm down because the reason for the distress will pass or be forgotten.

***Aggression***  Aggressive behavior on the part of a person with AD is considered to be a form of agitation. Verbal aggression such as cursing or screaming may arise from feelings of anxiety, fear, or depression and may be the only available form of communication for a person who is unable to express feelings adequately with words. Sometimes people with AD make gestures that seem threatening, waving their arms, making a fist, or grabbing someone, although actual physical aggression rarely occurs. If a patient does become physically aggressive, the caregiver may be justifiably frightened. At that moment, the caregiver should keep his or her distance from the patient. For example, a patient may lift a knife in a threatening way. While the patient is agitated, the person being threatened should not try to take the knife away. Rather, the best solution may be to get out of sight, since the patient is likely to forget why he or she is so angry.

When a behavior is potentially dangerous, caregivers need to know what steps to take to mitigate the danger. Caregivers may fail to take precautions or make any changes, even in the face of a potentially dangerous situation, thinking that they have exaggerated the meaning of the act. It is probably better to err on the side of safety. For example, sharp objects such as knives should not be left where the patient can use them unsupervised.

The caregiver should speak calmly, using reassuring words. The patient will respond to the anger implicit in a raised voice and may become even more upset. The caregiver should be encouraged to use reassuring nonverbal communication such as patting the person's hand or hugging. It may be possible to divert the patient by talking about someone who is important to him or her or giving the patient a picture of a grandchild or something soft to hold. It may also help for the caregiver to say that he or she is going to leave the room and then go out for a short time. If the person does not calm down and the caregiver continues to feel threatened, it may be necessary to call the police, although this should only be done if all else fails, since the interaction with the police may further upset the patient.

The caregiver should try to figure out the cause of the outburst to reduce the likelihood of a recurrence. Perhaps the caregiver felt frustrated or was in a hurry and ordered or tried to physically force the patient to do something. People with AD, like everyone else, respond better to an invitation than to a command.

***Sleep Disturbances***  Alzheimer's disease can cause disturbances of circadian rhythms. As a result, insomnia or sleep-wake cycle disturbance is common in AD and occurs in up to 20% to 40% of patients. In addition to the neurological effects of the disease, boredom, sleeping most of the day, lack of routine, lack of activity or exercise, diet or timing of meals, need to go to the bathroom, anxiety, and/or depression may cause people with AD to be awake all or most of the night. Patients who are confused about what time it is or where they are may insist on leaving home in the middle of the night to go to work. This can cause significant distress and sleep deprivation to family caregivers who are awakened at night and may have to be vigilant to prevent wandering away from home or self-injury of the patient.

Although this problem cannot be entirely avoided, it is helpful to keep the patient as active as possible during the day and encourage daily physical activity. The patient should go to the bathroom before going to bed. Sometimes music or a cup of warm milk will induce sleep. A favorite pillow, blanket, or robe may be comforting. If the patient does not want to sleep in bed, another comfortable and safe place may do just as well.

If the patient awakens during the night, he or she may go back to sleep if the caregiver reminds him or her that it is still night. If the patient stays awake at night and is not in danger, it may be necessary to accept that this is a symptom of the illness at this stage and may abate in time. If the patient insists on leaving home at night, the caregiver should install locks the patient cannot open or other security measures to be sure the person cannot leave while the caregiver is asleep.

Caregivers who do not sleep at night are likely to get emotionally and physically exhausted. If the patient does not sleep at night, the caregiver may want to sleep in a separate room. For some caregivers, a home health aide paid to be with the patient at night may be a solution. There are now a few day care programs that function during the night for patients who cannot sleep. It is also possible that the patient's physician can prescribe a medication to help the patient sleep.

Ted had been getting up five or six times a night for several weeks, and Millie was totally frazzled. It seemed like every time she fell asleep, he was turning on the light and getting up. He would ask her to go with him to the kitchen for a glass of milk or go out for a walk in the park. The next time she took Ted to his doctor for a checkup, she told him about Ted not sleeping well. The doctor gave her a prescription for a medication he said would help Ted sleep. She filled the prescription but didn't use it. A few days later she called her counselor and told her she didn't want to give the medication to Ted because she was afraid it was bad for him to take sleeping pills. Her counselor asked, "Did you tell the doctor of your concerns?" Millie, said, "Yes, and he said it was okay." The counselor said, with humor in her voice, "Well Millie, I suggest you either give the medicine to Ted or take sleeping pills yourself. Either way you'll sleep better. If you take them yourself, though, he might get himself into trouble while you are asleep and you wouldn't wake up to stop him." Millie laughed but got the point. "You're right," Millie said. "I'll give him the medicine and maybe then we both can get a good night's sleep."

***Hallucinations, Delusions, and Paranoia*** A delusion is a false belief and in and of itself represents no threat or problem. However, the most common delusions in AD are paranoid and misidentification delusions and can cause the patient to behave in a dangerous manner. For example, a person with dementia who believes that he is several decades younger than he actually is, and remembers his wife as the age she was then, may think she is a stranger and become fearful or even attempt to escape. It is not useful to contradict the patient, because he truly believes his delusion. Rather, the caregiver should try to sympathize and offer comfort and protection.

## Lifestyle Adjustments

Bertha and Sam had been married for 40 years. He was in the moderately severe stage of dementia. One day she called the counselor in anguish. "Yesterday, Sam told me that I wasn't his wife. He wanted to know why I was there. I kept telling him I was Bertha, but he refused to believe me. Then this morning he asked me why I let that strange woman in the house. He said, 'What is the matter with you? You let her wear your clothes and even your perfume, and she slept in your bed last night.' I told him there was no strange woman and that I had been there all the time. What does this mean? Why won't he believe me?" The counselor sympathized and said that she understood it must be dreadfully sad for her that Sam didn't know who she was. She told Bertha that it would not be possible to talk him out of the idea of the strange woman, and that she would only upset herself and him more by trying. The counselor suggested she might say, "I'm going to tell that woman to leave you alone. I'll protect you from her and I won't leave you."

Hallucinations are false perceptions of objects or events that involve a patient's senses, causing him or her to see, hear, smell, taste, or even feel something that is not really there. They are caused by changes within the brain that result from Alzheimer's disease. People with AD are more likely to have visual than auditory hallucinations. The person may see the face of a person in the folds of a curtain or hear people talking to him or her and may even talk to the imagined person. Because vision and hearing disorders may predispose a person with AD to sensory hallucinations, a thorough examination of vision and hearing is important for identification and correction of potential contributing factors. Caregivers should be aware that external stimuli (such as television) can sometimes be misinterpreted by patients with AD.

AD patients may become suspicious of people. If they think someone is trying to harm them, they may call the police; they have been known to accuse a devoted spouse of infidelity. The paranoid behavior is likely to be related to the memory deficits intrinsic to the disease. For example, if the person puts an object away for safekeeping and then forgets having done it, he or she may accuse the caregiver or someone else of taking it.

The caregiver should understand that the paranoid thought is real to the patient and that there is no point in trying to reason or argue with him or her. Instead, it may be helpful to calmly offer to help him or her find the missing object. If, for example, the wife who is a patient accuses her husband of stealing her purse, he can try saying something like, "Let's look for it together." Perhaps he can figure out where she might have put it and actually find it, or he can distract her and hope she forgets about it.

When delusions or hallucinations occur that are not distressing to the patient, they probably do not have to be treated. A person with AD may, for instance, believe that characters in a television show are real and are guests in the home and may be very pleased to have visitors. The caregiver does not need to join in the delusion by telling the person that he or she can hear or see whatever it is that the person is experiencing but can let him or her enjoy the experience.

When the person with AD is upset or frightened by the delusion or hallucination, the caregiver can be reassuring ("I won't let anything happen to you.") or distract the person ("Let's go in the other room and have tea."), knowing he or she will forget the frightening event if a little time goes by.

When delusions and hallucinations or paranoid thoughts are very disturbing to the person with AD and these techniques are not successful, the counselor can refer the caregiver to a physician who can evaluate the situation and prescribe appropriate medication. If this is not the patient's regular physician, the caregiver should tell him or her about any other medications the patient is taking and provide a complete medical history before any additional treatment is undertaken to be sure that the person is not ill or in pain or having an adverse reaction to a medication.

## COUNSELOR CHECKLIST

### Understanding and Responding to AD Symptoms

☐ Remind the caregiver that he or she will need to find the appropriate level of stimulation for the patient and be prepared to adjust the environment as the patient's needs change over time.

### An AD-Friendly Environment

☐ Provide the caregiver with guidelines for creating a safe environment for the patient.

☐ Help the caregiver understand that a simple, calm physical environment will reduce stress on the patient, which will ease the caregiver's role.

### Changing Lifestyles

☐ Suggest to the caregiver that the patient will generally be more comfortable in small gatherings of close friends and family.

☐ Suggest that a patient in the moderate stage will need to limit the length of time spent at social activities.

☐ Help the caregiver keep the patient's interests and abilities in mind when choosing activities.

☐ Give the caregiver guidelines for planning tasks for the patient.

☐ Help the caregiver develop strategies to make communication easier with the patient who is losing his or her verbal abilities.

☐ Help the caregiver decipher nonverbal communications from the patient.

☐ Explore caregiver reluctance to assume new responsibilities and offer support as new roles are assumed.

☐ If a patient is driving when it no longer seems to be safe, suggest a driving evaluation and identify alternative means of transportation.

☐ Help the caregiver understand the emotional aspects of a patient's needs for assistance with activities of daily living.

### Difficult Behaviors

☐ There are medications to control some difficult behaviors. Remind the caregiver to ask the doctor about how best to administer them to minimize side effects.

☐ Urge the caregiver to register the patient in the Alzheimer's Association Safe Return Program.

☐ Suggest a thorough medical evaluation of an agitated patient to rule out another illness as a cause of the symptoms.

☐ Counsel the caregiver on the appropriate steps to take when confronting aggressive behavior.

☐ Suggest medical and psychosocial evaluations of sleep disturbances and modifications of the environment to keep the patient safe and reduce the impact on the caregiver.

☐ Poor vision or hearing can contribute to the patient misinterpreting environmental stimuli and should be evaluated and remediated if possible.

☐ Suggest that the caregiver be reassuring and possibly distract the patient who is experiencing hallucinations or delusions.

☐ Refer the caregiver to a physician to evaluate the patient if the delusions or hallucinations are very disturbing to the patient or the caregiver.

# 10

# MEDICAL CARE FOR THE PERSON WITH ALZHEIMER'S DISEASE

**P**roviding medical care for the person with Alzheimer's disease (AD) presents special challenges for the caregiver. AD patients are not immune to the mundane inconveniences of a cold or the life-threatening situations that car accidents, cancer, or heart attacks cause. However, a caregiver may avoid taking a person with AD to the doctor because of the difficulties associated with the visit, such as getting the patient ready on time, arranging transportation, and worrying that, once they get there, the patient will not cooperate with the medical personnel. In this chapter we will discuss the importance of routine health care, as well as how to prepare the caregiver for a medical emergency and how best to help the caregiver cope with the special demands associated with hospitalization of the AD patient.

## Routine Health Care for the AD Patient

People who have Alzheimer's disease are generally elderly and have all the health problems of other people their age. Regular preventive measures, many of which are partially or fully paid for by Medicare, are as important for them as for anyone else who is elderly. In addition to following a good diet and getting enough exercise, they should have regular medical checkups, including cancer

---

This chapter was adapted from Mittelman MS, Epstein C. *How to Get the Best Medical Care for Your Relative with Alzheimer's Disease, In and Out of the Hospital.* New York, NY: Silberstein Institute of Aging and Dementia, 2002.

screening, dental care, eye examinations, hearing evaluations, and annual flu vaccinations.

The caregiver may need counseling to help him or her decide whether to take the entire responsibility for providing for the relative's medical well-being or whether it is possible to delegate some of the tasks to other family members or paid help. If the caregiver shares the tasks with others, he or she will have to arrange to get feedback from the health care provider or the person to whom the task was delegated.

## The Importance of Routine Care

Counselors should make the caregiver aware of the importance of routine health care for a relative with AD. During routine office visits, the doctor may identify medical problems about which the person with AD may be unable to communicate. The caregiver should be advised to take the person with AD to the doctor at the first sign of illness or change in physical functioning, as discomfort from physical illnesses can be responsible for behavioral problems and increased confusion. A functional change, such as incontinence or inability to walk, may not necessarily be a sign of the progression of AD but may be due to another illness.

There are generally no obvious physical manifestations of AD in the early stages. However, as the disease progresses, some people begin to have poor balance and to show signs of muscle rigidity, which increases the risk of falling and possibly breaking a bone. Regular exercise can postpone some of these physical symptoms of the illness.

*Nutrition* The patient's diet may need to be controlled to avoid excessive weight gain or loss or nutritional deficiencies or because he or she has another illness such as diabetes or high cholesterol. Foods the patient should not eat should be kept out of sight. A person with AD who lives alone may stop shopping, not realize when food is spoiled, or be unable to cope in the kitchen. He or she also may forget having just eaten and eat again or forget to eat at all. If the patient is in the early stage of AD, the caregiver may be able to arrange for him or her to eat at a senior center or to have a service such as Meals on Wheels deliver food to the home to ensure that the patient has enough food available. The caregiver may also want to leave a selection of prepared food in the freezer. When the person's illness becomes more severe, someone else will have to be responsible for preparation and serving of food.

*Substance Abuse*   People with AD may have had problems with alcohol abuse or recreational drugs before they became ill. These substances can sometimes cause dementia or make the symptoms worse. If the caregiver reports that his or her relative uses alcohol or recreational drugs and is unwilling to stop, the counselor should suggest that the caregiver make sure these items are no longer easily available. This may mean asking family members, friends, and anyone else who interacts with the person with AD not to give in to any requests for alcohol or drugs. Smoking poses special hazards for people with AD, who may forget that they have left a cigarette or a match burning and cause a fire. Caregivers should try to encourage quitting to restrict access to smoking materials and make sure someone is present when the person uses them.

## Addressing the Problems of Visiting a Doctor

The stage of dementia will affect a person's ability to attend to his or her medical care needs and to cooperate with health care providers. In the mild stage, the caregiver's role will mainly be to remind the person with AD of doctors' appointments, perhaps to ensure that the person doesn't get lost on the way to the doctor's office, and to help him or her follow the doctor's instructions. At this stage of the illness, the dementia may not be immediately obvious to a doctor who does not know the patient well, and the caregiver should be advised to tell doctors that the person has memory problems. In the later stages of AD, the caregiver will have more responsibility for the person's medical well-being and will have to go along to the doctor, prepare or give medications, and generally make all medical decisions on the person's behalf. If someone with AD is physically ill, symptoms of dementia—confusion, anger, suspicion, fear—may be more severe than usual, making it more difficult to get to the doctor. Nevertheless, this visit may prevent the new illness from getting worse.

## Health Care Issues

Larry, who was in the mild stage of AD, had always taken care of his health care needs on his own and considered them to be a private matter, not even to be shared with his wife, Martha. After he developed AD, it was very difficult for his wife or children to go with him to the doctor. He insisted on being alone with the doctor during his examination and became very angry if his wife or children tried to talk to the doctor. "This is my business," he would say. The doctor understood Larry's need for privacy, but he also knew that Larry could no longer be fully responsible for meeting his own health care needs. He suggested that Martha call him before Larry's appointment to discuss the reason for the visit, and he said that she could call him again after the visit to discuss the results of the examination and any recommendations he might have. Martha said, "I don't feel comfortable checking up on Larry, but I guess it's the best way to be sure he stays healthy."

Suggestions to give the caregiver of a patient in the later stages of AD to make the visit to the doctor easier:

- Leave plenty of time to get to the appointment, because it is difficult to hurry a person with AD.

- Get dressed and ready to leave before getting the patient ready, since it is hard for people with AD to wait for someone.

- Avoid talking about the appointment before getting to the doctor's office.

- Try to bring another family member, a friend, or a home health aide along to help reassure or distract the person with AD.

- If the patient is in the moderate or moderately severe stage of AD, pack a bag with a change of clothes, incontinence products, a snack and a drink, and some activity to occupy him or her while waiting in the office.

The caregiver should try to take care of as many administrative details as possible in advance of the visit, filling out forms, for example, to be able to give full attention to the patient in the doctor's office. The person with AD may not be able to sit quietly and wait for his or her turn to see the doctor but may wander around, touch things that belong to other people, or try to talk with other patients who are not interested in a conversation. The caregiver can try to keep the patient occupied by looking at magazines together or eating a snack. The caregiver should also try to make an appointment at a time when the office is unlikely to be busy and waiting times are more likely to be short.

The patient may refuse to go into the examining room. The caregiver can wait a few minutes and try again or suggest a visit to the restroom and then go directly to the doctor's examining room rather than returning to the waiting room. It may be possible for the doctor to do the examination in a consultation room, which may be less frightening than an examining room.

It is often tempting to talk in front of someone with AD as if he or she were not there. People with dementia can pick up on the tone of what is being said even if they do not fully understand the words and become confused or unnecessarily frightened. If the caregiver has questions to ask the doctor, this should be done when the patient cannot hear them. In deciding whether to go into the examining room with the patient or to help the person with potentially difficult procedures such as providing a urine sample, the caregiver must balance the patient's self-esteem and wish for privacy against the doctor's need for accurate information and cooperation.

It is important for caregivers to remember that if patients become agitated or uncooperative, it may be because they are not able to say that they are uncomfortable or feel pain. If the patient is uncooperative, the caregiver should ask the doctor to perform only those procedures that will provide essential information or to try again at another time.

## *Medication*

People with dementia may have trouble understanding or following instructions for taking medicine. They may forget to take it or forget that they have taken it and take it again. Caregivers should know what medications are prescribed, whether they come in a form that is easy for their relative to take, and how they are to be taken.

People in the mild stage of AD may deny or not be aware that they are having problems taking their medication, refilling prescriptions on time, and following their medical treatment plan. If the caregiver does not live with the patient, the caregiver should be advised to check for empty or full medicine bottles and spilled pills on the floor when visiting. The caregiver should be alert to changes in mood or orientation when speaking to the person on the phone, because they may indicate an illness or adverse reaction to medication. If other people take care of the patient part of the time, the caregiver will have to make sure they know the medication schedule, the diet to follow, and treatments to give.

## Health Care Issues

Helen, who was in the early stage of AD, lived alone. She was supposed to take medication for high blood pressure and diabetes every day. Her daughter visited Helen three or four times a week. At each visit, she checked the medication bottles to make sure that Helen had taken her pills. For quite some time, Helen seemed to be doing well, but recently, Helen's daughter noticed that the number of pills in the bottles did not seem to change from visit to visit. Her mother complained that her heart was beating too fast and that she would sometimes suddenly feel weak. When her daughter went with her to the doctor, he said her symptoms suggested that she was not taking her medication regularly. The doctor, who had warned her several times before that it was unwise for her to leave her mother in charge of her own health care, said, "Your mother has several conditions that could make her seriously ill if she doesn't take her medication as prescribed.  She needs someone to give her the medication on schedule. I suspect she isn't eating regularly, since she has lost 5 pounds since her last visit. A carefully monitored diet and regular meals are very important for a person with diabetes. I suggest you get her home care, at least part-time. If you lay out the medicine, the home health aide can give it to her. She can also prepare her meals. You should find out whether your mother is eligible for Medicaid, which may pay for some of this care. My assistant can give you the names of some home health care agencies you can call. Make an appointment to come back with your Mom in a month so I can see how she's doing."

Medicines should be kept where they can be found by a responsible adult, but they must be kept out of the reach of the person with AD. To ensure that they are taken on schedule, the caregiver can lay out the pills in a box that has sections marked for each time of day and each day of the week. Some medicines can be put on a napkin next to the plate at mealtime so the patient will remember to take them. In the more severe stages of dementia, people sometimes get into a stubborn mood and simply refuse to take their medication. A counselor can suggest that it may help to say that he or she can have something special, like a cookie, after taking the medicine if the person resists. If the person refuses, the caregiver might wait a few minutes and try again.

Late in the disease, swallowing becomes difficult, and it becomes more difficult to give medicines to the patient. The caregiver might ask the doctor if the pills can be crushed or if the medicine is available in liquid form.

## Including the Patient in Making Medical Decisions

If a person with AD can express a preference for a certain kind of treatment, this preference should be followed if possible. There are no fixed rules about how much to rely on a family member with AD to make an intelligent or responsible choice when it comes to medical decisions. Nonetheless, it is always important to try to include a person with AD in the decision-making process. Even when the dementia is quite advanced, the affected person can make some choices if they are explained in simple terms.

It is important to keep in mind that unless a person has voluntarily given someone else permission to make decisions on his or her behalf, he or she has the legal right to continue to make them. Only a formal court procedure can limit a person's personal autonomy. Because it is inevitable that a person with AD will ultimately become incapable of making most decisions, legal documents in which the decision-making power is given to someone else should be discussed and completed when people with AD are still able to express their thoughts and feelings about the medical care they want.

## Deciding if Procedures Are Necessary

The patient's doctor may recommend tests or procedures that require a hospital stay. The counselor should suggest that, before agreeing to go ahead, the caregiver ask the doctor what the tests or procedure involves, whether it is absolutely necessary, what it will accomplish, and what might happen if the procedure or test were postponed or not done at all. It is also important to ask about the risks associated with the procedure or test. Another factor to consider is whether anesthesia will be used and what its effects might be on a person with dementia. The caregiver should also inquire about the recovery period and what additional care is likely to be required during that time. If the patient will not be able to follow the instructions for aftercare, special arrangements may have to be made.

The caregiver should know that it is sometimes possible to have a procedure done in a day surgery center, a same-day unit in a hospital, or a doctor's office to avoid the difficulties associated with hospital care for a person with AD. On the other hand, if the patient is very anxious or sensitive to pain or touch, it may be better for him or her to be treated in a hospital where there are more choices for pain management. It may also be preferable to have the procedure done in the hospital if the caregiver is afraid to take the patient home immediately after a procedure or if the person lives alone or with someone who is not qualified to care for him or her.

The caregiver should not hesitate to get several medical opinions to help understand the options and the pros and cons of each one. The caregiver may want to include other family members in the decision-making process.

If a decision has been made to have a procedure done, the caregiver should be cautioned not to tell the patient more than he or she can understand and not to discuss the procedure until shortly before it is due to occur.

## Medical Emergencies

### Preparing for the Medical Emergency

Having someone with AD suddenly fall ill or have an accident is one of the most difficult experiences for a caregiver. If the documents and personal belongings the relative will need in the hospital are prepared in advance, some of the stress of a medical emergency can be avoided. All the necessary information can be placed in an envelope with the patient's name on it. The person's Social Security and Medicare numbers; details about additional medical insurance, including the name of the carrier and the policy number; a photocopy of insurance cards; the person's date of birth and address; the names of several people to contact in an emergency; copies of advance directives; a copy of the person's most recent electrocardiogram; a list of medications and dosages, including prescription and over-the-counter medications, and herbal or nutritional supplements should all be included. A written description of the person's abilities and limitations will help medical personnel know whether the symptoms they observe are new or chronic if the primary caregiver is not available as an informant. The phone number of the person's primary care physician should be posted near the telephone. It is also a good idea to post the number of the poison control center, a taxi or car service, and the name and location of the hospital to which the caregiver prefers the person with AD to be taken.

The counselor should advise the caregiver to arrange in advance for someone who lives nearby to have a key to the house or apartment to be able to go to the hospital with the person if the caregiver is unavailable. Anyone who is caring for the person with AD should also have clear instructions about what to do in an emergency.

## In a Medical Emergency

When a person who has Alzheimer's disease has a medical emergency, the caregiver may panic and call the counselor. The caregiver may be alone with the person or away from the patient's home when it happens. If the caregiver contacts the counselor in these circumstances, the caregiver should be told to call 911, the police, or the fire department. The caregiver should tell the emergency medical technicians (EMTs) that the person has AD, because if the patient is in the mild or moderate stage of AD and is not extremely ill or unconscious, he or she may give the EMT inaccurate information.

Millie and Ted had gone for a walk in the neighborhood one winter day. He slipped on the ice in the driveway and fell. He was able to sit up, but his leg was in a peculiar position and he clearly wasn't able to stand. Millie's first reaction was panic, but seeing how fright-ened Ted was, she calmed herself down. She looked for someone to help her, but no one was around. She had no choice but to leave Ted alone to go into the house and call an ambulance. After she had called the ambulance, she called her neighbor Sue Ann and asked if she could come out and help her look after Ted. Her counselor had advised her to always have a bag packed with Ted's personal care items, a set of pajamas, and, most important, a list of his medica-tions and photocopies of his insurance information. She went to the hall closet, got the emergency bag, and went back outside to wait for the ambulance. She was relieved to see that Sue Ann was already sitting with Ted and had wrapped a blanket around his shoulders. The ambulance arrived shortly afterward, and the EMTs put Ted on a stretcher and took him and Millie to the hospital.

## Caring for the AD Patient in the Emergency Room

When the patient first gets to the hospital, staff members will be focusing on the serious medical problem that has caused the hospi-talization. The caregiver should tell the doctor who examines the patient that the patient has Alzheimer's disease. Sometimes the med-ical problem can be diagnosed more quickly and treated more effec-tively if the caregiver informs the doctors about the severity of the patient's dementia and the extent to which the confusion they observe in the patient is chronic and not a new symptom. If the symptoms of dementia have suddenly gotten much worse, that should also be reported, as it may be a sign of delirium.

The caregiver should try to stay with the patient as much of the time as possible, explaining to the staff that because the person has Alzheimer's disease, a familiar face and voice may keep him or her from getting more confused and upset. (The caregiver should be aware, however, that the rules of the hospital, the way the staff members prefer to work, and how many other patients are waiting may make it difficult for them to permit this.) If the caregiver explains to the staff of the ER that noise and activity are frightening to the patient, it may be possible to have the patient put in a rela-tively quiet place.

When they reached the entrance to the emergency room, the EMT workers got the stretcher out of the ambulance and into the emergency room. EMTs and the care team quickly exchanged information with each other. All Millie overheard was that they suspected that Ted had sustained a broken hip. She didn't hear them say anything about Ted having AD. She tried to stop a nurse, who looked like she was going to listen at first but then went to assist with another emergency patient who was being wheeled in. Millie tried to find out which cubicle Ted was in, but no one was available to ask. Millie remembered her counselor's instructions about what to do in a situation like this, and she briskly walked over to the triage nurse and said, "I am the wife of a patient in the ER. He has Alzheimer's disease. It would help things to go smoothly if I could be with him. Otherwise, he is likely to get agitated and be more trouble for the staff." The nurse said she would inquire. She came back and told Millie that, unfortunately, right then Millie could not be with her husband because the ER was too crowded, but that she had notified the care team and they would try to let her be with Ted as soon as it was possible. Millie thought, "I'll wait a few minutes and ask again."

## Hospitalization of the AD Patient

Alzheimer's disease affects every aspect of hospital care. The hospital, with all its strange noises, people, and equipment, may make people with AD more confused and can bring on symptoms and behaviors that are more severe than those seen at home. There will be many people they do not know, and this may make them feel anxious. Even though they have trouble adjusting to disruptions in their normal daily routine, they will be expected to adjust to the hospital's schedule. They may not realize that they are ill or in the hospital and, not understanding what is happening to them, may feel attacked or threatened when forced to undergo painful treatments and examinations. They may not understand that they now need to ask for help with things they usually do on their own—something as simple as finding the bathroom in a new place and then finding the bed again may be difficult for them and make them feel frustrated and irritable. Counselors should alert caregivers to the special problems that people with AD will have in the hospital and to the need for them to explain their relatives' strengths and limitations and be advocates for them.

## Special Problems AD Patients Have in the Hospital

Hospital staff may mistakenly believe patients with mild dementia to be cognitively intact and expect them to be able to remember and follow instructions. They may then be puzzled or irritated by the patients' apparent noncompliance. People in the moderate and moderately severe stages of AD are more confused, forgetful, and frightened and need constant supervision and reassurance to cope with the demands of a strange setting like a hospital. People in this stage may be disturbing to other patients and staff. They may become aggressive, shout, or cry for no apparent reason, or they may have hallucinations or delusions. People in the severe stage require a great deal of time-consuming physical care.

People with Alzheimer's disease, who may not initiate exercise on their own, are very vulnerable to physical decline caused by immobility. The caregiver should try to make sure that the patient is out of bed as much as his or her condition allows and that he or she receives the appropriate exercises and physical therapy. When a person is kept in bed and does not move around, muscles quickly begin to tighten. Range-of-motion exercises, which gently move each joint, can prevent this loss of flexibility and the development of contractures (the decrease of 50% or more of the normal passive range of motion of the joint). A contracture develops when the normally elastic connective tissues become replaced with inelastic fibrous tissue; this makes the tissues resistant to stretching and prevents normal movement of the affected area. The chance that a person will fall is greater if muscle tone has been lost as a result of spending a great deal of time in bed. The risk is increased by the side effects of certain medications, which interfere with balance, and from the neurological symptoms of AD.

If possible, the caregiver should urge the staff to try to avoid the use of a catheter, which might be pulled out by a confused patient. If the patient was able to use the toilet before coming to the hospital, the caregiver should ask the staff to let him or her do so again as soon as possible so that the habit is not lost.

Tests and other procedures can be especially frightening to a person with AD, because he or she is unable to understand why they are being done, what people are saying, and what is happening to the other patients in the room. The counselor can suggest that the caregiver offer to help the patient stay calm enough to cooperate with treatment and make it easier for the doctors and other hospital staff members to communicate with the patient. The caregiver should be sure to tell the staff anything that has worked in the past to calm the patient and get his or her cooperation.

The caregiver should suggest to hospital staff that they wait until shortly before the procedure to tell the patient about it, because when information is given too far in advance, it may be forgotten, or the person with AD may become anxious and ask the same ques tions over and over or become too upset to cooperate. Either the caregiver or a nurse should explain, one step at a time and in very simple language, what is going to be done or what the patient needs to do. If possible, procedures should be scheduled for a time of day when the patient is most likely to be cooperative; the late afternoon and evening, when people with AD frequently get agitat ed and irritable, should be avoided. The caregiver can ask to be with the patient when he or she is being transported from one place to another and to stay during procedures, so the patient will be more cooperative and less frightened.

## The Caregiver's Role in the Hospital

Caregivers of people with AD worry about how to keep them from being frightened, how to comfort them, how to help them know where they are, and how to make sure that, in their confusion, they do not put themselves in danger.

It is the caregiver's role to alert hospital staff to the special AD-related needs of the patient and to meet some of those needs personally. The caregiver's role runs the gamut from making major decisions about medical care to helping with day-to-day tasks and finding safe and interesting activities to pass the time. After checking with the staff, the caregiver may be able to provide some of the care, perhaps feeding the patient or helping the patient do range-of-motion exercises.

The caregiver should offer to help the staff understand and inter pret the patient's efforts to communicate and explain what the patient is trying to say to the hospital staff. The caregiver should be cautioned, however, to try to let the patient do the talking whenever possible.

People with AD need company and supervision virtually all the time while they are in the hospital, even though this will require a major commitment of time and emotional resources for the caregiver and other family members. To avoid exhaustion, the caregiver should enlist the help of other family members, friends, or paid help. It is important to maintain a balance between the patient's and the caregiver's needs. The caregiver should be encouraged to consider how much he or she can and wants to participate in the care of the family member who is in the hospital. For example, if the caregiver feels it is important for a family member to feed the patient or to be in the room with the patient at night, the caregiver should be encouraged to take frequent breaks, to ask other family members for help, and to hire additional help if he or she can afford it. The caregiver should be cautioned not to be so zealous about caring for the ill relative that a job or relationships with other family members are jeopardized.

### Helping the Caregiver Communicate With Hospital Staff

It is important for the caregiver to establish and maintain a good working relationship with the hospital staff. Once the patient is assigned a room, the caregiver should try to arrange a meeting with the nurse who is in charge of the unit and coordinates patient care to explain the special needs and limitations of the patient caused by AD. The caregiver should ask about the routines and regulations and the role of each staff member and let the nurse in charge know how much help he or she can provide for the patient. Here are some tips the counselor can give the caregiver about how to communicate effectively with the hospital staff:

- *Pick the time carefully.* Caregivers should approach staff about meeting when it is convenient for both them and staff.

- *Prepare ahead of time.* Caregivers should write down questions or concerns in advance, even when they believe they know what they want to say.

- *Approach the staff with a positive attitude.* Caregivers may feel overwhelmed, embarrassed, frustrated, or just tired, but should try to bring a positive attitude to their interactions with all staff members.

■ *Acknowledge the staff's needs and priorities.*

■ *Offer suggestions in a constructive way.* If staff is having difficulty feeding the patient, for example, the caregiver might suggest something that has worked at home. Caregivers should be aware, however, that the hospital has rules and restrictions that may prevent staff members from always doing what the caregivers would like.

■ *Ask only for changes that are absolutely necessary to the patient's well-being and care.* Caregivers who ask for something that is not normal procedure, such as accompanying a patient to tests, should explain why they believe their request will make a situation easier for everyone. Caregivers should be prepared to accept that their request cannot be met.

■ *Be available to staff in between visits to help resolve any difficulties that arise.*

■ *Explain the patient's needs, way of communicating, and behavior management strategies that have worked for the caregiver in the past.*

■ *Know the responsibilities of each staff member in order to know the best person to talk to when a problem arises.*

It is sometimes difficult for caregivers to decide when they should provide the staff with information and when the patient can speak for himself or herself. While it is probably best for caregivers to give vital information to staff themselves, they should try to have the patient answer so that his or her dignity is preserved and so that the staff will view the patient as an individual.

> Ted was taken to the radiology department to have his hip X-rayed. Millie was able to accompany him as they wheeled him on the stretcher, and she kept him calm by talking to him and holding his hand. He did have a broken hip, and he was scheduled for surgery that night. Millie told the surgeon and every other staff member that Ted had AD. The nurses monitored Ted's level of confusion after the surgery to be sure that it wasn't significantly greater than it had been before. When he was taken to a regular hospital room, Millie went to the nursing station and asked for an appointment with the nurse in charge of the unit. When Millie met with the nurse, she told her about

the symptoms and difficulties caused by the fact that Ted had AD. She also gave the nurse a list of the medications Ted normally took. The nurse told Millie what she could expect to happen next and how long he would likely be in the hospital. She also gave Millie the names of the care team members and assured Millie that she would alert the staff to Ted's special needs. The nurse did, however, warn Millie that the hospital could not spare anyone to supervise Ted all the time. She asked if Millie could make arrangements with family or friends to be with him. The nurse suggested that Millie might consider hiring a private companion or aide to be with him at night so the family could go home and sleep.

***Addressing Problems With Medication***  People with Alzheimer's disease are particularly sensitive to the effects of medication and may have paradoxical reactions. The caregiver should know what medications have been prescribed, their purpose, when the patient is supposed to take them, and possible side effects. The caregiver should tell the doctor about adverse reactions the patient has had to medications in the past, because the patient may not remember.

Although the hospital staff will be looking out for reactions to medication, they may miss signs that the caregiver is more likely to notice, such as changes in behavior or level of confusion. If the patient becomes unusually confused and upset, the caregiver should ask the doctor to reevaluate the prescribed medications.

Sometimes people with AD will insist on holding and playing with their pills, or they might hold the pill in their mouth and then spit it out later. The caregiver should ask the nurse to give the patient the pills one at a time and make sure each is swallowed. It may be helpful for the caregiver to tell the staff how the patient takes pills at home.

The caregiver should be cautioned not to give the patient medicine from home. While in the hospital, patients can take only medicines prescribed by hospital doctors and only on the hospital's schedule.

***Helping a Caregiver Make Decisions for the AD Patient***
In the early stages of Alzheimer's disease it is often difficult to determine the person's competence. As the illness becomes more severe,

the person will clearly no longer be capable of making decisions about medical care. The caregiver may find it distressing to have to act on the patient's behalf. If the patient has signed advance directives, the caregiver will have the legal right to make these decisions, although it may still be emotionally stressful to do so. The counselor may have to support the caregiver in following these wishes. It may help to remind the caregiver that the advance directives state what the person would have wanted, even if it differs from what the caregiver would choose (see Chapter 13 for a discussion on advance directives).

If there are no advance directives, the medical staff will generally turn to the spouse or adult child to make decisions. If there is serious disagreement about a decision among family members, or the family and the doctor, and there is no advance directive, it may be necessary to involve the hospital ethics committee or have a legal proceeding in which someone will be appointed by the court to be the patient's guardian.

The caregiver may be asked to make decisions about diagnostic or treatment procedures. Before giving or withholding approval, the caregiver should try to understand what the risks and benefits are likely to be, the consequences of not doing the procedure or treatment, whether the procedure will improve quality of life or chances of recovery, and what alternative treatments are available. The caregiver should be advised to try to get as much information as he or she needs to make an informed decision by talking to the doctors and the health care team involved in the care of the patient. Other people who can help a caregiver make a decision include hospital chaplains, as well as spiritual advisors outside the hospital, friends, family, and even the patient, if he or she is able to participate. If the caregiver is concerned that certain tests or treatments are not being done, he or she should be encouraged to ask why not. The decision may have been based on the person's age, medical condition, stage of dementia, or cost of the tests. It may be helpful for the caregiver to request another doctor's opinion about how to proceed if the patient's doctor will not agree to the tests.

One of the first decisions the caregiver may have to make when a relative is admitted to the hospital is whether to sign a "do not resuscitate" (DNR) order or "do not intubate" (DNI). If a DNR is not signed, then hospital personnel are obligated to do everything possible to save the patient's life. The caregiver can cancel a DNR at any time and make another one if circumstances change. The caregiver may also have to decide whether or not to continue treatments that may prolong life in a condition that may not seem to be worthwhile. If the person has not made his or her wishes clear, the caregiver may have to decide about the use of a feeding tube if the patient can no longer swallow, mechanical ventilation to assist breathing, and medications that may relieve pain but possibly shorten life.

***Supervising a Person With AD in the Hospital*** A caregiver may think of a hospitalization as a chance for respite and not realize that it will be necessary to spend more time than usual, rather than less, with the person with AD. People with AD in the hospital need more help than other patients. Very simple things may be confusing for them: they may not know how to use the call button or remember how to use it and may need someone to push it for them. They may not realize that the IV in their arm is attached to a pole that they need to take along with them when they get out of bed. Someone needs to push the IV pole for them and make sure they do not leave it behind or hurt themselves with it.

Normal daily activities such as eating and toileting are more of a problem in the hospital than at home. Patients with AD may not understand how to fill out the menu and may not be able or want to eat the food brought to them. They need someone to help them make appropriate food choices or do it for them. They cannot be expected to refuse foods they are not supposed to eat. They may also need more help eating than the hospital can supply. People with AD may not be able to find the bathroom or remember to call for help if they need assistance getting there. They may get off the toilet by themselves because they usually do so at home, not understanding that they are now too weak to do so without help. They should have someone to accompany them to the bathroom to prevent them from falling and help them if they are no longer capable of using the toilet on their own.

People with AD may not remember the instructions they are given and will need them to be repeated over and over again. They may try to get out of bed when their treatment plan calls for complete bed rest. They may try to climb over the side rails, which are intended to keep them safely in bed, and fall. If people with AD are able to get up and walk around, there is a risk that they will wander away and get lost. Not being able to understand hospital rules, they may go places and touch things they should not. Patients with AD have been known to leave the hospital floor or go into a maintenance closet, a linen chute, or other dangerous places. The best way to guard against this is to be sure they are supervised at all times and distracted with safe activities. Sometimes seating a patient in a geri chair (a chair with an attached table) will keep him or her securely contained, without giving a feeling of being tied down. If the caregiver or someone else cannot be there all the time, the counselor can suggest the caregiver try to have the relative assigned to a room that requires him or her to pass the nursing station before getting to an exit.

The caregiver, another family member, or a hired companion who understands the patient may be able to calm or distract him or her and may make it possible to avoid the use of physical or chemical restraints. Physical restraints can make people angry and frightened, even causing them to injure themselves while struggling to break free, although there are times when, for the patient's own safety, physical restraints are the best alternative. Medications that act as chemical restraints are sometimes given to patients with AD if they become agitated or noisy or cannot sleep. Although such medications are meant to have a calming effect, they may have a paradoxical effect on a person with dementia, making him or her more confused and, in some cases, more agitated.

The caregiver should be encouraged to ask family and friends to help provide supervision for the patient and not try to do it all alone. Sometimes, even family and friends cannot provide all the care and supervision needed, and it is necessary to hire help. It may be possible for the caregiver, friends, and relatives to provide supervision during the day and in the early evening hours. It is during the night, however, that people with AD often need the most support— more support, in fact, than can realistically be met by the hospital's night staff. If no one among family and friends is available to stay overnight, it will be necessary to hire help for these hours, especially if the patient has been staying awake most of the night and needs constant reassurance or has to go to the bathroom frequently.

Hospitals often have a private-duty nurse office that will help families hire additional help for patients in the hospital. If the caregiver wants to bring in someone who was taking care of the patient at home or from an outside agency, it will be necessary to check with the head nurse or nurse manager about hospital rules and procedures, which may include a review of the credentials and insurance of companions who are not on staff. The choice of the type of help to hire depends on the patient's needs.

After talking to the nurse, Millie got together with Carol and Tom to work out a schedule so that some member of the family would always be with Ted. They decided that Carol would spend the mornings with him, and Millie would leave work early and relieve Carol. Tom would come in the evening and spend the night. The nurse had mentioned that a cot could be set up if someone wanted to stay with Ted at night. They decided not to hire an aide because they preferred to have a family member stay with him. When Matt called to find out how his father was doing, Millie told him about the plan for the family to take turns being with him. Matt said, "I still have a few vacation days left. Why don't I come down and help. I can stay with Dad some of the time, too."

***Making the Patient Comfortable in the Hospital Room*** Many things about being in a hospital room can be upsetting, or even terrifying, to a person with Alzheimer's disease—voices heard over the intercom system, pictures on the wall, the view from the window, or the patient in the next bed moaning, screaming, or receiving many telephone calls and visitors. These strange sounds and activities might be upsetting to anyone, but they can be overwhelming to a person with Alzheimer's disease. Dim lighting can cause curtains, furniture, and moving objects to cast frightening shadows. Clutter on the tables or too many chairs and tables will make it hard to get to the bathroom or even to get from the bed to the chair. This confusing environment may cause the patient to become agitated. The nurse in charge of the unit may permit the caregiver to make some changes that will simplify the patient's environment.

Here are some suggestions the counselor can give the caregiver:

■ Ask what equipment can be removed, put away in closets, or hidden behind a curtain; the caregiver should put items in drawers that the patient does not use all the time.

■ Lower the volume on the telephone ringer.

■ Ask that the intercom be used as little as possible or that its volume be lowered.

■ Ask if a bright light can be left on near the patient's bed.

■ Cover or remove pictures.

■ Limit the number of visitors.

■ If the patient is upset by the view from the window, close the curtains.

■ Leave eyeglasses and other essentials within easy reach.

■ If possible, ask that the bed be pushed against the wall so the patient can get out on only one side.

■ Close the curtain that surrounds the bed to make a more private space that may feel safer to the patient.

■ Do not let magazines, leftover juice, and wilting flowers accumulate.

***Problem Behavior in the Hospital***  A few simple measures can be taken to alleviate some common problems. If the patient is picking on bandages or pulling out IV lines or other tubes, the caregiver can ask the nurse if these items can be placed in a less accessible place (such as high on the dominant arm) or concealed under the gown. If the patient refuses to take a bath, the caregiver can ask the aide to try again at the time he or she is regularly bathed at home and to respect his or her modesty and privacy as much as possible. If the patient wants to keep his or her clothes on, the caregiver can ask that this be allowed. If the behavior that is considered "strange" by the staff is not dangerous and will not require more staff time to accommodate, the caregiver can explain that the behavior is due to the patient's dementia.

It is possible that AD patients will become agitated or withdrawn or behave inappropriately because of fear of being in a strange place or pain that they are unable to communicate. They may also become confused and think the hospital room is their home and try to get the "strangers" to leave. The caregiver should explain the cause of the behavior to the staff and other people in the room.

If the patient is shouting or cursing or makes gestures that seem threatening, such as waving his or her arms, making a fist, or grabbing someone, it may frighten the staff. It may help to explain that the patient has not hurt anyone when behaving in what seems to be a threatening way. The presence of the caregiver, who is familiar to the patient, may be calming.

If the person with AD cannot tolerate being in a room with another patient, the caregiver might consider changing to a private room, even though there will be an additional charge. Sometimes, if no one intervenes, a person with Alzheimer's disease will forget what was so upsetting and calm down.

People with Alzheimer's disease feel pain, although they may not be able to say so in words. They may show it by becoming agitated or angry. If the patient is screaming, the caregiver should ask the nurse to check if he or she is in pain or has received pain medication.

A counselor can suggest many methods to a caregiver that may reduce agitation:

- Change the amount of light in the room; experiment with increasing and decreasing the light level and reducing glare and shadows.

- Try to distract your relative by involving him or her in a pleasant activity, such as looking through a magazine or listening to music, folding napkins, or arranging objects on the bed table.

- Seek out special services, such as music, massage, and recreation therapy; activities and materials for patients with dementia may be available in the hospital.

- If the staff says it is okay, take your relative out of the hospital room to a sunroom or lounge, or you can sit in the lobby for a few minutes for a change of scene.

- Speak calmly, pat the person's hand, use reassuring words, offer him or her a treat, or talk about someone who is important to the patient (perhaps giving him or her a picture of a grandchild or something soft to hold) to divert the patient.

- If the patient is not in pain, it may be best to try to ignore the behavior or leave the room for a short time.

- If the patient had been taking medication for this behavior prior to the hospitalization, the doctor should be informed.

- Ask the staff to help you figure out what caused the outburst; find out what happened just beforehand (sometimes a routine event, such as taking temperature or blood pressure, can upset a person with dementia who does not understand what is being done).

Matt and Tom decided to take turns sleeping in the hospital with Ted. On the first night, as Matt dimmed the lights for Ted to sleep, Ted started waving his arms around and shouting, "Go away, lady." When the same thing happened the next night, a nurse came into the room and noticed that Ted was looking at a painting on the wall. The nurse took down the painting and said, "See, Ted, the lady's gone away." Ted began to calm down. The nurse said, "I've noticed that when lights are dim, people with dementia are frightened by pictures, shadows, or even folds in curtains."

## Preparing for Discharge of the Patient

People with Alzheimer's disease are at significant risk for cognitive and functional decline during an acute hospitalization. Although some regain their previous level of functioning, for others the decline is permanent. While the patient is in the hospital, the discharge planner will meet with the family caregivers to discuss after-care. The hospitalization may provide an opportunity for a professional and the family to evaluate the safety and appropriateness of the patient's previous care plan. Seeing the patient in the hospital setting may alter the caregiver's perception of the patient's condition. Sometimes family caregivers benefit from the objective view of their care plan and, as a result, consider making changes, such as hiring more help, enrolling the patient in day care, or even placing him or her in a nursing home. Counselors can help caregivers to assess the viability of altering the care plan and then help them adjust to the change.

The hospital discharge planner may suggest that the person with AD be discharged to a nursing home. Counselors can prepare caregivers not to take the suggestion as an indication that they are not doing a good job. In fact, in many cases a person can return home after a hospitalization if the family is willing and able to provide care. Ultimately, the decision is up to the caregiver.

It is common for patients with AD to be referred to a subacute facility after hospitalization. Many need skilled nursing care. Others require rehabilitation and would not be able to tolerate the intensity of the demands of an acute rehabilitation facility.

The day after Ted's surgery a social worker came to talk to Millie about the discharge plan. "Already," Millie exclaimed. "Ted just got here. I can't think about that yet." The social worker explained that from the time a patient is admitted to the hospital the discharge is being planned so that all the arrangements will have been made by the time the patient is ready to leave. She told Millie that she thought it would be necessary for Ted to go to a subacute facility because he would need physical rehabilitation to be able to walk again. Millie was disturbed to learn that the subacute facility was part of a nursing home, although it was in a separate wing. She was sure that Carol would be upset as well. She talked to her children about it, and they agreed that it was a sensible plan and there was no reasonable alternative. Since the facility was nearby, it would still be easy to visit Ted regularly.

If the patient was formerly living alone, the caregiver may decide to have the patient move into his or her home. This alternative is discussed in Chapter 11. The caregiver may agree to have the patient transferred to another facility on a permanent basis upon discharge from the hospital. The counseling issues associated with choosing and moving the person with AD into alternative living situations are discussed in Chapter 12.

## COUNSELOR CHECKLIST

### Routine Health Care for the AD Patient

☐ Explain the importance of routine health care for the person with AD.

☐ Advise the caregiver to take the patient to the doctor at the first sign of illness.

☐ When behavioral disturbances occur, suggest a medical evaluation to rule out remediable physical causes.

☐ Provide guidelines to make medical appointments less stressful.

☐ Advise the caregiver to keep track of medications prescribed for the patient and to make sure that the medication schedule is followed.

☐ Advise the caregiver to have the patient assign legal and medical decision-making powers while the patient is still able to express his or her wishes.

### Medical Emergencies

☐ Counsel the caregiver to keep a bag packed with copies of the patient's insurance documents, a list of current medications, advance directives, and personal belongings in case of a medical emergency.

☐ Advise the caregiver to always tell medical emergency personnel that the patient has AD.

### Hospitalization of the AD Patient

☐ Counsel the caregiver that the AD patient will need supervision and assistance while he or she is in the hospital.

☐ Encourage the caregiver to enlist the aid of family members, friends, or paid help to contribute to the additional care needed by the AD patient.

☐ Give the caregiver suggestions on how to communicate effectively with the hospital staff.

☐ Suggest ways to simplify the patient's environment while in the hospital.

☐ Suggest methods to reduce patient agitation.

☐ Caution the caregiver not to give the patient any medications from home.

☐ Support the caregiver in following the patient's advance directives.

☐ Counsel the caregiver to be as informed as possible when deciding whether to consent to medical treatment.

☐ Help the caregiver assess the viability of the discharge plan and adjust to any new responsibilities and changes in the patient.

# 11

# CARING FOR THE PATIENT AT HOME

A person with Alzheimer's disease (AD) can be cared for at home throughout the course of the illness with adequate support, if that is the family's choice. The caregiving tasks will become numerous as the disease progresses, including supervision, help with activities of daily living, ensuring good health care, providing for safety, and finding appropriate and stimulating social and recreational activities. Caregivers almost always need formal services to help them carry out these tasks unless there are sufficient informal resources, such as other family members.

The counselor can guide caregivers through the process of deciding where the person with AD should live and can provide emotional support as well as information about appropriate resources. This chapter first discusses the decision to care for the patient at home. It then provides an overview of the different types of formal services available for people with Alzheimer's disease, including home care, community respite services, and health care services.

## The Decision to Care for the Patient at Home

There are many reasons why families decide to care for their relative with AD at home rather than placing him or her in a long-term care facility. These reasons fall into two general categories, personal conviction and practical considerations. The decision in each individual situation is usually based on a combination of the two. Families should be advised to consider the logistics and consequences of each of the arrangements they are considering before making a decision to keep the person at home.

The counselor's role, in addition to offering education, emotional support, and assistance in problem solving, is to help the caregiver obtain appropriate formal services, as well as the informal support of family and friends. Of course, if the counselor feels that the well-being of the patient or caregiver is in jeopardy, he or she should urge the caregiver to consider alternative options. If the situation seems immediately dangerous, it may even be necessary to enlist the aid of protective services.

## *Personal Convictions*

Most often the tasks involved with care are seen as a natural extension of family roles, and family members may not even realize that they are stepping into a caregiving role. This is especially likely when the patient lives with a family member rather than alone. Family members in this instance do not consciously make a choice to care for a patient at home instead of in an alternative residence, but rather, the patient gradually declines in his or her own home and the caregiver provides care accordingly.

For many families an emotional connection or previous promise to the patient precludes the notion of placing the person in a residential facility. For instance, people who have lived with their spouses for many years prefer to be together with their husband or wife, even though their partner may be severely impaired. It feels comforting just to know the person is in the house or sleeping beside him or her.

The decision to care for a person with AD at home may be tied to ethical, moral, or religious beliefs and cultural values. For many people, the idea of taking someone out of his or her home and putting the person in a residential facility is inconsistent with their idea of what is right or of what a person's obligations are to his or her family.

### Care Choices

Hannah was annoyed by the fact that neighbors, friends, and her husband's physician continued to insist that she place her husband in a nursing home, even though she had told them she was determined to keep him at home. She told her counselor, "I take very good care of Carl. No one denies it. Even his doctor says he is getting great care. Still, everyone keeps telling me I should put him in a nursing home for my sake. They say I shouldn't put myself through this kind of stress and that I'm sacrificing my life for him. It's true he's often up and pacing around half the night and sometimes yells at people only he can see." The counselor asked, "Why do you want to keep Carl at home?" Hannah thought for a moment as tears rolled down her face. "Because I love having him with me. Even though it's hard caring for him, I like holding his hand. Why is that so wrong?" "Hannah," the counselor said, "it isn't wrong. I know you take good care of Carl, and I know it makes you happy to be able to have him at home. There is really no good reason why you can't continue to do so. It's your decision; you are obviously comfortable with it, and the problem is how to deal with the other people. Perhaps if you tell them what you told me, they will understand. If they persist, let them know you've made a decision and you would appreciate their support rather than suggestions for change."

## *Practical Reasons*

A caregiver may decide it is a high priority for the patient to have one-to-one care, because it will give him or her the highest quality of life and maximize the maintenance of functional capacity. In order to do this in a residential facility, the caregiver would have to pay a private aide to stay with the patient at all times in addition to the cost of the facility. At home, caregivers may have other options. In addition to providing care themselves, they may be able to enlist support from family members, friends, or volunteers and supplement this support with formal services at a lower overall financial cost than that of a residential facility.

There may be times when family members care for a person at home because there are no suitable facilities within a reasonable distance that would enable them to visit as often as they would like. In some areas, there may be few facilities from which to choose, long waiting lists for a bed, eligibility requirements that a patient may not meet, or financial requirements that a family cannot meet. In these cases, the counselor can help the family find ways to make it possible to keep the person at home, either for the long term or while they are waiting for a bed in a facility to become available.

Some families care for the person at home to avoid the cost of a residential facility. People with limited savings may fear that what they have will be entirely expended on patient care. Some family members may want to conserve their inheritance. Sometimes disagreements about how money should be spent or saved may cause conflict in the family. In many of these situations, there is no right or wrong. The counselor's main concern should not be about how the money is spent, but rather that the patient receives adequate care, the caregiver's well-being is not jeopardized, and family members continue to support each other even though they may disagree.

## Care Choices

Diane's mother, who was in the severe stage of AD, lived at home in Florida with her brother Ralph, who did not have a job and took complete care of her. Their mother no longer recognized them, was incontinent, and needed to be fed and bathed. Diane, who was a teacher, lived far away and could only visit on school holidays. One day Ralph called Diane to say that he had taken their mother to the hospital because she seemed to be in pain. Diane immediately flew down to Florida. The hospital kept her mother for observation for a few days but could find nothing to explain her symptoms. The hospital social worker advised them to have their mother discharged to a nursing home, thinking that her care was too much for Ralph to handle. Diane agreed with the social worker. She suspected that Ralph was keeping their mother at home to save the cost of the nursing home, assuming he would inherit the money as a reward for all his efforts. She was also concerned that Ralph had no life of his own, since taking care of Mom was occupying all his time. When she voiced her concerns, Ralph said, "You're right. I do want to save the money for myself. But I take very good care of Mom. She's used to me. It makes me feel good to be useful for once in my life." The social worker said that Ralph had come to the hospital every day and stayed for hours. The staff had told her that, indeed, their mother ate much more when Ralph came to feed her than when they tried to do it, and she even occasionally smiled when he was there. She said that since Ralph and Diane shared power of attorney, they should try to come to some agreement. Diane realized that Ralph was going to continue to have the major responsibility for their mother, unless she moved her to a nursing home near where she lived. She also came to the conclusion that Ralph deserved to inherit their mother's money, since he had spent many years caring for her. She said, "All right, Ralph, if you want to take her home, I'll agree to it. But please, if it gets to be too much for you, promise to reconsider."

## Choosing Living Arrangements

Once the decision has been made to keep the person with AD at home, additional questions have to be considered. Where will the person live, in his or her own home or another relative's home? And what are the consequences of each of these decisions to the lives of the patient, the caregiver, and other family members? Working out living and care arrangements requires planning and creativity, and the counselor can be available to caregivers to suggest appropriate care options, help families weigh the benefits and risks of each decision, and provide support when difficulties arise.

## *Deciding in Whose Home the Patient Will Live*

A person with AD may be able to live in his or her own home throughout the course of the illness if he or she already lives with someone who can provide care or if his or her home is large enough to accommodate hired live-in help when this becomes necessary. In many instances, however, the patient lives alone and it is not possible to hire sufficient help. Family members may then have to consider other living arrangements. Some family members decide to move the patient into their own homes, because they have the space to do so or because they believe that this will be a better alternative than hiring help. Some people decide to move into the patient's home. For example, an adult daughter may move into her parents' home because her own apartment is small and her parents' home is bigger, more luxurious, or closer to work. Another reason might be to spare the patient the stress of moving. The counselor should help the caregiver weigh all the options and be aware of the consequences of the choice he or she is making.

The counselor should suggest that the following factors be considered:

- The stage of the illness and the symptoms

- The physical condition of the patient

■ The caregiver's availability to provide care directly or supervise hired help

■ The availability of family members or friends to assist in care

■ The wishes of the person with AD and other family members

■ The suitability of the environment

■ The availability of formal services in the area

■ Financial consequences

## Care Choices

Vanessa and her husband, Mike, went to see the counselor because Vanessa was thinking about renovating a room in the basement so her grandmother could live with them and she could keep an eye on her. "It seems a lot nicer than leaving her in her own home with only her aide to talk to when she has a family. I'm sure it's a good idea because my grandma and I have always been close, and it will be so much better than having to worry about what she's doing and supervise from miles away. It won't be any trouble to cook for one more, and it will be nice for the kids to have Grandma around. Besides, we won't have to pay someone to stay with her. Don't you think that's a good idea?" The counselor said that Vanessa had many arguments in defense of this idea but wondered if she and Mike had thought about the negative aspects. Mike said, "I can answer that. First, we have four children, two of whom don't go to school yet. Also, her grandmother sometimes acts up. She'll be in everybody's way. She'll scare the kids. Should I keep going?" The counselor said that his perspective seemed clear enough and turned to Vanessa. "Vanessa, your grandmother has been living alone for many years with the help of an aide. Why do you want her to move in with you now?" Vanessa started to cry. "A few weeks ago, I was cleaning out the attic and found all the old family stuff—photo albums, letters—I just started thinking that Grandma is the only person I have left on my side of the family and that I should do more to help her, to be closer to her, to give the kids a chance to know her before she dies. But I guess Mike is right. It doesn't make sense to bring her into our home. I just wish I could help her more."

## *Understanding and Adjusting to the Living Arrangements*

Altering living arrangements may cause major changes in the caregiver's life. Some caregivers can take the patient into their own homes and are able to adjust to the situation. Many people make this choice because they think it will reduce their need for formal services or make caregiving more convenient. They may not anticipate the impact living with their ill relative can have on their family relationships, social life, and work. The caregiver may no longer be able to invite friends into the home because of the patient's behavior or to work late or go out to a movie after work because he or she has to rush home to be with the patient. The decision may cause great family upheaval. If there are other family members in the household, they may have agreed to this arrangement but nevertheless resent losing their privacy and sharing the space and the attention of the caregiver. They may also find the behavior of the patient difficult or embarrassing. When more than one family member will be affected by the new living arrangement, the counselor can facilitate their involvement in the decision-making process.

Caregivers should also be made aware that when their relatives are living in their own homes with the help of an aide, they still will have to supervise the care. This can also interfere with a caregiver's family, social, and work life. The caregiver should be aware that he or she may have to interrupt other activities in response to the needs of the patient or to solve a problem.

If a caregiver is living at a distance from the person with AD, the problems of supervising home care are more acute than if the caregiver can be available on a regular basis. A social worker employed by a community agency or a care manager who is hired privately can provide case management for a patient who is living alone and cannot be visited on a regular basis by a relative. Case management generally includes instituting and supervising services to ensure that the person has regular meals, consistent health care, secure housing, contact with the community, and access to entitlements, as well as adequate home care.

The process of making the decision about where a person should live or which services a patient needs can evoke strong emotions in the caregiver. It may force the caregiver to look more closely at the conditions in which the patient has been living and, for the first time, truly acknowledge the impact of the illness on the person with AD. The realization of the severity of the patient's illness can be very distressing. While the caregiver may have long been aware of the patient's diagnosis, he or she may not have put together the signs that the living arrangement was no longer safe. For example, the caregiver of a person living alone may have assumed that the person could adequately care for himself, only to discover that the refrigerator is almost empty and the person is disheveled and unkempt. This discovery may make the caregiver feel guilty about not having realized how bad the situation had become.

Changing the patient's living arrangements may also mean having to sell the patient's house or apartment and dispose of many possessions. For many family members this may signify the end of a chapter in the family's history and be extremely upsetting to them. The wife of an AD patient, for instance, may decide for practical reasons that the couple should sell their house and move into a smaller apartment that would be easier to manage and is closer to their children who could help with the patient's care. This move, however, may mean losing the house that the couple moved into when they first married many years ago. It may mean moving away from the few close friends they have. Or it may signify the end of any hopes or dreams that were built while the couple was living in that home. Counselors can provide caregivers with emotional support, an opportunity to talk about their sadness, and advice about the practical aspects of making the change.

For some caregivers, thinking about changing the patient's living arrangements can force them to be aware of financial limitations, which may be a painful and upsetting reminder of missed opportunities earlier in life or of the wider choices available to those with greater financial resources. Before making any suggestions or comments about the benefits and pitfalls of any particular living arrangement or formal service, the counselor must be aware of the family's circumstances in order to avoid making recommendations that are not feasible.

## Care Choices

Sofia and John had immigrated to the United States rather late in life. They left their careers and sold their home in their native country for what seemed like a small amount once they arrived in America. The great jobs they believed they would get so easily did not materialize, so Sofia and John were never able to save much and often struggled to make ends meet. John was diagnosed with AD just 10 years after they arrived, when he was only in his mid-50s, and lost his job shortly thereafter. For several years Sofia felt comfortable leaving John home alone, but now she was becoming increasingly worried about whether this was still safe. She had to continue to work because she was their sole source of support. Sofia called the counselor at the Alzheimer's Center where he had been diagnosed to make an appointment to talk about what to do. The counselor reviewed their file before Sophia came and noted that they had very limited financial resources and no family in this country. She told Sophia that there were two options she generally recommended. "Either someone can stay with John or he can be enrolled in a day program." Sophia said she had looked at some brochures of day care centers and home health agencies and realized she couldn't afford them. "Why did we ever come here? We don't have money for all of this. In our country we had a house. We had family, friends. What am I going to do now? I'm on my own. We don't even have insurance." The counselor said, "I can see how hopeless the situation looks to you. I'm not saying it's going to be easy, but I think I can help you to work something out. You may not be aware of some of the benefits that are available. There are day care centers that accept payments on a sliding scale. The government has programs that sometimes pay for help at home. In the meantime, let me contact some local organizations that have volunteers." Sophia said, "Thank you so much. I was afraid you were going to tell me that I would have to put him in an institution."

## Formal Services to Support In-Home Care

Many formal care services for people with AD have the dual benefit of providing care for the patient and respite for the caregiver. Formal services in which someone else cares for the patient for a period of time, giving the principal family caregiver some temporary relief, can be characterized as respite care. Short-term respite care can range from a few hours to a few days to several weeks and can be required when the caregiver becomes ill, has to travel, wants to go on a vacation, or simply needs relief from caregiving. In general there are three kinds of respite care services: (1) home health aides, homemakers, and companions; (2) community activities and adult day programs; and (3) overnight respite care in a residential facility such as an assisted living residence or nursing home. In this section, we briefly discuss the benefits of respite care and then discuss each type of care in detail.

Respite can reduce burnout and isolation for caregivers by allowing them personal time. It provides relief from the physical and emotional stress of caring for a person with Alzheimer's disease and helps caregivers rebuild their energy to continue caring for the patient. Caregivers who use respite services are able to take a break or take care of other responsibilities with the peace of mind that the person with AD is receiving care and supervision while they are away.

Formal services outside the home offer opportunities for socializing, recreation, physical activities, change of scene, and emotional support for patients. Without these services, patients may become isolated, rarely leave their homes, and be at risk for excess disability due to lack of stimulation. It is difficult to provide comparable experiences for the patients at home.

Caregivers using formal services for the first time need to learn how to get the most from the services and also to tolerate their limitations. Generally, no single service is adequate to accommodate all the needs of caregivers and patients, and a combination of formal care services may be necessary. Sometimes, a formal service solves existing problems but creates new ones. For instance, the transportation provided by the local day care center may be inconvenient, and caregivers may need to either make special arrangements or take the patient to and from the center themselves.

In some areas few formal services are available. Counselors may have to help caregivers find alternative services where there are no specialized dementia care options available. The local chapter of the Alzheimer's Association can usually direct counselors to appropriate alternatives.

Caregivers, especially those who have never before had the experience of caring for an ill person, are often unaware of the formal services available to patients living at home and try to take on the burden of care by themselves. Some caregivers may do without formal help until quite late in the illness and may even have thought that a medical evaluation was not required to assess the cause of the patient's cognitive problems.

## Home Care Services

Home care services can give respite to a caregiver. Home care personnel can provide a range of services for the patient, from companionship and homemaking to personal care. They supervise the patient so that caregivers are able to carry out other responsibilities, keep appointments, do errands, or just take a break from caregiving tasks. Home care attendants assist the patient with personal care such as bathing, grooming, and dressing, as well as basic nursing care such as helping a patient take medications, exercise, or move safely around in and outside the home. They may also help with errands, shopping, light housekeeping, meal preparation, or laundry and assist with social and recreational activities.

***When Should Home Care Be Initiated?*** Home care is generally initiated when the patient is in the moderate stage of AD, although some people in the early stage may need home care if they live alone or have a physical disability that makes it difficult for them to manage on their own. In the moderate stage of AD, a person can no longer be safely left alone and needs considerable hands-on care. If the family and other informal caregivers cannot supply sufficient supervision and care, paid help may be a viable option.

The decision to hire outside help is often precipitated by the increasing severity of the patient's symptoms or an illness or hospitalization. Sometimes hiring help occurs as a result of an event that upsets the previous caregiving arrangements, such as the caregiver's illness.

Several weeks after falling and breaking his hip, Ted was home from the subacute facility. Millie called her counselor. "Up until now I have always managed to care for Ted without hiring help. He was able to go to the day care center while I was at work, and our children have always been able to help with this or that, but now Ted needs much more care, he isn't able to get around the house as easily by himself, and he can't go back to day care yet. What do you think about my hiring someone?" "I think it's a wonderful idea," the counselor answered. Millie said she wanted to meet with the counselor to discuss the details. The counselor suggested that, before they met, Millie should make a list of what she would like the person to do.

***What Kind of Home Care Should Be Provided?***  If the person lives alone and is beyond the early stage of AD, he or she may need a live-in aide to provide 24-hour supervision and assistance. If the patient is still in the early stage of AD, the caregiver may want to hire someone to run errands or accompany the patient or do housekeeping as a way of monitoring the patient's safety when the caregiver cannot be available. Caregivers may also decide to have someone stay with the patient when they are at work or tending to responsibilities and then take over the care themselves.

Counselors can help caregivers decide the number of hours per day or week and specific times of the day they would like to have home care (for example, when they are at work), taking financial circumstances into consideration. When deciding what type of care is needed, caregivers may find it useful to make a list of specific chores and duties to be done throughout the course of a typical day or week. This list then can be used as a job description and help caregivers to select the appropriate provider. Some providers are restricted or willing only to give personal care to the patient; some will also do the patient's food preparation, laundry, and other patient-related chores; others will only do homemaking chores; and some will do all of these tasks.

Millie came to her counseling session with the list of tasks for the home health aide. She pulled out of her bag four loose-leaf pages filled with notes and began checking to see if she had gathered all of them. She looked up at her counselor, who was watching the process, and laughed, "I know, I know. It looks like a lot, but I just wanted to make sure I didn't miss anything." Together, they came up with a plan in which the aide would be needed from 8 AM to 4 PM. The aide would be responsible for Ted's personal care, giving him breakfast and lunch and engaging him in activities throughout the day.

If the caregiver has not been actively involved in day-to-day care, the counselor can suggest that he or she spend some time with the person with AD to see firsthand what kind of assistance will be needed. Some issues to consider include:

■ What level of care is needed? What can the patient do for himself or herself? With what does he or she need supervision? With what does he or she need complete care?

■ Are medical procedures such as insulin injections, physical therapy, or infusion therapy required?

■ What type of care and supervision can the caregiver provide?

■ Does the caregiver have set hours during which help is needed because of a job or other responsibility?

■ Are there certain tasks that the caregiver cannot tolerate, eg, changing a soiled undergarment?

■ Does the patient require the aide to speak a foreign language?

Caregivers who hire aides privately will have the most flexibility in choosing the hours of care and the tasks that an aide is assigned. The immediate costs are also often lower than when working through an agency. However, caregivers should understand that this option comes with many additional responsibilities and fewer safeguards. For instance, caregivers will be responsible for paying taxes and workers' compensation, abiding by state regulations regarding the employment of a home care worker, and monitoring the quality of care the patient receives.

Caregivers who choose to hire an aide through a home care agency and those who have aides paid for by either long-term care insurance or government insurance such as Medicaid will have to work within the guidelines of the agency or the insurance plan. Caregivers should, however, always remember that they have the right to ask for another aide if the one the agency sends is not working out.

When caregivers are able to hire an aide privately, they will have had the opportunity to interview the person, present their needs, and get a sense of the person's capabilities and limitations so that when the person begins his or her job, caregivers have had some time to get used to the idea of this person caring for the patient. When the aide is working for an agency or is paid for by insurance or entitlements, both caregiver and patient will probably be meeting the aide only after he or she begins working. It is important that the home care personnel be reliable and compatible with both the caregiver and the patient. The process of finding the appropriate person and developing a trusting relationship can take time and may involve a number of false starts before the right person is found.

***Orienting the Home Care Person***   When the aide first comes to the home, the caregiver should review his or her tasks and show the aide around the house. The caregiver should also discuss how he or she approaches the patient, decisions the aide is permitted to make, and when the caregiver should be consulted. It is important that the caregiver give the aide a clear understanding of the patient's needs, abilities, daily routine, habits, and—especially—triggers for behavior problems, as well as techniques that seem to help avoid or manage them. The aide should have a list of the patient's medical conditions and medications and know what symptoms indicate the need for a phone call to the caregiver or physician for advice or additional help. The aide should also have a list of telephone numbers to call in an emergency, including the number of the caregiver, another relative, and the patient's doctor, and the name and address of the hospital to take the patient to in an emergency.

Counselors can remind caregivers that the process of integrating home care personnel into their homes and daily lives takes time. The patient, caregiver, and other family members will have to accommodate to the new person in the home, and the home care worker will have to learn how the household and patient function. Home care personnel should be encouraged to ask questions as well as initiate new care strategies—as long as they clear them with the caregiver first. Many times, good help is sent away because of misunderstandings that could have been cleared up.

Several days after Millie hired an aide, she called her counselor and said, "Do you know any good reliable aides? This one isn't working out." The counselor asked what had happened, and Millie said, "Every time I come home, I find Ted very frustrated and irritable. When I ask the aide what happened during the day, she says everything is fine and he ate all his lunch. She must be doing something wrong. Otherwise why would he act like that when I come home?" The counselor suggested that Millie get some more detailed information from the aide about how the day went. "Maybe Ted needs some more time to get used to the aide." Millie called the counselor back the following week and said in a much calmer and more optimistic tone, "I think we solved the problem. I had given the aide a list of activities and a menu for each day. The aide thought she had to follow the list to the letter. She thought she had to take him outside every day, and getting him ready was such a hassle that he became irritable. She didn't want me to think that she was having a problem and so kept saying everything was fine. I guess I just assumed that she would know that these were just suggestions, and she could use her judgment about how many things to do. No wonder Ted was so upset. He hates to be forced into anything."

*Getting Used to Having Help in the Home*   Caregivers may contact a counselor after they have hired someone to help at home and they are having trouble managing the situation. They may be new to having help in the house and have unrealistic expectations of what an aide will do. In addition, after caregivers have help at home, they may become aware that they do not know how to use the free time they have gained.

## Care Choices

Abigail had finally hired an aide to help take care of her husband, Ray, who was in the moderately severe stage of AD. She called the counselor after the aide had been working about a week and said, "What do I need her for? She just sits next to Ray and watches TV with him. I thought she would clean and do the laundry, but I still have to do all that." The counselor told Abigail that aides are expected to take care of the patients and not to be housekeepers. "I didn't realize that." The counselor asked Abigail why she didn't go out while the aide was there. Abigail said, "Because I have to be sure she's doing things the right way, and if I leave, who will watch her? Besides, where would I go?" The counselor asked Abigail to think about some pleasant activity outside the house she used to enjoy before Ray got too sick to go out with her. "I guess I could go to the mall with my friend Agnes for the afternoon. I haven't done that for ages. But I look such a fright! Maybe I should go to the beauty parlor first."

### Helping Caregivers and Patients Accept Home Care

Although it may seem obvious to counselors that home care is beneficial, many caregivers find it difficult to accept the need for this type of assistance. Some caregivers, especially spouses, feel that they must provide all the care themselves. Others feel that no one can care for the patient as well as they can. Caregivers may have to be eased gently into the idea of hiring help and be assured that it does not reflect negatively on their ability to care for the patient. Understandably, there is also often a great deal of concern about the cost of such care.

## Care Choices

After his children had begged him to do so for years, Mr Berns finally agreed to hire an aide to help him care for his wife, who was bedridden and required a great deal of help with eating, toileting, and dressing. Mr Berns had been caring for his wife himself and, in spite of his exhaustion, had resisted getting help, insisting that no one could care for his wife as well as he could. Mr Berns' daughter, Alison, told the family counselor, "Dad fired the first aide after a few hours because he was not satisfied with the way she fed Mom. The next aide quit because Dad followed her around and was constantly looking over her shoulder, telling her what to do. The next aide cleverly asked Dad to show her exactly how he wanted her to care for his wife. 'Finally,' we thought, 'Dad had found someone who would listen to him.' He fired her, too, saying, 'She should know what to do without my telling her.' If this new aide didn't last, I don't know who will. What are we going to do?" The counselor suggested to Alison that it was a good sign that Mr Berns finally hired help and that he continued to search for someone satisfactory, despite not being happy with any of the aides. "I know that you understand how much it means to him to care for your Mom himself, even though it is clearly too much for him. It may take time for him to be fully comfortable with someone else doing what he feels is his job, so you may have to be prepared for another round of hiring and firing until he really accepts the idea of having help."

Sometimes it is not the caregiver but the patient who resists having help in the home. It may be especially difficult to persuade a patient who lives alone and has been independent to accept help in spite of an obvious need. In these situations, the counselor can help the caregiver find a strategy for bringing help into the house. It may require ingenuity to figure out how to overcome the patient's objections.

Some patients will be less resistant if they think the person is hired to help the caregiver or someone else rather than themselves. Some respond to the idea that they will have fewer responsibilities if an aide is hired. Others will accept a particular aide if her personality is to their liking. Some people may accept home care only if they believe that it is free of charge; this is especially true of those who have lived through an economic crisis or worry that they do not have enough money to live out their lives comfortably. Counselors can help caregivers determine what the best strategy is for a particular patient based on their past history, lifestyle, and personality.

## Care Choices

Mrs Allens, who was in the moderate stage of AD, had always lived alone and was very independent. Her brother, Thomas, was working with a counselor to get Mrs Allens to accept having a home health aide. She refused help adamantly, and the last time Thomas tried to introduce a home health aide, she had thrown Thomas and the aide out of the apartment, threatening to call the police. "What should we try next? I have to do something. Her apartment is filthy, she looks like she hasn't taken a bath in a month, and, although I see traces of food wrappings in the apartment, she has lost a tremendous amount of weight. If I don't do something soon . . . I don't even want to think about it." The counselor asked Thomas if there was any gift his sister really liked. Thomas said she loved tulips. She suggested that he accompany the next aide to Mrs Allens' house and that the aide bring tulips and sandwiches with her. He could introduce the aide as a friend of his who wants to meet her. Thomas said it didn't make much sense to him but he'd try it. The counselor said, "It's not about making sense. It's about finding a way that your sister can accept a stranger into the house. In fact, the aide should just sit and chat with your sister the first few days." Thomas called the counselor the following week and said, "Well, the house is still a mess, but my sister is letting the aide in the house, and she and the aide are shopping for groceries together. I think this may work out."

## Health Care Services at Home

There may be instances when someone other than a home care attendant needs to be involved in the care of a patient. This may happen as the result of a medical illness other than AD, after a hospitalization, or when the patient advances into the moderately severe and severe stages of Alzheimer's disease and needs more skilled care. When health care services are started as the result of an illness or hospitalization, the doctor caring for the patient or the hospital care team will determine the services that are appropriate for the patient. These services may include nursing, social work, occupational therapy, nutrition or dietetics, and physical therapy.

Knowing the value of maintaining functional capacity for a person with AD, counselors may suggest that family members request that the patient's doctor consider making a referral for rehabilitative services at home. When insurance will not reimburse for these services, caregivers may choose to pay for them privately if they can.

*Registered Nurse* Caregivers of patients with serious medical conditions that require skilled care, such as those with diabetes that requires insulin shots, may require the services of a visiting nurse. Occasionally, people trained as nurses can be hired privately to perform the services of a home health aide and skilled care as well.

*Physical Therapist* A physical therapist can provide passive exercise for a patient who is in the later stages of AD, who can no longer initiate physical activities, helping the patient exercise muscles or maintain physical strength and endurance in order to prevent muscle rigidity and contractures.

*Occupational Therapist* An occupational therapist can be consulted for a patient whose gait has become unsteady or whose coordination is poor and who needs to find new ways to move around the home or perform activities of daily living. They also perform home assessments and recommend adaptive devices such as grab bars and raised toilet seats to make the home safe for the patient.

*Nutritionist*  A nutritionist can make recommendations on how to help the patient maintain a healthy diet despite difficulties with eating that result from AD.

*Speech Therapist*  Some speech therapists specialize in helping patients with dementia or other illnesses when they have swallowing difficulties.

## Community Services Appropriate to People in the Early Stages of AD

People in the early stages of AD can participate in many activities appropriate for other elderly people if those activities are carefully selected. When helping caregivers choose activities and programs in which their relatives can be involved, it is important to stress that early stage patients may be able to continue many of their regular activities or join in community programs for the general population. Movies, ballgames, concerts, or arts and crafts classes may be suitable, especially if the person has had a prior interest in these activities. Counselors should advise caregivers to include patients in the process of choosing an activity.

### Care Choices

Patricia was concerned that her mother, who had been recently diagnosed with AD, was spending a lot of time alone at home. Patricia called the counselor and asked her if she should send her mother to day care so she could meet other people. The counselor said it sounded like her mother did not need day care yet and asked Patricia what her mother used to like to do before she became ill. Patricia said that her mother had always enjoyed music and, in fact, used to play the violin when she was younger. The counselor suggested that Patricia look for a music appreciation class. Patricia found one she thought her mother would like at the YMCA. She told her mother about it, and her mother said she was willing to try it if Patricia went with her. A few weeks later, Patricia drove her to the first class. As they were walking from the parking lot, they saw another older woman walking with her daughter. After they all got inside the building and went to register, the two older women looked closely at each other and realized they had both been teachers at the same elementary school. They had never been particularly friendly then and did not remember each other's names, but they felt a connection that needed no further articulation. Patricia called the counselor a few weeks later and said that she hoped the two women would become friends and keep each other company. "My mother is desperate for companionship," she said. "Anyway, she loves the music class. I didn't realize my mother could still enjoy a class even though she has AD."

***Senior Centers and Other Community Programs***  Senior centers, sports clubs, religious institutions, art centers, and other organizations in the community can provide recreation, education, or social programs in which persons in the early stage of AD can participate, unless the activity is dependent on a particular skill that has become impaired. In many cases, people with early stage AD can select programs and activities in which to participate with guidance and encouragement from family members.

Counselors should caution caregivers to be sensitive to the cognitive abilities and social skills of their relatives and to choose programs that are not too difficult and in which their presence will not disturb others. For example, discussion groups and educational classes whose purpose is the acquisition of new skills or information may be inappropriate because they may be too stressful or highlight the memory impairment and make the person feel inadequate. Sometimes the person may accept his or her limitations, but other participants may be uncomfortable in his or her presence. They can become upset and reject the person with AD. It is important to help caregivers understand when an activity is appropriate and also to know when the patient's dementia has progressed to the point at which special activities for people with dementia would be more suitable.

## Care Choices

Roland, who was in the early stage of AD, saw an advertisement in the newspaper for a discussion group for seniors starting at the local community arts center. He told his wife he wanted to attend. His wife, Harriet, worried that because he often forgot words or used the wrong word, he would be laughed at or rejected by the rest of the class. Feeling the need to protect him, she immediately began to discourage Roland, who said he really didn't care if people had a problem with his speech difficulties. "They will just have to wait until I get my words out, or if I feel I am having a bad day, I won't say anything." Harriet, who was still concerned, called the counselor at the Alzheimer's center. After listening to the problem, the counselor said, "Harriet, I know you want to keep Roland from being hurt, but it sounds like he is aware of the difficulties he may face at the class and is prepared to deal with them. Maybe you should let him try the class since he really wants to do it, and be ready to support him in case your fears are confirmed." Harriet said, "Maybe you are both right and I am just being overprotective. I should probably be happy that he is still willing to go out and do things instead of sitting around depressed."

***Early Patient Support Groups***   People in the mild stage of AD may benefit from joining an early patient support group. These groups provide members with the opportunity to discuss both emotional and practical issues regarding their illness with others who are dealing with the same condition. Members can discuss their feelings about the diagnosis, exchange strategies for carrying out tasks or facing challenges, or talk about positive or painful experiences in a supportive environment that can help them through the early years of the illness. Caregivers may be relieved that the support groups provide a venue for their relatives to meet with others like themselves to help them to come to terms with the illness. In some areas, early patient groups and caregiver groups are held at the same time and in the same place to facilitate the attendance of both patient and caregiver.

Before making the suggestion about a support group, counselors should get a sense of the patient's level of functioning so they are not recommending a group to someone who will not be accepted. People interested in joining an early patient support group will be interviewed by the group leader, who will determine the person's eligibility. Groups are generally open to people who have some insight into their illness and have an interest in sharing their experience with others. They are also screened for their ability to communicate verbally and to participate. When participants are no longer eligible, they will usually be asked to leave the group; this can be quite traumatic for both patient and caregiver. When this happens, every effort should be made by the support group leader or the counselor to find a suitable ongoing service, such as an activities program, that does not require the same level of communication skills or attention span.

---

### Care Choices

After being diagnosed with AD, Rupert seemed to lose confidence in himself. He stopped doing a lot of the things he used to do and went out of the house less and less. His wife, Joan, told her support group leader that she was worried that Rupert had stopped doing everything he used to enjoy and was spending too much time alone. The leader said that there were support groups for people in the early stages of AD and she thought he might benefit. Joan hesitantly presented the idea to her husband and told him how much help she got from her group. To her surprise he agreed to try it. After several weeks, Joan started seeing a change in his mood. He seemed more confident. He told Joan, "The group members have told me about things they do to help them remember and have helped me to stop worrying so much about what other people think when I forget a word. One of the members plays golf and invited me to join him. Maybe I will."

---

## Community Services for Patients in the Moderate Stages of AD

*Adult Day Centers*  Adult day centers can provide respite for caregivers while offering meaningful experiences to patients and enhanced patient care. There are two types of adult day centers, medical model and social model. Both provide a planned program that includes structured social and recreational programs with activities that provide mental stimulation and physical exercise. Medical model day centers also provide health care services. Adult day centers are most appropriate for patients in the moderate stage of Alzheimer's disease, who may no longer be able to stay safely at home alone or initiate meaningful activities or social contacts themselves. Day centers may provide services exclusively to those with dementia or have activities for both cognitively impaired and cognitively intact frail adults.

Most centers are open five days a week, Monday through Friday, usually from 8:00 AM to 4:00 PM. Some have extended or weekend hours. Generally, people may attend the center as little as one day a week or as many as five. Some centers have policies about minimum attendance and prior notification of absences, late arrival, or pickup.

Medicare does not cover the cost of day care, which varies considerably by location. If the participant is enrolled in Medicaid, the costs may be covered. Financial assistance may also be available for those with low incomes and few assets through public sources such as the State Department on Aging or the US Department of Veteran Affairs. A sliding fee scale may also be available for those not eligible for subsidies. Private medical insurance policies sometimes cover a portion of day care costs when registered, licensed medical personnel are involved with the care.

***Selecting an Adult Day Center***   The caregiver should call the adult day centers in the area and ask for a flier or brochure, eligibility criteria, schedule of activities, a monthly menu, and application procedures. After reviewing the written materials, the caregiver should make an appointment to visit two or more centers that might meet his or her needs and those of the patient. When visiting a potential center, the caregiver can ask for references and speak to some families that use the center. The following site visit checklist from the National Adult Day Services Association (NADSA) can be a useful reminder of what to look for:

- Did you feel welcomed?

- Did someone spend time finding out what you want and need?

- Did someone clearly explain the services and activities the center provides?

- Did they present information about staffing, program procedures, costs, and what they expect of caregivers?

- Was the facility clean, pleasant, and free of odor? Were the building and the rooms wheelchair accessible?

- Was there sturdy, comfortable furniture? Loungers for relaxation? Chairs with arms? Is there a quiet place for conferences?

- Is there a place to isolate sick people?

- Did you see cheerful faces on staff and participants?

- Do volunteers help?

- Are participants involved in planning activities or making other suggestions?

There are practical constraints to the use of adult day care, such as waiting time for transport and length of the journey to and from the center, as well as the time taken by the family caregiver to help the person get ready to attend the center. Getting to and from some centers may consume a large part of the caregiver's day and be stressful to the relative with AD. Some centers offer pickup and drop-off transportation services and provide transportation for outings and medical appointments.

The center should fit the needs of both caregiver and patient. Sometimes when caregivers visit a center that is less than adequate, they get discouraged and do not want to continue searching for an appropriate facility. Some caregivers become upset when they first visit a day care center and realize that their relative is as ill as the other people there. They may have to visit several centers before they are comfortable with the idea.

## Care Choices

The first time Sue went to visit a day care center she looked around and felt sure it was not the right place. The participants were sitting in a circle, heads bent or staring into space, while music blared. Sue told her counselor, "That certainly didn't seem like the right company for Mom. She is still so full of life. I couldn't send her to day care. She's nowhere near as sick as the other people there." The counselor wondered if once again she was hearing the typical reaction of a family caregiver visiting a day care center for the first time and Sue was not ready to take this step, or if indeed this was the wrong center for her mom. She asked Sue if she would be willing to visit another center. Sue agreed. The following week Sue called her counselor and told her with great optimism that she had enrolled her mother in the second center she had visited. "I know you thought that I wasn't facing reality and that I think my mother isn't impaired like all the other patients. Well, probably that is somewhat true," she said, "but in the second center, in spite of all their disabilities, the members seemed to be enjoying themselves, and so did the staff. I felt I could trust my mother to their care." Several months later Sue commented to the counselor that the day care center provides her mother with a social setting in which she feels comfortable and that she, too, felt welcome and cared for when she visited.

***Helping the Patient Adjust to the Day Center***  Caregivers often ask how to approach the subject of day care with their relative. Counselors can suggest that they avoid telling the patient too much about going to the center too far in advance to keep the patient from becoming anxious. The caregiver should approach the subject of day care with the patient in a positive, calm, and reassuring manner. A simple statement is best, such as, "We are going to visit a new center today. I think you'll like it." If the caregiver thinks it is a good idea, the patient is likely to go along with it. It is customary to try a day center for 3 to 5 days and is generally suggested that the caregiver stay at the center for a few hours to facilitate the adjustment. Some people with Alzheimer's disease will react well to their first visit to an adult day care center, while others may be resistant, frightened, or upset by the new and unfamiliar environment. Staff will help the patient to feel comfortable. After an initial period of adjustment, most people with AD enjoy the experience and look forward to attending.

## Care Choices

Ellen enrolled her father in a day care program, but every day it was a struggle to get him to go to the center and stay there. Each day he would argue, "I don't want to go there, I have to go to work. How am I going to pay my rent?" Ellen spoke to the social worker at the center and said that she had tried to tell her father that he is retired and that this is a program to help him enjoy life, but he continues to worry that if he doesn't work, he won't be able to pay for his apartment. The counselor said, "Well, we'll just have to put him to 'work.' The center actually has several participants 'on the payroll.' We choose a task or an activity that the participant enjoys doing and make that his job." Ellen was appalled. "How can I lie to him like that?" The counselor said, "Look at it this way. Your father is telling you that he is worried about paying his rent. At his stage of AD, there is no way that you will be able to convince him that he is retired and doesn't have to work. It is kinder to let him believe he is working."

It is important for caregivers to keep in mind that their relatives may not be able to recall the day's activities. Staff members who are involved with the care of the patient generally schedule regular meetings with the caregiver to give the family feedback on the member's adjustment, interests, and participation and to set goals for the next several months. Problems that are occurring at home or in the center will also be addressed. If caregivers have questions or think their relative is having a problem, they should ask for an additional conference. They should also be encouraged to visit with their relatives at the center. They can share an activity and allow their relatives to be the host. After the initial adjustment period, it is probably better to wait before visiting again until the patient feels comfortable at the center. Caregivers should let the staff know in advance that they plan to come.

## Institutional Respite Care

Assisted living facilities and nursing homes usually have rooms available to take a patient in for several days or weeks. This form of respite can provide caregivers with essential time to take care of their interests. Caregivers can be encouraged to use this service when they become ill themselves, when they need a break or want to take a vacation or need to go on a business trip, or when the patient cannot stay at home for some other reason, such as a renovation. This service can provide a stimulating atmosphere for the patient, as the activities programs and services available to all residents of the facilities are also available to those who are there temporarily.

Caregivers may be reluctant to use this service. They may not want to subject their relative to a change of surroundings and unfamiliar people. The staff will not know their relative, and caregivers may fear that they may not know how to care for him or her. Facilities that provide this kind of respite may have a minimum length of stay, which may be too long and costly for the family. In some areas, respite beds are in short supply and may not be available when needed. Institutional respite may have to be paid for privately and can be costly, although it is sometimes covered by entitlements. Some caregivers express feelings of guilt for leaving the patient in an institution, even for a short time or when the stay is necessary.

## Care Choices

Nettie's sister, Ruth, was turning 90, and her children were throwing a huge party; they invited the whole family, including all grandchildren and great-grandchildren. Since Nettie was Ruth's only surviving sibling and Ruth's health was failing, the children insisted that Nettie come. They sent her an airline ticket and asked her to write a speech about family history that only she would remember. Nettie accepted the invitation. This might be her last opportunity to see Ruth. Nettie had only one problem. Who would take care of her husband, Theo, who was in the moderately severe stage of AD? She called her counselor and said, "I can't leave Theo with the aide because she is scared to be with him alone for so many days with no family member nearby to call in case an emergency comes up. I can't take him with me; the trip would be way too much for him. Help me think of something. I have to go to this party—my whole family is counting on it." The counselor suggested respite at a nursing home and helped Nettie make the arrangements. A day before the trip, Nettie called the counselor and said, "How could I be so selfish and leave Theo to go to a party? I am going to cancel the trip. What if something happens to him?" The counselor comforted Nettie, saying he understood that it was difficult leaving Theo in order to enjoy herself. Nettie replied, "I guess I panicked. This is the first time I am leaving Theo alone since he got sick and it doesn't feel right. But it's not like I'm doing it just for fun. My family needs me and I want to see Ruth one more time." The counselor responded, "Have a great time and let me know how it went when you get back."

## COUNSELOR CHECKLIST

### Choosing Living Arrangements

☐ Highlight the factors the caregiver should consider in deciding where the patient will live.

☐ Facilitate the involvement of all affected family members in the decision about where the patient will live.

☐ Advise the caregiver that if the patient is living in his or her own home with the help of an aide, the caregiver will nevertheless still need to be responsible for the supervision of care.

☐ Provide emotional support to a caregiver who is selling the patient's home and possessions because the patient is moving elsewhere as a result of the illness.

### Home Care Services

☐ Help the caregiver decide how much home care is needed and the tasks that should be performed by the aide.

☐ Remind the caregiver that integrating home care personnel into the daily routine may take time and flexibility.

☐ Counsel the caregiver on how to facilitate the patient's acceptance of home care.

### Community Services for Patients in the Early Stage of AD

☐ Advise the caregiver to include the patient in the process of choosing appropriate activities and programs in the community.

☐ Caution the caregiver to be sensitive to the cognitive level and social skills of the patient when choosing these activities.

☐ Help the caregiver assess his or her relative's suitability for a patient support group.

### Community Services for Patients in the Moderate Stage of AD

☐ Adult Day Centers

■ Offer the caregiver a checklist of what to look for in an adult day center.

■ Advise the caregiver to choose a center that meets the patient's and his or her own needs.

- Counsel the caregiver on how to help the patient adjust to day care.

- Help the caregiver find alternative services if no specialized dementia care options are available.

☐ Institutional Respite Care

- Encourage the caregiver to use institutional respite care when it is essential for him or her to have time away from the patient.

# RESIDENTIAL CARE

Changes in the patient or caregiver over the course of Alzheimer's disease (AD) may ultimately make it necessary to place the person in a residential facility in which care will be provided by professionals. This represents a major turning point in the lives of both patient and caregiver and is often a cause of personal distress and family conflict.

Counselors should be aware that the degree to which caregivers feel comfortable with the decision to place their relative depends on their having had sufficient time to adequately plan, the extent to which both the caregivers and patients have been involved in the decision-making process, the exploration of alternative possibilities, and the caregivers' receipt of sufficient information on which to base an informed decision. Knowing this, the counselor should focus work with caregivers on those factors that are likely to lead to a positive outcome.

Counselors can help caregivers throughout the process of placing their relatives in a residential facility. They can help family members understand the options available to them, help them think through the decision and its likely effects, and offer both information and emotional support to cushion the impact of the placement.

This chapter discusses the decision making process and includes a review of the residential care options available and ways to help caregivers choose the right facility. It concludes with the actual placement process and the role of the caregiver after placement.

## The Decision to Place a Relative With AD in a Residential Facility

The decision to place a relative in a residential facility is rarely easy for caregivers. Even when there are many reasons in favor of the move, caregivers often feel reluctant to make it, and counselors can help them to think through the decision and feel comfortable with it.

### *Reasons for Placement*

The decision to place a person with AD in a residential facility can be made for practical, psychological, and/or medical reasons. Caregivers may have to place their relative in a residential facility because of their own personal health, such as exhaustion or an emotional or physical illness. Symptoms such as incontinence or aggression may become too difficult or unpleasant for the caregiver to manage. The caregiver may not be physically able to provide assistance with activities such as bathing or transferring from bed to a chair. Insufficient support and respite from family members can make it difficult for a caregiver to keep the patient at home. Frequently, other family members persuade the caregiver to place the patient in a facility because of concern that the caregiver is overburdened. Sometimes a placement occurs because of the death of a caregiver, after which there may be no other family members available or willing to provide or supervise care. Health care professionals should recommend placement in a residential facility when the home care plan seems inadequate and either the patient's or the caregiver's well-being seems in jeopardy.

There may come a time when the patient needs more supervision or skilled care than can be provided at home. There may be inadequate space for home care providers, or it may not be financially feasible to provide sufficient care at home. In some areas, suitable paid home care providers may not be available.

Some caregivers may choose to place their relatives in a residential facility because the patients need more care than they are willing to provide or supervise. Choosing their own aspirations or needs over caregiving may be a painful but necessary and legitimate decision.

Residential placement can be precipitated by an event that clarifies the need for change, such as an accident that makes it clear the patient is not safe at home, or a sudden change in the health or life circumstances of the caregiver that has an impact on his or her ability to provide sufficient care at home. If the patient is hospitalized, the staff may recommend placement when the patient is discharged.

## Caregiver Reluctance to Agree to Residential Placement

The decision to place a relative in a residential facility is rarely easy and can be the source of much internal personal struggle for caregivers. Sometimes caregivers are torn between a practical need to place the person in a facility and a prior promise they have made to "never to do such a thing."

### Placement Decision

Carrie's mother had asked her to promise never to put her in a nursing home no matter what happened. Now her mother was in the moderately severe stage of AD and living alone with an aide a short drive from Carrie, who looked in on her every day. Carrie called her counselor to say she was torn with indecision, because the company she worked for had offered her a big promotion if she would relocate. She really wanted the job, because it was an exciting opportunity and would help her pay off her debts. "I can't take Mom with me. I would have to buy her a new house or have her live with me. I can't leave her here because there is no one but me to manage her care at home." The counselor said, "It looks like you've ruled out all the options but putting her in a nursing home." Carrie responded, "But how can I put her in a nursing home when I promised never to do that?" The counselor said, "You made the promise at a different time, and it was impossible to anticipate that she would be in the condition she's in now. If she could have foreseen it, she might not have asked you to make that promise." Carrie said, "Well, I'm going to find the best place for my mother, and I hope I can live with the decision." The counselor said she could still visit her mother in the nursing home. She wouldn't be entirely giving up her caregiving role. Carrie said, "Well, Mom keeps asking me where she is, so maybe it won't be so hard for her to be in a nursing home."

Caregivers may be reluctant to place their relatives in a residential facility for fear they will receive poor care or be neglected. Fear about unacceptable care in residential facilities is fueled by occasional media headlines about poor treatment or neglect in such places, bad personal experiences of friends or family members, and personal convictions that "no one can provide the care that I can." Counselors can assure caregivers that they can still have an effect on the type of care the patient receives in the facility. By making an informed choice of facility and by consistently interacting with staff at the residence, caregivers can continue to have a role in the care of their relatives and in seeing that their needs are met.

Sometimes well-meaning family members, friends, or health care professionals put pressure on primary caregivers to make the decision to place their relative in a facility before they themselves are ready to do so. Part of the counselor's role is to make sure that the caregiver is comfortable with (or at least reconciled to the necessity for) the decision and that it is not being made solely in response to pressure from others.

Ted was never able to walk well after his hip operation, and he couldn't get from one place to another on his own. Several years later, Millie needed to have an operation that required several months of recuperation at home afterward. While she was in the hospital, Tom and Carol took turns staying with their Dad at night after the aide left. After Millie was discharged, Tom and Carol continued to take turns coming over each evening. This was the first time they really understood how hard caregiving could be. Ted was incontinent and became agitated when his clothes had to be changed. He woke up frequently during the night and called out for someone to help him get out of bed. Everybody was feeling exhausted, and Millie wasn't recuperating because she couldn't get a good night's sleep. All three children got together to talk about what to do, and even Carol admitted it might be time to begin to think about placing Ted in a nursing home. When they told Millie, she said she was shocked that they could even suggest such a thing. She had never expected to get to that point and found it very distressing to even consider it. The children told her she wasn't getting better and they were wearing themselves out, and they thought it would be easier for Dad to get proper care in a nursing home.

Family members can also disagree about whether the person should be placed in a residential facility. The counselor can meet with the caregiver and other family members to help them resolve these differences in a way that is in the best interests of the caregiver and the patient. People with AD should be included in the decision-making process to the extent that they are able.

Some caregivers seek a counselor's support and guidance because they are uncomfortable bearing the sole responsibility for making such a major decision for another person. They may need to discuss the decision with a professional to feel confident that they are making the best decision possible under the circumstances.

Caregivers may find it easier to make a decision about placement if they are reminded that the move does not have to be permanent. A patient can always be moved to another facility or return home if a placement does not work. Most facilities even recommend that people keep their home or apartment for at least 3 months after placement in case they decide that a long-term facility is not suited to their needs.

After several discussions with her counselor and her family, Millie became more comfortable with the idea of placing Ted in a nearby nursing home. One day, however, she called the counselor sounding extremely upset. "I can't do this. What if he gets worse when I put him in the nursing home? They don't know him like I do. They won't understand what gets him upset. I know he would never do such a thing to me—he always took such good care of me before he got sick." The counselor said, "This is an exceptionally difficult decision. No one can guarantee that there won't be problems once Ted is at the nursing home, but he seemed to get along when he was there for rehab. Besides, you know that you can always change your mind and bring him back home. You have put a great deal of thought into this move; you and your family have done a lot of research into the options. You have always taken good care of Ted, and I know you will continue to do so, whether he is in the nursing home or at home. You and your family have come to this decision because it seems like the best way to provide for Ted's well-being at this time."

# Choosing a Residential Facility for a Person With AD

Once the decision has been made that the person can no longer live at home, the caregiver will have to choose among the available facilities. In some areas of the country, a wide array of possible facilities is available to people with AD, and while this may allow for greater choice, the process of selecting the appropriate place can be confusing and exhausting. In other areas, there may be only one facility suitable for a person with AD, and the family will have to accept its limitations.

Most caregivers feel unprepared to select a long-term care facility. Counselors can assist in selecting a facility that is acceptable to them and appropriate for the person's stage of dementia and physical condition. Counselors often have to explain the different options available and help caregivers determine the type of facility to look for. It is important for caregivers to have a realistic expectation about the care their relative will receive or that the facility can provide. There are organizations that publish information about nursing homes. It is also possible for caregivers to consult a geriatric care manager to help with the selection process.

## *Assisted Living or Nursing Home?*

At present, the options available to people with AD include two types of facilities—assisted living facilities and nursing homes. Assisted living facilities usually serve people who can function relatively independently, while nursing homes provide care to those who need skilled nursing and/or personal care.

Some assisted living facilities and nursing homes provide several levels of care so that the person can stay within the facility as his or her care needs change, rather than moving to a different facility. The fact that one facility may be able to provide for the care needs of the patient for the rest of his or her life may be comforting to both the family caregiver and the patient.

*Assisted Living Facilities*   *Assisted living* is a broad term that includes senior residences, enriched housing and board-and-care facilities, group homes, adult homes, and other types of congregate housing. Assisted living facilities are generally reserved for elderly people who can function relatively independently and do not have any serious medical or physical needs, but who may need some supervision or help with activities of daily living. They offer congregate meals, personal or custodial care, and recreational activities to their residents.

Facilities that cater to the general elderly population may not provide the level of care that a person with AD needs. For instance, people in assisted living facilities are free to go in and out unattended whenever they please, which may prove problematic for a person who has a tendency to get lost. Some assisted living facilities, however, have created specially designed AD units, and some are now being built specifically for people with AD. They differ from other assisted living facilities in that they provide more supervision and hands-on care and security to ensure that the person with AD does not leave the facility unattended. They also offer activities specifically designed for people with cognitive impairment.

Assisted living facilities generally accept people with mild or moderate stage Alzheimer's disease. Caregivers should be aware that once a person reaches the moderately severe stage of the illness, he or she may be asked to leave. Caregivers of people who are already in the moderate stage of AD will have to evaluate the appropriateness of the particular assisted living facility for the patient. They should be advised to consider the value of placing the person in a facility that he or she may have to be transferred out of relatively soon. Caregivers of patients who are at a more severe stage of dementia may have difficulty coming to terms with the fact that their family member does not meet the criteria for admission to assisted living, which may seem like a more attractive alternative, but will need the services of a nursing home that can provide a higher level of care.

## Placement Decision

Several years after Christina had placed her father in an assisted living facility, the administrator of the facility told her her father could no longer stay there. He said she should place him in a nursing home and recommended a place nearby. Christina was devastated. Her father loved the place. How was she going to tell him he had to move? And where was she going to place him? Certainly not in that dreary facility the administrator had suggested. Christina wanted her counselor to help her convince the administrator to keep her father where he was. The counselor did not say no, but instead asked Christina what reasons the administrator gave for wanting him moved. Christina said, "He told me that while they used to have no problems with Dad, he was now in need of more care than the facility could offer. It's true Dad wandered outside and got lost several times, and other residents complained he went into their rooms uninvited and took their belongings. Every time the phone rings, I get chills thinking it's another call about a problem with my dad. Plus, I keep having to run over there to help the staff look for my father when he disappears and return the things he takes from people. What happened? I thought that was the perfect place for Dad." The counselor pointed out that the administrator was right, and while the place had been good for him in the past, her father had progressed to a stage that required a different kind of care. If he stayed where he was, the problems would just continue to get worse. Christina agreed that she would have to come to terms with the fact that her father's dementia had become more severe, and another facility better suited to his current condition might be necessary.

*Nursing Homes*  Nursing homes provide housing, meals, personal and custodial care, as well as social and recreational activities. Their residents generally need medical care or physical help with most activities of daily living. Many residents are cognitively impaired. Nursing homes tend to look and feel more like a hospital than a home because they are structured according to a medical model of care. They are usually less appealing to caregivers than assisted living facilities because they cater to a more ill and frail population.

In some nursing homes, residents with AD or other cognitive impairments live together with those who are physically frail. Other facilities offer special Alzheimer units with a physical layout designed for people with cognitive impairment; they may offer special recreational and social programs and have staff trained in the supervision and care of people with AD. Counselors should caution caregivers that the designation of a particular unit as a special AD unit does not always mean better or more care for their family members. They should encourage caregivers to ask specifically about the services the person with AD will be getting in the special,

as opposed to a regular, unit. Although nursing homes are highly regulated and must conform to federal, state, and local guidelines, each
facility has a different philosophy of care.

## Placement Decision

Theresa visited several nursing homes in her search for a place for
her brother, Aaron. She could not believe the disparity she saw in
the programs, services, and layouts of the facilities. She commented
to her counselor, "I thought you said that nursing homes are highly
regulated. How can these facilities be so different? In one place I
saw people in a huge day room sitting around doing nothing, while
at another, the activity director had several assistants who were
helping residents with individual projects." The counselor said that
although the facilities are indeed regulated, there is a great deal of
room for interpretation about what is appropriate care. She said,
"That is why I suggested that you tour each of the facilities you are
considering and talk to staff and family members of residents. In
fact, you should visit more than once at different times of the day
and evening, if possible, to be sure that there is adequate staff
coverage and activities at all times."

## *What to Look for When Choosing a Residential Facility*

Caregivers should feel comfortable that they have chosen an appropriate facility for their relatives, and the best way to achieve this is
to visit a number of facilities rather than make a choice based on
looking at one or two. Most caregivers will need some guidance
about what to expect at residential facilities. What is an appropriate
standard of care? Are residents getting sufficient care? Counselors
can suggest what to look for and what to ask in order to make the
best possible choice. The first visit to a facility may be very distressing to caregivers. By visiting a number of residences, caregivers can
form a realistic view of what these facilities can provide.

## Placement Decision

Dawn realized that her father could no longer care for her mother at
home when her mother was admitted to the hospital because she
had developed bedsores and was dehydrated. Dawn went to visit a

nursing home she had heard was very beautiful and took a tour of the facility, which had expensive artwork on the walls. This did not distract her from the image that kept coming to her mind of her mother in a wheelchair, sitting among all the frail old people she saw. She made an appointment to see the hospital social worker the next day, who confirmed her understanding that her mother would need to go to a nursing home when she left the hospital. Dawn said, "Yesterday I visited what I heard was the best place around, and I feel sick at heart." The social worker said, "I see you really weren't prepared for what you saw. I know the first time that someone visits a nursing home, it is very upsetting. You may find that, after you look at several of them, you will get used to the idea and become sensitive to the ways in which they differ. As difficult as this process is, it will help you to make the best choice for your mother. I'll give you a checklist of what to look for."

Having seen what is available, caregivers will have to develop a set of priorities and decide which characteristics or services are important to them and which they are willing to do without. For instance, a family may choose a facility that is close to home but is less appealing to the eye over a facility in a beautiful setting and more activities that is inconvenient for them to visit. Some of the issues that should be explored when looking for either an assisted living facility or nursing home are:

I.  What services are offered?

    A.  What kind of medical supervision is available?

    B.  What recreational and social services are offered?

    C.  How much assistance do residents receive with personal care?

II. What are the eligibility requirements for a new resident?

    A.  Are there any cognitive or physical limitations that would exclude a person from eligibility?

    B.  What are the financial requirements?

    C.  What is the placement process?

D. Does a person need to leave the facility when the disease progresses?

III. Is the staffing appropriate?

A. What type of staff is available? Are there registered nurses, aides, social workers, psychologists, physical therapists, etc?

B. What is the staff-to-patient ratio during the day and at night? Who is on night duty?

C. Is the staff trained to work with AD patients?

D. Can additional help be hired by the family to help a person to stay in the facility?

IV. What is the philosophy of care at the facility?

A. What do staff do to ensure that a new resident adapts to the facility?

B. Are people free to stay in their rooms during the day, or are they required to stay in a day room or other places in the facility?

C. When a person is upset or acting out, what is the normal course of action for the staff? Do they believe in using chemical or physical restraints and, if so, under what circumstances?

D. When a person is ill, what is the normal course of action? Who is called for consultation? A doctor? A nurse? When is the family notified?

E. How much personal attention does a person receive? Does the facility staff seem to understand the patient's interests, likes, and dislikes?

F. Does the staff welcome family involvement in care? When is the family consulted about patient issues?

G. Are the cultural and religious norms of the facility in keeping with those of the family?

V. Is the physical setting suitable for an AD patient?

A. Is the facility locked, or can people walk in and out on their own?

B. Is there room for residents to move around safely?

C. Is the setting clean?

D. Are there any odors?

E. Is there an outdoor area that is safe for residents? Are residents taken outside by staff of the residence, or does a family member or additional paid help have to be there for the patient to go outside?

VI. What are the total costs of the residential facility?

A. What are the monthly costs of the facility? Are there different levels of service and different fee structures associated with each level?

B. When are payments due? What happens if a payment is late?

C. How much of the cost will be paid by long-term care insurance, if available? Are any costs payable by Medicare? What will happen when the patient's assets are gone? Will Medicaid cover the same services?

D. If family members are expected to contribute to the payments, are all in agreement about the decision? What will happen if one of the family members is unable to make their contribution?

Asking these questions will not only help caregivers choose an appropriate place for the patient but also make them aware of what the residence will supply, what services are available, and what they can request. They will also get a sense of the services they may have to provide through other means, by either hiring help or assisting the patient themselves.

It is not enough to ask questions. Caregivers should observe how staff interact with each other and the residents. How do they talk to the residents? Are they impatient and brusque or nurturing and considerate? Do the staff talk mostly to each other or to the residents? Does the facility have a warm, homelike feel in which the individual needs of residents appear to be of high priority?

Family members may have different views about the facility that is the most appropriate. In these cases, counselors can meet with family members as well as the patient and help them to agree to a plan that best satisfies the needs of all concerned.

Caregivers will probably feel more comfortable leaving the patient in the facility if they are familiar with it beforehand. However, there are times when the choice will have to be made very quickly, either because the patient is being discharged from a hospital to a nursing home and insurance will not cover a prolonged hospital stay or because the caregiver cannot continue in that role because of illness or other circumstances. In these situations caregivers often take the first available place or base their selection on relatively superficial criteria, such as appearance or decor. Caregivers can be reassured that this placement does not have to be permanent, and they can always look for another facility if they are dissatisfied.

Sometimes the place the family prefers does not have a bed available. It may be possible to continue the current care plan until a bed becomes available in the facility of choice. If there is a critical need for immediate placement, it may be necessary to choose another place.

## The Placement Process

Once the patient has been accepted into a facility and the date of placement has been set, the caregiver will have to get the patient ready for the move to the residence. Counselors can be a resource, and the facility staff can make recommendations about how to prepare the patient for their particular facility and should be regularly consulted before the day of placement. Many facilities have social workers and supportive services for family members and patients to help ease the transition.

### Telling the Patient About the Placement

Caregivers commonly ask what to tell a person with AD about the move to a long-term care facility and when to do so. There is no consensus among professionals about how caregivers should approach the subject. The counselor will have to make individual recommendations on a case-by-case basis. For instance, if the patient is in the moderate stage of AD and has a tendency to worry about every new piece of information he or she hears, the caregiver may not want to tell the patient about the move until very close to the day of placement. If the patient is in the moderately severe or severe stage, it is difficult to predict what the patient will understand and how he or she will react.

The patient's reaction will depend in part on what the caregiver chooses to reveal and how it is done. It may be preferable to suggest that the change is being made to create a better environment for the person rather than to focus on anything negative. The patient's initial reaction to being told can range from apparent indifference to agitation, but the reaction upon admission can be very different. Ultimately, the caregiver will have to make the decision as to how or whether to tell the person, based on circumstances and knowledge of the patient.

> On Wednesday, the nursing home that Millie and her children had chosen called to say there was a bed available and Ted could be admitted that weekend. She put the phone down and started to cry. Millie called her counselor and said, "We haven't said a word to Ted. What can I say to him now? I can't just pack him up and move him." The counselor suggested that Millie might want to tell him that she was going to take him to a nice place to stay until she had fully recuperated from the operation. She also said it might be best not to tell him until Friday and to have one of her children there for support. On Friday, Tom and Carol came over to Millie's house and brought dinner. After dinner, Millie said to Ted, "You know how my back has been killing me lately. The doctor said I had to get complete rest for a few weeks. I found a really nice place where you can stay while I get better." Ted just said, "Okay." Millie was relieved that he didn't get upset. Carol said, "I wonder if Dad understood." Tom said, "I don't know whether to hope he did or didn't."

## *What the Patient Should Take to the Facility*

Outside of the obvious, such as clothing and toiletries, the amount and type of personal belongings that a patient brings to the facility may depend on the facility itself. Some long-term care facilities allow residents to bring selected pieces of furniture, such as a chair or dresser, and almost all allow residents to have familiar items such as photos or knickknacks that make them feel at home. It may ease the transition to the new place for the patient to have familiar items on the night table and photos of the family on the wall.

Caregivers should be cautioned that personal belongings may get lost or misplaced and are not the responsibility of the facility, so they should choose the items that they take to the facility for the patient carefully. Lost or misplaced items are very common in Alzheimer's units, because residents will often walk away with someone else's belongings, thinking the items are their own or because they no longer understand the concept of personal possessions. It may be best for the caregiver to bring the patient's belongings gradually, starting only with some of the basic necessities until it is clear how to protect items of value.

## The Day of Placement

When a nursing home informs a caregiver that a bed has become available, it may be necessary to bring the patient as soon as the next day. Despite all the preparation, this is the first time that the caregiver is faced with the reality of placement. All the doubts come back. "Why am I doing this?" "Should I do it?" A counselor who has been working with the caregiver during the process of placement can tell the caregiver to anticipate these reactions and inform him or her that they are normal and do not mean that it is the wrong decision. No amount of counseling can completely counteract these feelings. Caregivers often say, "This is the hardest thing I've ever had to do."

The day of placement is often both hectic and emotionally difficult for caregivers, so they should plan to have some friends or family members on hand for either physical help with whatever has not been brought over or put in place at the residence or for emotional support once the patient is at the facility.

The counselor can meet with caregivers after the placement to help them adjust to the decision they have made. The counselor can also explain that the patient will go through a process of adjustment and that, although the patient may be initially distressed, this feeling usually abates within a few weeks.

Millie was advised by the counselor to have her son Tom accompany her when she took Ted to the nursing home. While they were going to the nursing home, she got very upset and told Tom to turn the car around and go back home. Tom said, "No, Mom. You know you're still not well. Dad will be fine." He continued to drive to the nursing home. When they got there, Millie started to cry and said, "How can I leave him?" The intake nurse put her arm around Millie and called another nurse to go upstairs with Ted and Tom, while she stayed with Millie. The intake nurse told Millie that her feelings were completely understandable. "You need to give yourself time to get used to it." She said Millie could call her any time she wanted. "We're going to serve lunch soon. You can eat with him if you like or come back later." Tom came back downstairs and said, "Dad's doing fine. He has a nice roommate. I know this is a hard time for you, but I think he will be okay. Why don't we have lunch with Dad, and then we'll go to Carol's house to see the kids." When Millie went to her support group the following week, she said, "I feel so sad," and asked, "Did I do the right thing?" They reassured her by saying that he was in a safe place, she had selected a very good nursing home, and she could visit him as often as she wanted.

## The Caregiver's Reaction to Placement

The magnitude of the act of placing a relative in a residential facility can cause strong emotional reactions, including guilt, loneliness, sadness, worry, and a sense of powerlessness, as well as relief. Often the caregiver experiences more than one of these emotions by turns. Knowing that this might happen, counselors can anticipate possible feelings with the caregiver and should be available after the placement as well as before.

Caregivers may find it difficult to become accustomed to the change in their lives brought about by having the person in a residential facility. They either had direct responsibility for care or supervised others who provided the care. They may find it difficult to relinquish the previous caregiving role and be uncertain about how to be involved with their relative's care in the new setting. If the person lived with the caregiver, especially if the person was a spouse, the adjustment to living alone may be difficult.

Many residential facilities have support groups for family members of patients, and caregivers should be encouraged to join them so they will be able to share their feelings with others who are experiencing the same transition in their lives.

## The Caregiver's Role After Placement

Many caregivers worry that they will have no role in the care of their relatives with AD when they are placed in a long-term care facility. For others, it may come as a relief to think that the problems and responsibilities of caregiving will be over. The caregiver should be aware that he or she is more likely trading in one set of responsibilities for another when the patient is placed in a residential facility. While the day-to-day, hands-on care and supervision of the patient will be the responsibility of the facility, it is in the best interest of the patient for the caregiver to visit regularly and make sure the patient is well looked after.

### *Reasons to Visit*

The caregiver's visits serve many purposes. One important function is to maintain a relationship with the patient through regular contact. The patient can benefit from the sound of a familiar voice and the sight of a familiar face at any stage of dementia. The counselor can suggest activities such as looking at old family photos or sharing special snacks that will give pleasure to both caregiver and patient during visits. Caregivers may want to ask other family members to visit as well.

When a person in a residential facility has dementia, the visit of a family member is essential to his or her well-being. The caregiver can help the staff see the patient as an individual. More than anyone, the caregiver and other family members know the patient's history, habits, likes, and dislikes, which they can share with the staff. They can tell staff about what the patient used to be like before the illness. It may be helpful to bring a picture of the patient from the past and describe his or her former interests, hobbies, and so on. The caregiver can ask if the patient can participate in activities that match previous interests.

Caregivers should talk to the staff regularly to stay up-to-date on the patient's status and find out about any problems related to the patient's care. They may be able to help staff deal with behavioral problems because of their knowledge of the patient and strategies that worked at home. The family should try to build a relationship with the staff and treat them respectfully and with appreciation, since the patient may be unable to do so.

If a caregiver feels that additional help may solve a problem or provide a more personalized level of care, he or she may want to hire additional help if it can be afforded and is acceptable to the facility.

When a caregiver visits, he or she may want to check for weight loss, abrupt changes in functioning, and bruises. If the patient is incontinent, is he or she changed regularly? If the patient is immobile, the caregiver may also want to periodically check for bedsores. To get the best sense of whether the patient is well cared for, it is a good idea to visit at different times and on different days of the week.

## How Often Should a Caregiver Visit the Patient?

There is no right answer to the question about how often a caregiver should visit. Caregivers will become involved with patients' care to varying degrees after placement. A counselor might want to suggest that visits should fit comfortably into the caregiver's schedule, not interfering with other interests or obligations or, most important, with the caregiver's health and well-being, and should be frequent enough that the caregiver has consistent knowledge of the patient's condition and care. Caregivers should also consider the patient's schedule, so as not to interfere with the routines of the facility or the patient's participation in activities.

Some, especially spouse caregivers, will visit the patient every day for many hours, bringing homemade meals, taking care of the patient in place of staff. Although this provides an opportunity for maintaining the bond with the patient after placement, this type of behavior may be driven by something other than a desire to see the person and should be explored by the counselor.

## Placement Decision

Dorothy had been caring for her husband Darrell for many years. Then he developed chronic diarrhea that could not be treated, and it was an around-the-clock task to keep him clean. She decided she had to place him in a facility. She found a place within easy driving distance of her home. She visited Darrell every evening after work and brought his dinner. She fed him and stayed until bedtime. The social worker at the nursing home noticed how tired and thin Dorothy looked and suggested she see her doctor. She went to the doctor and said, "I've lost 15 pounds and people say I look terrible. I'm exhausted all the time." He asked her about her daily schedule. She said that when she got home she was too keyed up to eat, and it took several hours for her to calm down enough to go to sleep. The doctor suggested she might consider visiting less often, but she said she felt terrible about putting Darrell in the nursing home and couldn't just abandon him to the care of strangers. The doctor examined her and ran some tests to be sure nothing was physically wrong. He asked her if she had talked to anyone else about these problems. When she said no, he said, "I think you would benefit from therapy. You can't go on this way," and gave her the name of a colleague.

Counselors may also discover that some caregivers may not know how to fill the void that the patient's placement has left in their lives, so they continue their caregiving role by going to the facility to be with the patient. They may feel that their lives are empty without the patient and are accustomed to spending all their time with him or her. While they have transferred the responsibility for supervision and hands-on physical care of the patient to the facility, they may either think they can do a better job caring for their spouse, feel guilty about what they view as abandonment, or have nowhere else to go.

Many caregivers, especially spouses of patients, derive pleasure from spending time with their relatives and still being able to participate in their daily lives. They may volunteer in the nursing home, becoming involved in the day-to-day activities and visiting other patients as well as their own relatives.

## Placement Decision

Steve's counselor suspected that his frequent visits to his wife, Joanne, in the nursing home were being driven by something other than the desire to be with her. When she asked Steve why he felt he needed to visit her so often, Steve responded, "What else would I do if I didn't go see Joanne?" The counselor realized that after 10 years of being a caregiver, Steve felt a void that he was naturally filling by spending time at the nursing home. Steve added, "I feel useful there. After I spend some time with Joanne, I visit the other patients. Sometimes I bring them little treats. I love to make them smile. Lots of the residents never have any visitors but me." The counselor realized that Steve, who was retired and had relied on Joanne to arrange his social life before she became ill, was probably lonely, but that helping the people in the nursing home was a good way for him to compensate for Joanne's absence from home and seemed to give meaning to his life.

Some caregivers may not want to visit the patient at all or may visit only on holidays or special occasions. Caregivers may find it painful to visit, too sad to see so many ill people and the patient among them. Some may feel guilty about the placement and may find it hard to face the person. Others may not visit because they do not know what to do with the patient or say during the visit. They may feel that they have no contribution to make to the care.

If the caregiver expresses concern about this behavior, the counselor may help the caregiver explore the reasons for not visiting or visiting the patient infrequently. The counselor can remind the caregiver that it is important to the welfare of the patient that the staff of the residential facility be aware of the family's ongoing interest. The counselor may suggest activities that might provide pleasure for both the caregiver and the patient to make it less tedious or distressing for the caregiver to visit.

After patients have been placed in a nursing home, caregivers will go through a continuing process of adjustment as their needs and those of their relatives change. If they become more confident and trusting of the facility's care, they may visit less frequently. Or, if their relative becomes physically ill or has a significant change in level of functioning, they may visit more often. Counselors can offer continual support and guidance through this phase of caregiving.

## COUNSELOR CHECKLIST

### The Decision to Place a Relative in a Residential Facility

☐ Explain how the caregiver can continue to play a role in the care of a relative living in a residential facility.

☐ Explore whether the decision to place the patient has been made freely and is not the result of pressure from friends or family.

☐ Remind the caregiver that the placement does not have to be permanent.

### Choosing a Residential Facility

☐ Explain the different options available and help the family members to determine the most suitable facility.

☐ Explain the level of care that can be provided in an assisted living facility and the possibility that when patients need more care they may have to move to another type of residence.

☐ Suggest that the caregiver ask about how the special AD unit of a nursing home differs from the regular unit.

☐ Offer the caregiver a checklist of issues to explore when visiting a residential care facility.

☐ Encourage the caregiver to visit several facilities before selecting one.

### The Placement Process

☐ Advise the caregiver about how to make the move acceptable to the patient.

☐ Caution the caregiver that personal belongings should be labeled to prevent their being lost or misplaced.

☐ Be available after placement to offer support to the caregiver.

**The Caregiver's Role After Placement**

☐ Remind the caregiver that regular visits help to ensure good patient care.

☐ Suggest that the caregiver talk to the staff regularly to stay up-to-date on the patient's status.

☐ Discuss with the caregiver the appropriate frequency and length of visits.

☐ Suggest activities that might provide pleasure to the caregiver and the patient during a visit.

# 13

# THE END STAGE OF ALZHEIMER'S DISEASE, DEATH, AND BEREAVEMENT

The final stage of Alzheimer's disease (AD), GDS 7, lasts for an indeterminate amount of time, and it is very difficult to know how close the person is to death. People have been known to live in this stage for as long as 7 years. A patient in this stage is likely to develop problems for which medical treatment may involve ethical, religious, and moral dilemmas.

Unless an acute illness such as a heart attack or pneumonia intervenes, the patient will ultimately die from what appears to be a complete shutdown of vital organs. However, many people with AD do not live until the final stage but, instead, die of other causes.

In this chapter, we discuss the issues caregivers face during the end stage of AD, the death of the patient, and bereavement and the ways in which these issues can be addressed and mitigated by professional and family support.

## The End Stage of AD

It is important for the counselor to understand the characteristics of a patient in the last stage of Alzheimer's disease and the caregiver's reactions to this stage before offering guidance and support to the caregiver and the family.

### The Patient's Condition

During the course of the severe stage, people with AD will lose the ability to speak and to walk, they will not be able to sit up without support, and eventually they will not be able to hold up their heads. They no longer have control over their bowel or bladder. Eventually they need to be fed, and they develop trouble swallowing. They will be completely dependent on others to perform all the activities of daily living for them. It is important to remember that patients in this stage may feel physical pain that they cannot express in conventional ways.

Patients in the severe stage become increasingly immobile and, as a result, are at risk for contractures (the inability of the joints to open to their full extension), skin breakdown, and bedsores. Inadequate nutrition and hydration as well as incontinence increase the risk of skin breakdown and bedsores. Swallowing difficulties can lead to malnutrition as well as aspiration of food into the lungs rather than into the stomach, resulting in choking. Patients in this stage who are bedridden are especially vulnerable to contracting pneumonia.

It is possible that symptoms such as inability to walk, sit unsupported, or feed themselves are at least partly due to the fact that the patient's joints have become contracted and muscles weakened due to inactivity. Exercises that maintain flexibility may delay the onset of contractures. Caregivers should be made aware of the fact that professional training is necessary, at least initially, to safely and effectively conduct these exercises.

All of these conditions associated with the end stage of AD can potentially be minimized with sufficient attention and care. Providing this level of care will require an enormous commitment of time and/or money, and even with the best of care, they may not be entirely preventable.

## Caregiver Reactions to the End Stage of AD

Caregivers have a range of reactions to a person in the end stage of AD. Some continue to feel great love and compassion, and having taken care of their relative for many years, approach this stage of caregiving with acceptance and adjust to the new level of care required. Many caregivers feel overwhelmed or intimidated by the amount and extent of physical care the patient needs. Some may feel helpless or frustrated with their inability to communicate with a person who makes sounds and motions that are difficult to understand. It is very painful for many caregivers, especially those who have had a close relationship, to see a relative in such a dependent and vulnerable condition.

One of the many difficulties for a caregiver of a patient in the end stage of AD is not knowing how long this stage will last. "I could stand it if I knew it was only 6 months or a year. It's the fact that I have no idea when it's going to end that makes it hard to tolerate." Some caregivers may try to maintain a connection with their relatives despite the fact that they know it could be severed at any time, while others may try to loosen the connection for the same reason.

It is not surprising that, under such trying circumstances, caregivers experience mixed feelings toward the patient. On the one hand, they may want to do everything possible to keep the person alive. On the other hand, they may really wish the person would die, so as to not prolong his or her suffering as well as their own. Some make every effort, even though it seems futile to do so. Some caregivers may feel anger and hostility toward the patient and the caregiving situation, and they may feel guilty for having these thoughts about a person who is severely ill. Caregivers may feel that it is inappropriate to share these feelings with friends and family or worry that if they do so they will be criticized or misunderstood.

Caregivers who are struggling with mixed feelings toward the patient may be afraid to trust their judgment when making life and death decisions. They may compensate for their ambivalence by making decisions that prolong the life of the patient when this is no longer in the patient's best interest. Alternatively, caregivers who are deeply bonded to the patient may be unable to take steps that represent letting go.

In counseling, caregivers can express and explore their feelings without fear of condemnation and get relief from the pressure of containing them. Caregivers can gain insight into why they are having these feelings and come to terms with them. This may enable them to make the many very difficult decisions they are likely to face at this stage without misattributing them to the negative feelings. Support groups can provide a venue for working through these feelings as well.

Ted had now reached the end stage of AD. Millie continued to visit him in the nursing home three times during the week and every Saturday and Sunday. Millie called her counselor and said, "Ted can't speak. He lies in bed and can barely move. He hardly ever responds to my voice or touch. I don't think he knows I am there most of the time, but I still want to be with him, so I go to visit as often as I can. I sit with him, hold his hand or put my arm around him, and tell him about the kids, work, and the things that need to be done around the house. Sometimes I bring a tape recorder with his favorite music. Do you think that is crazy?" The counselor asked, "What do you think?" Millie answered, "You know, sometimes I think it is crazy, since he doesn't really acknowledge that I am there, but who knows, maybe he does feel my presence. I think of all the wonderful years that we were together and the love that we shared. I want to be with him to the end. If I were in his position, I would want him to be there for me." The counselor said, "That doesn't sound crazy to me, and perhaps what you're doing really is soothing to Ted."

## The Caregiver's Role at the End Stage of AD

Some caregivers may question whether their personal involvement in patient care at this stage has any value. Counselors can help these caregivers to see that they can still have an effect on their relative's quality of life at this stage of the disease. By helping them to appreciate the emotional, spiritual, and physical needs of their relatives and understand how they may satisfy these needs, counselors may enable caregivers to continue to provide sensitive care. Also during this stage, caregivers may have to make many decisions regarding medical treatment or, in some cases, actually withholding medical treatment and allowing the patient to die. Counselors can provide guidelines to help caregivers prepare for and make these difficult decisions.

### Maintaining an Emotional Connection With Patients

Although people in the severe stage of AD can no longer speak, they emit a variety of sounds such as moans, screams, and groans that suggest that they may be attempting to draw one's attention to something or that they are in pain or discomfort. They also communicate with body language. Grimaces or restless movements may be signs of discomfort, need, or pain. Each person will have his or her own way of communicating, which the caregiver will learn to interpret with experience. One person may turn his head when he is annoyed; another may try to communicate by making sounds.

Even the most experienced caregiver may not always know whether he or she is reading the signals correctly. Counselors can encourage caregivers to value the efforts that they are making on the patient's behalf, even though they cannot be sure how they are being received.

Some caregivers naturally continue to relate warmly to their relatives, while others may need some guidance and support as they try to maintain an emotional connection at this stage. Caregivers will have to learn to use body language and vocal intonation themselves to communicate with relatives in the severe stage, and provide sensory stimulation to give them pleasurable experiences and maintain a connection. Family members can speak gently to their relatives, massage and hold them, play music that they used to like, or use scented candles or oils to create a pleasant smell in the room. Since end stage patients may have different reactions to these stimuli, counselors should prepare caregivers to be sensitive to their relatives' reaction to these activities and not to be disappointed if they do not seem pleased and respond positively. Some patients at this stage appreciate touch, while others avoid it. Some indications of pleasure could be a smile, a sound, or turning in the direction of the caregiver.

The physical care of a patient at the end stage of AD can be performed in an indifferent, mechanical way or in a sensitive, engaged way. If physical care tasks are used as an opportunity for emotional contact with the person, they can become a kind of social interaction. It may be difficult to feel motivated to behave this way because patients cannot respond in a conventional fashion. Nevertheless, caregivers can talk to the patients while they are feeding, dressing, bathing, or moving them, which can personalize the interactions and make them more respectful. Counselors can help all caregivers, whether family, friends, or paid helpers, find ways to provide physical care in a sensitive and humane manner.

## *Deciding Where the Patient Will Live*

Many patients whose care is not complicated by other medical conditions remain at home until they die. While the physical and emotional toll can be enormous, it can be made easier for the caregiver to manage if adequate formal and informal support is available. The family caregiver will usually have had either professional or other help in caring for the patient earlier in the disease that will continue as the need shifts to providing complete hands-on care. If caregivers are not physically capable of accomplishing the tasks associated with the end stage on their own, it may be necessary to change the care plan, perhaps getting additional help at home or placing the patient in a nursing home. Providing medical care to the person in the end stage will require making arrangements with home care agencies or doctors who come to the home, as it will be extremely difficult to bring the patient to the doctor. If the patient is enrolled in hospice, these problems will be significantly mitigated by the services that will be brought into the home.

Adult children frequently worry that their well parent will become exhausted by the physical requirement of caring for a patient at the end stage of AD and may not understand why their mother or father is so determined to keep the patient at home. Perhaps they cannot appreciate the value to a spouse who has lived with a person for many years of just having the physical presence of their ill spouse in the house, in spite of the advanced stage of their disease. The children may realistically fear that the well parent will become ill from the strain of caregiving and that they will lose both parents as a result of the sickness of one. Counselors can help parents and children to empathize with each other's perspectives even though they might continue to see the situation differently.

If the patient has been living in a nursing home, it is likely that he or she will remain there, although caregivers occasionally choose to bring their relatives home at this stage, since the difficult behaviors that are frequently the cause of placement in the moderate stage will have abated. Sometimes a patient who has been cared for at home is transferred to a nursing home at the end stage because more care is needed or the family is not comfortable having the person die at home. These caregivers will have to learn how to take care of their relative in the new setting at a most difficult time. A counselor can help them to orient themselves and direct them to supports that are likely to be available.

If a person has been living at a nursing facility for many years before entering the end stage of the illness, there are potential opportunities for support for the caregiver from staff members, other caregivers, and other residents with whom they may have long-term relationships. Staff may understand the way the patient communicates and help family members maintain a connection with the patient during visits. The facility may offer a range of services for patients in this stage and their family members, such as palliative and hospice care, support groups, spiritual or religious guidance, and counseling by a social worker or psychologist. In many cases caregivers spend so much time visiting their relatives in the nursing home that the people there become a kind of surrogate family.

## Addressing Medical Care Issues

At the end stage of AD, decisions frequently need to be made about the amount and kind of medical procedures that are most beneficial to the patient at this point; whether to insert a feeding tube or to treat pneumonia or to intubate to help the patient breathe are examples of such decisions.

The main reason these decisions are so difficult to make is that they may shorten or lengthen the person's life. Some caregivers may find themselves wondering whether it is worth lengthening life if it means diminishing or not enhancing its quality. Other caregivers may choose to lengthen life at all costs, because either they believe it is the right thing to do, they are implementing their relative's expressed wishes, or they don't want to let the patient go. The process of making these decisions may involve more than one person, and opinions may vary as to what to do.

There is no certainty about the outcome of many of these decisions. Even though the caregiver may decide to forgo a specific treatment and let the patient die, he or she may nonetheless survive for an indeterminate amount of time. The caregiver may be forced to make similar decisions more than once.

***Difficulties Feeding the Patient***   When the patient begins to have trouble swallowing, a caregiver may become distressed or frightened. It is possible that the caregiver has consulted a doctor who may have recommended a change in diet or even a feeding tube. The counselor should be aware that the decision not to use a feeding tube does not necessarily mean that the patient can no longer be fed. The counselor can suggest that the caregiver ask the doctor to make a referral to a specialist to evaluate the patient's condition and to identify the cause of the problem.

Questions the caregiver can ask the doctor include: Can the patient still eat if he or she is fed very slowly? What consistency of food would be easiest to swallow? Would thick, smooth liquids be appropriate? It is possible that with skillful feeding techniques and sufficient time spent, the swallowing difficulty may be delayed? The dilemma for caregivers may be whether they are willing to invest the time it takes to feed a person who is in this stage or to hire someone else to do so. A caregiver may be motivated to spend the necessary time to feed a relative who seems willing to eat. If no remediation of the swallowing difficulty is possible, the caregiver faces the dilemma of whether to insert a feeding tube or not.

## End Stage Decisions

Jenny was in the early part of the severe stage of AD when she was hospitalized for a broken hip. After she was operated on, she was fed with an IV. When the staff tried to get her to eat, the nurses became concerned that she was in danger of choking because she was not always able to swallow her food properly. The doctor told one of her daughters, Susie, who was visiting, that he recommended a feeding tube to ensure that Jenny be properly nourished. Susie said she would discuss it with her sisters and let him know their decision. Her sisters objected, saying that their mother had made it very clear to them that she did not want to stay alive if she had to depend on machines. Susie said, "You mean you want to let Mom die?" Finally, one of her sisters said, "Maybe the social worker can help us sort this out. When Mom was admitted, she said we could call her if there was a problem." The social worker suggested that she be part of a meeting with the doctor and the daughters. At that meeting, Susie's two sisters reiterated their reluctance to putting in a feeding tube and asked, "Isn't there a chance something else can be done?" The doctor said, "I can order a swallowing evaluation, and there may be some chance that, with proper feeding, you can postpone putting in a feeding tube, but there are risks involved."

The results of the evaluation indicated that their mother did have some problems swallowing, but the specialist said that some of her difficulty might be due to the aftereffects of the surgery. The daughters were told that if she was positioned correctly while she was eating, the consistency of the food was modified, and she was fed very slowly, she could continue to receive adequate nutrition without a feeding tube, although some risk of choking remained. The daughters agreed that it was worth the time and trouble to take turns feeding their mother to follow her wishes.

When a person is at the stage of AD at which swallowing is no longer possible, some would argue that the body may already be shutting down and the feeding tube may not prolong life but perhaps increase suffering. If the patient has prepared advance directives or appointed a health care proxy who knows his or her wishes, the decision regarding the use of a feeding tube may already have been made. In the absence of advance directives, the closest family member will need to give consent to have a tube inserted.

***Treating Pneumonia***   It is common for patients in the end stage of AD to suffer repeated episodes of pneumonia, resulting in multiple trips to the hospital for treatment. These hospitalizations are tremendously exhausting for the patient and the caregiver and may begin to feel like a futile battle against the inevitable. As a result, some caregivers decide that they will not treat the next episode, knowing that this decision may result in the death of the patient. Others will not be willing to commit themselves to a plan for future treatment or may want to continue to treat each episode to prolong the life of the patient.

Ted had gone through several bouts of pneumonia, each of which left him weaker. The day he returned to the nursing home after his last hospital stay, Millie left work early, went to the nursing home, and sat with Ted for the rest of the day. Toward the evening, she dimmed the lights in the room and sat at the edge of the bed. "He looks so tired, so drained," she thought to herself, and just then, she thought she saw Ted look directly at her, as if he could hear her thoughts and was agreeing. She decided that she would no longer agree to aggressive treatment for Ted, but rather she would talk to her counselor about how to enroll him in hospice so that he could spend his last days as comfortably as possible. As she was driving home that night, she realized she would have to tell the children. But how? The next day she called her counselor and informed her of the decision. "I need to talk to you about how to tell the children," she said.

***Cardio-Pulmonary Resuscitation (CPR)*** CPR was originally developed to rescue victims from sudden death, not to save people whose death is expected. However, in the absence of a DNR (do not resuscitate) order, CPR is routinely administered by emergency medical technicians and hospital personnel to anyone whose heart has stopped. Because CPR is difficult for a body to withstand, people in the end stage of AD who receive CPR are in a more debilitated condition if they survive. A DNR order, which must be signed by a doctor, can be prepared in advance for use at home. In the hospital, the patient or caregiver will be asked to sign a DNR upon admission if it appears that the patient would not be a good candidate for CPR.

***Hospitalization*** A patient at the end stage of AD may develop a condition that requires him or her to go to a hospital for treatment, and a decision has to be made about whether this is appropriate considering the patient's overall condition. When the patient has been repeatedly hospitalized for the same condition, caregivers may decide that the stress and discomfort of this kind of medical intervention is no longer warranted. If the patient is living in a nursing home, caregivers should provide specific written instructions about the conditions under which they want the patient not to be hospitalized. If the patient is living at home, these decisions should be made in conjunction with the patient's physician.

## End Stage Decisions

Janet and her father came to see the counselor who had been working with them periodically throughout the course of Mrs Burten's illness, usually when an important decision had to be made. Mrs Burten was living in a nursing home and had been hospitalized three times in the last year. First she had a urinary tract infection that did not respond to usual treatment, then she had a fever of unknown origin, and the third time she had an infected bedsore. Now she had sepsis and Mr Burten felt that it was time to let go, to let his wife die in peace at the nursing home without another trip to the hospital. His daughter Janet essentially agreed with him but had some reservations. She said to the counselor, "All our decisions up until now have been to keep my mother alive. Now I am making a decision that will bring her life to an end, and I keep asking myself whether I'm ending her life so that I can get mine back or whether this is really the right thing to do for my mother." The counselor felt deeply touched, as she always did by the profundity of the questions caregivers face. She said, "Let's consider some questions that may help you think this through. First, though, I wonder why you think you are being selfish now, when you have been devoted to your mother for so many years." Janet answered, "I feel like I shouldn't want my mother to die."

***Palliative Care and Hospice***   There is no single definition of palliative care; however, some common principles inform all of them. Palliative care signals a shift in goals from acute care to supportive care. It is a service for people with terminal illness such as end stage AD and their family and friends. Its aim is not to cure but to give the patient the best possible quality of life. Palliative care includes services designed to relieve pain, provide medical treatment when necessary, reduce stress, and provide emotional support, information, and referrals for the patient and family members. Palliative care can be instituted at home or in a hospital.

Some families may feel that their needs and those of the patient can be better met when care is provided under the umbrella of palliative care rather than traditional medical services, although the length of time until the death of the patient cannot be predicted with any certainty. When the patient's status changes and he or she is believed to have 6 months or less to live, a referral to hospice might be appropriate.

When death is imminent, caregivers may consider how to make it as dignified and comfortable as possible. For some, hospice may offer the kinds of medical care and supportive services that the patient and family members need. Others do not feel the need to seek out additional support.

Hospice, a form of palliative care, is a service designed to meet end-of-life care needs. When the person with AD reaches the very severe stage and aggressive medical treatment is no longer seen as beneficial or desirable, hospice may be appropriate. In a hospice program, doctors, nurses, social workers, home health aides, clergy, and volunteers guide and support the patient and family throughout the final stage of life and after the patient dies, through bereavement. Hospice may make it possible for the family of a dying person to feel that instead of withholding treatment, they are giving their family member with Alzheimer's disease the best possible care until the last moment of life.

Hospice has generally not been thought of as a service that could be used for people with AD, because a person can live in the end stage of AD for an indeterminate amount of time, and it is difficult to know when a referral is appropriate. In response to this problem, special criteria have been developed for people with AD. Medicare guidelines require that the patient be in the FAST stage 7 (see Chapter 1) and have suffered from an acute illness such as pneumonia or a urinary tract infection during the past 12 months. Since these guidelines are subject to change, the current requirements should be checked. This information can be obtained directly from Medicare and institutions that provide hospice service. Family members, physicians, and other health care providers can enroll a patient in a hospice program. Hospice services can be provided in some nursing homes, in the patient's home, and in designated sections of some hospitals. Equipment and medications are provided as needed. Hospice care is usually covered by both Medicare and Medicaid.

In some cases, patients or families may not subscribe to the values implicit in hospice care. They may want to continue aggressive treatment and may always choose the intervention they feel is most likely to prolong life. Some doctors may be reluctant to give up trying to cure their patients even when there is almost no chance of success.

There may be situations in which hospice is not an appropriate referral for a family. Families who already have home care paid for by a government insurance may find the number of home care hours provided by hospice insufficient for their needs and may prefer not to exchange their current services for hospice care. Others may not feel comfortable with the idea that their family member may be disenrolled from hospice if he or she no longer qualifies (does not die within 6 months and remains stable within the 6-month period). They would prefer not to have a service, get used to it, and then have to discontinue it. Because of the limitations of a service such as hospice, counselors should advise caregivers to meet with a representative of the local hospice program to see if the program is right for their particular needs.

After talking to the counselor, Millie felt that she needed her to be there when she told her children about her decision. She arranged for a family counseling session and even called Matt and asked him to fly in. When everyone was gathered in the counselor's office, Millie told the children that she no longer wanted to subject Ted to painful tests and treatments to keep him alive in his current condition and said she was going to enroll him in hospice at the nursing home. Carol gasped and said, "How can you do that, Mom? What are you thinking? You're going to let him die?" Tom snapped at Carol, "How can you say that to Mom?" Matt stared out the window silently. Carol turned to the counselor and asked, accusingly, "Did you put her up to this? Mom would never do this on her own." Millie said, "No, Carol. It was my decision. Your father has been through so much. He is tired; he's weak. I am doing what I think is best for him. I can't ask you to agree with me, but I would like you to trust that I am doing this out of love for your father." The counselor said, "This was a hard decision for your mom to make." She encouraged the family to talk about what it meant to them for Ted to be going into hospice.

## Making Treatment Decisions

While there are decisions to be made at all stages of AD, some decisions that need to be made in the end stage may result in prolonging or ending life and therefore can be the most emotionally draining a caregiver has to face. Even the language that is used to describe the discontinuation of life-extending treatment, such as "hastened death," "assisted suicide," and "euthanasia," has emotional overtones that may compound the difficulty of decision making. These terms have negative implications to some, while to others they might mean bringing an end to needless suffering or fulfilling the wishes of a relative. A family's cultural background, as well as whether they value the preservation of life despite pain and suffering, shape end-of-life decisions and may determine whether they have prepared advance directives.

***The Counselor's Role in Decision Making***   Counselors should never make decisions for caregivers; rather they can try to help them think through the issues and come to their own decisions. The counselor's previous experience, knowledge of where to turn for help, and ability to tolerate the anxiety and other strong emotions the family members are feeling can enable him or her to facilitate the decision-making process. By expressing an appreciation of the difficulty of making these kinds of decisions, counselors can reduce the sense of pressure for caregivers and enable them to come to a decision.

Counselors should not offer any medical advice or make other recommendations that exceed their expertise. In order to take into account the medical, psychological, legal, financial, ethical, and spiritual aspects of these decisions, it may be necessary for families to consult experts in these fields. Counselors can help caregivers understand the implications of treatment decisions by suggesting questions to ask and exploring the pros and cons of each choice.

***Guidelines for Helping Caregivers Make Decisions***   Even when advance directives have been prepared, caregivers may find it difficult to follow them, because the actual situation is never as clear cut as the one noted on paper. The following guidelines can be used by the counselor to help the caregiver make a treatment decision:

- Identify what the patient would have wanted. Has the patient left written instructions? In the absence of specific documentation, what other information has the patient provided? Has the patient ever said or done anything that would guide a decision? If so, is the caregiver following the patient's wishes? If not, why not?

- What has been the basis for previous decisions made by the caregiver? Were invasive procedures and hospitalizations avoided?

- What is the recommendation of the patient's doctor? Has a second opinion been sought?

- Explore the caregiver's view of how the decision will affect the patient's quality of life. Does the person appear to be suffering? Will the procedure cause him to suffer more or less?

- What are the financial ramifications of the decision? Are there issues around the cost of care, inheritance, loss of income, etc?

- Does the decision reflect a wish of the caregiver to be relieved of the burden of care?

- Do other family members agree with the decision?

- What are the consequences of the decision? What are the care problems? Will there be family conflict? How will the caregiver feel after implementing the decision—as if he or she has abandoned the patient or honored his or her wishes?

- Is the caregiver uncomfortable with having control over another person's life?

When there is time to explore these issues in advance, the process can be very beneficial in helping caregivers to clarify their thinking and in living with their decisions afterward. When the counselor is working with a family that is likely to confront these end-of-life decisions in the near future, he or she should raise these issues so that the family will have time to gather information and sort out their mixed feelings.

Counselors should be aware that, even with all the preparation and forethought, what people do when the situation actually arises may be different from what they planned. Many say that they will not agree to extraordinary measures. However, when they are actually confronting the decision to let the person die, they find it difficult not to take action to keep the patient alive. Caregivers in these situations may need additional support to live with the consequences of having changed their minds about the decision they had made in advance.

### Decision Making in the Absence of Advance Directives

Preparing advance directives is inconsistent with the values of some cultures, and there are individuals for whom planning for death is unacceptable or inconceivable. Death and dying are not openly discussed in many families. In the absence of advance directives, caregivers should try to do what they think the person with AD would have wanted. It may be necessary to review the history of the patient's prior decisions, religious beliefs, statements with regard to the care of others, and any information that will enable caregivers to identify what the patient would have wanted. If the patient is in the hospital, the patient representative can direct caregivers to mechanisms such as convening the ethics committee to help them to come to a decision. Physicians and other medical personnel can help caregivers by providing information on the medical implications and realities of the various options.

*Family Conflict About End-of-Life Decisions*    End-of-life decisions can cause conflict when some members of the family are in favor of letting the patient die and others want to continue with aggressive treatment. Especially intense emotional interactions may arise when a decision has to be made about withdrawing treatment. Disagreements can occur because of lack of understanding or differing interpretations of the medical situation and the implications of the choices. Individual family members may not have the same values and may not have articulated them in a way that other family members could understand. Sometimes family members disagree about what the patient would have wanted under specific circumstances that had not been anticipated.

Occasionally no one has been designated as the decision maker, and there are no written instructions. The family will have to decide whose decision should be followed if there is disagreement. It may be possible for the counselor to help the family agree about who has been closest to the patient and allow that person to make a decision. Among the considerations in trying to help the family agree about who should make the decision might be how much contact each person has had with the patient recently and in the past and the degree of involvement in the patient's care. There is a generally agreed-upon hierarchy of decision-making power in hospitals: beginning with the spouse, followed by adult children, then parent, next adult siblings, and, finally, a close friend. If there is a legal guardian, he or she has the greatest authority. If the patient is not in the hospital, the counselor can suggest that this hierarchy be followed if the family cannot resolve its disagreement.

A counselor can convene a family meeting to facilitate the decision-making process in a way that will bring families together and respect the patient's wishes and needs. The counselor can try to mediate disagreement to avoid escalation of family conflict and referral to other authorities. If there is no agreement or a decision appears to be based on conflict of interest, ultimately an ethics committee may be called in to resolve conflicts and facilitate decision making, or a judicial process may have to be invoked.

Sometimes caregivers are unwilling to risk a breach in their relationships with other family members and may feel they have to accede to their wishes in spite of their own beliefs and what they think is in the best interest of the patient.

## End Stage Decisions

Maurice's wife, who was in the severe stage of AD and could no longer walk, had been in a nursing home for 6 months when she developed a problem swallowing. The doctor at the nursing home suggested that she have a stomach tube inserted so she could be adequately fed. Maurice was opposed to taking this step but was unable to make this decision in the face of the doctor's recommendation. His wife had not signed advance directives, and they had never even discussed the subject. He brought his dilemma to his support group because he knew they would understand his problem and not judge him. Talking about it strengthened his resolve to do what he thought was right. When he told his children of his decision, they became very angry with him, and all three threatened never to speak to him again if he carried out his plan. When he went back to his support group the following week, he said, "I don't know what to do. I'm afraid of alienating my children." With the help of the group, he realized that his children weren't ready to let go of their mother yet and that he didn't want to cause them further distress. He decided to have the tube put in. His children were relieved by this decision, although Maurice himself was never entirely comfortable with it.

*Discontinuing Treatment*  The laws vary from state to state regarding who has the authority to discontinue treatment if the patient is deemed incompetent to make the decision. In the course of caring for a patient at the end stage of AD, it may seem clear to the health care professional that the patient is dying and that further intervention will only prolong the dying process. At this point, further intervention may be described by the doctor as futile, although caregivers may not be willing to accept this judgment, and there may be controversy among family members about whether this is indeed the case.

***The Use of Advance Directives*** Documents such as advance directives can be helpful in outlining the parameters of care the patient would want and guiding decisions. The person selected as health care proxy should have knowledge of the patient's wishes or sufficient understanding of the patient's values to make decisions on the patient's behalf that are consonant with them.

Advance directives are usually written a long time before they will need to be implemented. The caregiver may be concerned that the patient might not still make the same choices were he or she still competent. Even if advance directives have been prepared, unanticipated situations often arise that can cause indecision and conflict among family members. The patient's wishes set down in advance directives may make a situation more complicated rather than easier to follow. Caregivers may ask other family members for their opinions and discover that there is no agreement among them. Caregivers and their families who are dealing with any of these situations may turn to a counselor for information and support.

Implementing the prior decision of the patient, whether it was written or only verbal, is especially difficult for a caregiver who is opposed to it. Such caregivers need support to follow the wishes of their relatives. They should be encouraged to seek support from family, clergy, and friends, as well as the counselor.

## Death of the Patient

When death actually occurs, the finality is almost always a shock to the family, even if it has been anticipated and some of the ties to the dying person already have been severed by the effects of dementia. Caregivers will experience a variety of feelings, including sadness, loss, and relief that the patient is no longer suffering and the caregiving is over.

Some families will find consolation in being able to make a contribution to knowledge about Alzheimer's disease by consenting to an autopsy of their relative's brain. It is only after the death of a person with Alzheimer's disease that the diagnosis can be confirmed with certainty.

## *Caregiver Reactions to the Death of the Patient*

In most cases, no matter how much a caregiver may have built a life without the patient, whether through work, socializing, or enjoying recreational activities, he or she will react to the death of the patient. Some may be surprised at how much they are grieving over the person, while others may wonder why they are not aware of feeling more distressed.

Bereavement, or mourning, is a normal response to loss. Mourning helps the person separate himself or herself emotionally from the person who has died and to reinvest energy in the future. When a person dies, the reactions of family members will depend on many factors, including the importance of the person in the relatives' lives, the intensity and quality of the relationship, and how ambivalent the individual family members felt toward the person. It also depends on the circumstances of the death. There is generally a different kind of reaction to sudden loss than to one that is anticipated and comes after a long illness.

People with Alzheimer's disease rarely die from AD-related causes until the very severe stage. Usually, people with AD have been ill for a very long time, so that the immediate effect of the death may be less severe than if the death were unexpected.

People with Alzheimer's disease can, of course, die at any stage of the illness from accidents or diseases that afflict all older people. When this occurs, the issues for the family are likely to be similar to those of family members of other elderly people. Perhaps some family members will also feel that, though the death may seem untimely, at least the person will be spared the decline that is certain to follow. However, a counselor should never make assumptions about how given family members will respond to a death, but rather should understand its meaning to them in order to provide appropriate support. Caregivers have expressed great anger when well-meaning friends and family try to comfort them with the idea that it is better for the person to have died prematurely than to have lived to the later stages of the disease. Similarly, not all family members are relieved that a person in the severe stage has died. The personal experience of each mourner needs to be appreciated.

Counselors should expect that caregivers may have very mixed feelings when the patient dies. They may feel relief that the suffering of the patient is over, simultaneously with grief over the loss. They may be glad that the burden of care is finally lifted and also feel ashamed to have such relief. Some caregivers' reactions to the death of their relative will be complicated by guilt over the decisions they made or their wishes for the end of caregiving.

Although the hospice team had explained to Millie and the rest of the family what would happen after Ted was enrolled in the program, they still were a little surprised by the extra support they and Ted were offered. The hospice doctor and a physician's assistant examined Ted and explained to the family what they would do to keep him comfortable. Ted had already stopped eating, so no food would be offered. A very slow drip to hydrate the body just enough to preserve the integrity of his skin would be started. He would be repeatedly assessed for signs of pain, which would be immediately treated. The doctor said that he expected Ted would die within the next few days. Millie and their children took turns sitting beside Ted, who seemed very peaceful. A music therapist asked what kind of music Ted had liked and brought in some tapes that the family listened to together while they reminisced about the times when they had listened to these songs together. Later that evening a social worker invited the family to meet with her. They told her about how hard it had been to accept that Ted was dying but that they now felt that they had made the right decision when they enrolled him in hospice. The social worker suggested that they continue to talk to Ted. She asked each of them if there was something they had not yet said that they wanted Ted to hear. Tom said that he wanted to stay with his dad during the night and that he would use that time to tell him some of his thoughts. The social worker said that Millie looked very tired and encouraged her to get some rest. Millie said that she would go home since Tom was staying. It was a relief to know that a family member could stay by the bedside and that nurses would be available at any time if Ted needed care and Tom needed comforting. The family looked in on Ted before they left. When Millie came back in the morning, Ted looked much the same but his breathing was more shallow. The doctor told her that he could die at any time.

Millie called the rest of the family and they returned to the nursing home. Later that afternoon Ted died with his family close by. It was hard to say a final goodbye. The social worker invited the family into the lounge, where they wept tears of sorrow.

When a person with Alzheimer's disease dies, family caregivers may, for the first time in many years, have the opportunity to think back to who this person was before he or she became ill and the caregiver became caught up in the day-to-day practical aspects of patient care. They may regret having lost sight of that. Some caregivers express sadness at the death of the person and regret for the life he or she did not get to live. Some may look back on the events related to the person's illness and feel guilty about negative feelings they may have had or for not having done more for the patient. These caregivers may have more difficulty adjusting to the patient's death than those who are at peace with themselves and feel comfortable with the care they provided.

The death of the patient is a turning point in the life of the caregiver and may lead to other losses for him or her. The absence of caregiving and the daily routine it imposes leaves a gap that may feel difficult to fill at first. Coming home to an empty house may be difficult for spouse caregivers who have lived with the patient for decades. Many caregivers become attached to the home health aides with whom they have shared caring for the patient and miss them when the death of the patient ends the relationship. Caregivers who have never lived alone or have lived with the patient and may have devoted themselves to his or her care will need to redefine themselves and develop a whole new lifestyle.

Some caregivers lose the support system that was built around caregiving. If the patient has been living in a nursing home, caregivers may have developed relationships with family members or even other patients with whom they will no longer spend time on a regular basis. They may have to terminate with their caregiver support group and enroll in a bereavement group.

Millie and her counselor embraced. Millie said, "I feel like I'm falling apart. I've known for so long that Ted was dying, and now I just can't pull myself together. I hurt all over. Why did he have to die like this? It just isn't fair. I still need him." The counselor held Millie's hand as she spoke to her. "I know it's hard. You did indeed lose Ted too soon." Millie said, "Sometimes I think I lost him many years ago. I'm surprised I'm so upset now. I guess it's because I can't get used to the fact that now he's really gone. In fact, sometimes I feel like he's still in the room with me." The counselor replied, "When people are grieving they have all kinds of feelings that don't seem to make sense. Millie, you seem far away." "I'm sorry Gloria, I was thinking about my children. So much of our time was spent caring for Ted. I'm wondering if we'll have anything else to talk about now that he's gone. I'm pretty sure they won't be around so much anymore." The counselor said, "I see how worried you are. It may take awhile before you find new ways to be together, but you've always had a close relationship with them." Millie said, "But will I have to stop seeing you?" The counselor said, "No Millie, we can continue to meet for awhile."

Counselors can provide emotional and practical support for caregivers through the grieving process, normalize the strange and even frightening experiences that accompany grief, and when appropriate, express hope and confidence that the pain will remit in time. They can also make referrals for more intensive treatment for those caregivers who have severe reactions or whose grief does not abate. A caregiver who is unable to react to the death also warrants concern because unresolved grief may prevent the person from reengaging in life.

Many times counselors feel almost as though they have become a part of the family and also experience grief at the death of the patient. Caregivers sometimes invite counselors to attend the patient's funeral. If the counselor chooses to attend, he or she should clarify the role he will play, whether or not the caregiver wants to acknowledge their relationship, or if he is to be a silent supporter who blends in among the mourners.

## Autopsy

Since Alzheimer's disease can, at present, only be definitely diagnosed by autopsy, some people request that, when they die, an autopsy be performed, and they include this request in their advance directives. In the absence of written instructions, some families will want to have an autopsy performed to confirm the diagnosis. Another reason for requesting an autopsy is to contribute to research to expand knowledge about Alzheimer's disease and the search for a cure. Families should be made aware that most research centers prefer to receive donated tissue from their own patients.

If the patient has been enrolled in a brain donation program, the family member will need to contact the autopsy coordinator when the patient dies. The cost of performing the autopsy most likely will be paid by the program. If there were no prior plans and the family wishes an autopsy to be performed, they should inform the funeral home and then contact the patient's physician, their local teaching hospital, the local chapter of the Alzheimer's Association, or the Medical Examiner's office to inquire about where and how to request an autopsy. The family should understand that they probably will have to pay for the autopsy, as it is not covered by Medicare, Medicaid, or most private insurance.

Families can be reassured that an autopsy of the brain does not disfigure the body and that a funeral, even with an open casket, can be held without delay. Some people refuse an autopsy because of personal beliefs or because they want the body to remain whole or, because now that the person is dead, they no longer want further information. Some family members request that the diagnosis be confirmed in this way because they want to know about any genetic implications for themselves and the rest of the family, while others will not want the autopsy because they do not want to know that their relative died of a disease that they may have inherited. If a caregiver is being urged to allow an autopsy, but he or she or another family member is opposed, they have the right, in most cases, to refuse the procedure.

A year after Ted's death, Carol is in Millie's kitchen helping her mother do the dishes after their Thanksgiving dinner. She says, "Mom, you seem kind of sad just now. Are you doing okay?" Millie replies, "You're right, Carol, I am sad. With the whole family together today, I can't help but miss your father." Carol says, "I know, Mom, I miss him, too." Millie says, "You know, Carol, it was just over 10 years from the time your father was diagnosed with Alzheimer's disease until he died. I can't imagine what we would have done during that time without the support you kids gave us. And Gloria, too. She was a real gift to this family. I don't think we could have gotten through Dad's illness without her." Carol says, ""But Mom, how are you doing now that you're on your own?" Millie says, "Actually, I'm doing better than I expected. I've gotten back together with my old friends, and I've still got the friends I made in my support group. I've been learning to play bridge, and I play at least once a week. I've been spending a lot of time with Madge from next door. She wants me to take a bus tour to Amish country with her next spring. I think I'll go."

## COUNSELOR CHECKLIST

### The End Stage of AD

☐ Help the caregiver understand the special care needs of a patient at the end stage of AD.

☐ Acknowledge the profound implications of decisions at this stage.

☐ Create an environment to facilitate expression and exploration of the caregiver's feelings about decisions that need to be made.

### The Caregiver's Role at the End Stage of AD

☐ Help the caregiver understand how he or she still can affect the patient's quality of life at this stage.

☐ Suggest that the caregiver ask for a referral to a specialist to evaluate swallowing difficulties. Advise the caregiver to explore feeding options with the specialist.

☐ Advise the caregiver about the services provided by hospice.

☐ Offer guidelines that will help the caregiver make treatment decisions.

☐ Facilitate family discussions regarding treatment decisions if there is disagreement.

### Death of the Patient

☐ Expect that the caregiver may have very mixed feelings about the death of the patient.

☐ Offer support during the grieving process.

☐ Refer a caregiver who has severe reactions of grief for more intensive counseling.

☐ Explain the benefits of an autopsy to the caregiver.

# THE CAREGIVER ASSESSMENT BATTERY

The regular detailed assessments used in the NYU Spouse Caregiver Intervention Study consisted of structured self-report instruments, about both the caregivers and the patients. These instruments were selected, to the extent possible, from among those that have been published and for which reliability has been established. To assess outcomes such as depression and anxiety, we selected instruments used in large-scale studies for which population norms are available. This enables us to compare the relative efficacy in improving caregiver well-being of this and other interventions using the same instruments. Most of the instruments are designed for the general population, rather than for caregivers, enabling us to compare these caregivers to noncaregivers, as well as to caregivers of patients with other illnesses, and to estimate the burden of caregiving over and above the other burdens shouldered by similar people.

Since ad hoc counseling is continually available, counselors maintain logs of the amount of time spent in ad hoc consultation with each family to provide a measure of the utilization of this resource. If the patient is in a nursing home, a suitably modified version of the assessment battery is administered. If the patient dies, the caregiver receives only the assessment instruments that do not pertain specifically to caregiving (such as the depression scale) 1 and 2 years after the death of the patient.

1. **General Information.** The *Caregiver Questionnaire* was developed at the NYU-ADRC to provide comprehensive and detailed information about the caregiver: basic demographic information; family structure, questions about living arrangements, changes in

the caregiver's life, and new responsibilities taken on because of the patient's condition; the nature and amount of formal and informal support the caregiver is currently receiving and would like to receive; and financial difficulties due to the patient's illness, cost of home care, and use of Medicaid.

2. **Caregiver Psychological Status.** We include specific scales for several dimensions of psychological status that are sensitive to small but important changes over time.

   a. *Geriatric Depression Scale* ($\alpha$ = .94; Yesavage et al, 1983). This 30-item, yes/no depression scale was specifically designed for a geriatric population.

   b. *Short Psychiatric Evaluation Scale* (SPES; ICC = .68, Pfeiffer, 1975). This 15-item self-administered scale was developed for the elderly to indicate the existence and degree of functional psychiatric disorder.

   c. *Burden Scale* ($\alpha$ = .88; Zarit et al, 1985) consists of 22 questions that measure the specific stresses experienced by caregivers of dementia patients.

   d. *Memory and Behavior Problems Checklist* ($\alpha$ = .80; Zarit et al, 1985) consists of 30 questions regarding caregiver reaction to problem behaviors of the patient that are likely to be upsetting for the caregiver, as well as the frequency of occurrence of these problems. The scale of caregiver reaction is a primary source of information about caregiver appraisals of patient behavior problems.

   e. *Perceived Stress Scale* (PSS; $\alpha$ = .78 for persons over 65; Cohen, S, 1988) is a 14-item structured Likert scale designed to be sensitive to chronic stress.

3. **Caregiver Physical Health.** The *Caregiver Physical Health Form* is adapted from the OARS battery of questionnaires (ICC = 0.83; Duke Center for the Study of Aging and Human Development, 1978). It includes questions about number of visits to a physician and number of days sick and in the hospital in the last 4 months; number of medications used in the last month; current illnesses; and physical, visual, and hearing disabilities. Also included are several subjective ratings of the caregiver's

current physical health, each on a four-point scale (from excellent to poor).

4. **Social Support.** We conduct a detailed assessment of both positive and negative aspects of social support, which we hypothesize is a major mediator of the effects of the intervention on major outcome variables. It should be noted that, in addition to the measures listed below, the *Caregiver Questionnaire* (1, above) includes questions about specific categories of informal support received and desired, as well as types of formal support utilized.

   a. *The Stokes Social Network List* ($\alpha$ = .92; Stokes, 1983) measures the size and composition (ie, number of friends, relatives, and how many of each to whom the subject feels close) of the social network and the caregiver's *satisfaction* with various aspects of the social network (eg, assistance, emotional support). This includes the aspects of social support that research has suggested is important for mental health of caregivers.

   b. An additional *Social Support Assessment* was developed at the NYU-ADRC for this study to add in-depth information about social support provided by each member of the caregiver's social network who is listed in the *Stokes Social Network List.* It includes questions about the amount and helpfulness of specific types of functional support received from each individual.

   c. Family Cohesion. The 16-item cohesion scale from the *FACES III* instrument ($\alpha$ = .77; Olson et al, 1987) assesses the cohesiveness of the family (from the point of view of the primary caregiver).

5. **Caregiver Personality**

   a. *NEO Personality Inventory* ($\alpha$ = for the N, E, and O scales range from .89 to .93; Costa & McRae, 1988). The NEO measures five major dimensions of normal adult personality traits: neuroticism, extroversion, openness to experience, agreeableness, and conscientiousness. It has been used in several large longitudinal studies of community dwelling adults that included elderly subjects. The NEO has been used to study caregiver personality as a determinant of depression in response to caregiving stress. This instrument was administered only at intake.

b. *Orientation to Life Questionnaire* ($\alpha$ ranged from .82 to .95; Antonovsky, 1993) measures Sense of Coherence (SOC) (perception of the world as manageable and understandable). SOC has been found to be a strong predictor of health outcomes and life satisfaction in older adults.

6. **Patient Functioning**

a. The global severity of dementia of the patient is determined by the *Global Deterioration Scale* (GDS; $\alpha$ = .83; Reisberg et al, 1982), a semistructured rating of patient functioning by the counselor, based on the interview of the caregiver at baseline and at each follow-up interview. The *GDS* is part of the standard patient diagnostic evaluation at the NYU-ADRC and is used to characterize the *global* functional status of the patient. Patients with dementia have scores ranging from 4 to 7 on this scale.

b. The frequency of patient behavior problems is measured at intake and at every follow-up assessment while the patient is living at home with the *Memory and Behavior Problems Checklist* (*MBPC*; Zarit et al, 1985), which consists of a list of 30 common problems manifested by dementia patients.

c. Patient Physical Health. The Patient Physical Health Form is a caregiver-rated version of the self-rated physical health items in the OARS battery of questionnaires (ICC = 0.83; Duke Center for the Study of Aging and Human Development, 1978), which we have been using to rate patients in the spouse caregiver study since its inception.

7. **Home Environment Questionnaire.** This instrument, developed by members of our staff, consists of a series of yes/no questions designed to evaluate the safety of the home for both patient and caregiver. Questions are included about the accessibility of potentially dangerous objects such as knives and cigarette lighters, as well as the use of safety devices such as window guards.

8. **Assessments of Treatment Delivery and Caregiver Satisfaction With Treatment.** Attendance of family members at each counseling session was recorded. At each formal counseling session for caregivers in the treatment group, clinical notes were taken by the counselor. These included the areas in which family members requested help or resources, what each family member agreed to do, points of conflict and degree of resolution, and the resources advised by the counselor (eg, get respite, hire help, take specific safety precautions, or protect against the effects of incontinence). Whether the caregivers complied with this advice was recorded at the following session. Since control subjects can use services on their own, counselors ask caregivers in both the treatment and control groups whether and how frequently they have gone to support groups or used any other formal services.

   In addition, for several extended periods over the course of the study, counselors recorded the number and length of ad hoc requests for counseling (both telephone calls and in person) by caregivers, family members, and patients, and the reasons for these requests. This log is kept in a structured format and provides a record of counseling requests from caregivers and family members in both the treatment and control groups.

# RESOURCES

## *Organizations for People With Alzheimer's Disease and Their Families*

Alzheimer's Association
National Headquarters
919 N Michigan Ave, Ste 1100
Chicago, IL 60611-1676
800 272-3900
www.alz.org
Referrals to local resources for caregivers and people with AD, such as support groups, educational information, and seminars. It also maintains the nationwide Safe Return Program, which helps families find people with Alzheimer's disease who are lost or missing.

Alzheimer's Disease Education & Referral Center
PO Box 8250
Silver Spring, MD 20907-8250
800 438-4380
www.alzheimers.org
Educational materials regarding diagnosis and treatment of AD; patient care and caregiver supports; and education, training, and research related to AD. The staff will respond to telephone and written requests and make referrals to national and state resources.

Alzheimer's Disease Centers (ADCs)
www.alzheimers.org (Choose "Links to Other Federal Resources")
800 438-4380
Information about federally funded centers that provide comprehensive evaluation for AD, treatment, and services—in addition to psychosocial research and clinical trials of new medications.

Clinical Trials Information

www.ClinicalTrials.gov

This Web site was developed by the National Institutes of Health to provide general information about clinical trials and lists trials currently available for Alzheimer's disease and other conditions.

## Organizations That Provide Health Care Information and Assistance to the Elderly

Resource Directory for Older People

National Institute on Aging

Information Center

PO Box 8057

Gaithersburg, MD 20898-8057

800 222-2225

Available through the Administration on Aging Web site at www.aoa.dhhs.gov Information about long-term care planning, nutrition and fitness (including Meals on Wheels programs), health promotion, etc.

The Eldercare Locator

800 677-1116

www.eldercare.gov

A nationwide directory assistance service designed to help older persons and caregivers locate local support resources.

National Association of Professional Geriatric Care Managers

1604 N Country Club Rd

Tucson, AZ 85716-3102

520 881-8008

www.caremanager.org

An organization of private practitioners (generally social workers and nurses) who develop and implement care plans for older people and their families. A consumer directory is available for $15 from the national office.

National Hospice and Palliative Care Organization

1700 Diagonal Rd, Ste 625

Alexandria, VA 22314

800 658-8898

www.nhpco.org

Helps locate hospice services and runs a toll-free hospice referral line.

National Association for Home Care
228 7th St SE
Washington, DC 20003
202 547-7424
www.nahc.org
Helps locate accredited home care aide services and hospice information by area.

## Federal and State Agencies That Govern Health Care in the United States and Provide Health-Related Services to the General Public

The Department of Health and Human Services
200 Independence Ave SW
Washington, DC 20201
877 696-6775
www.hhs.gov
The principal federal agency that governs health care in the United States, providing over 300 health care programs such as Medicare, Medicaid, nutrition programs such as Meals on Wheels, support services, and health care research. The Department of Health and Human Services Web site gives an overview of all its agencies and links to agency Web sites. Below is a listing of some HHS agencies that may be helpful in providing care for your family member.

Administration on Aging
330 Independence Ave SW
Washington, DC 20201
General Information: 202 619-0724
Statistical and Gerontology Information: 202 619-7501
www.aoa.dhhs.gov
Contact information for state offices of the aging, the eldercare locator, long-term care ombudsman programs; resources for locating birth certificates, property deeds, and other records; resources for financial and legal planning and other topics of interest to the elderly.

National Institutes of Health
Bethesda, MD 20892
www.nih.gov
Information about current health care research, clinical trials for various
diseases and conditions, and research centers that provide evaluations for
Alzheimer's and other diseases.

National Institute on Aging
Bldg 31, Rm 5C27
31 Center Dr, MSC 2292
Bethesda, MD 20892
Alzheimer's Disease Information: 800 438-4380
Age-Related Publications: 800 222-2225
www.nia.nih.gov
One of the 25 institutes and centers of the National Institutes of Health
that focuses on the study of aging. It is the primary federal agency involved
in Alzheimer's disease research and provides a variety of information about
the topic to the public.

# BIBLIOGRAPHY

Aneshensel C, Pearlin, L. Caregiving careers and stress processes. In: Aneshensel C, Pearlin L, Mullan J, Zarit S, Whitlatch C, eds. *Profiles in Caregiving, the Unexpected Career.* San Diego, Calif: Academic Press; 1995:16-39.

Antonovsky A. The structure and properties of the Sense of Coherence scale. *Soc Sci & Med.* 1993:36;725-733.

Boss P, Caron W, Horbal J, Mortimer J. Predictors of depression in caregivers of dementia patients: boundary ambiguity and master. *Fam Process.* 1990;29:245-254.

Busse EW, Blazer DG eds. *Textbook of Geriatric Psychiatry.* 2nd ed. Washington, DC: The American Psychiatric Press, Inc; 1996.

Butler R, Lewis M, Sunderland T. *Aging and Mental Health: Positive Psychosocial and Biomedical Approaches.* 5th ed. Boston, Mass: Allyn and Bacon; 1998.

Coffey CE, Cummings J, eds. *Textbook of Geriatric Neuropsychiatry.* 2nd ed. Washington DC: The American Psychiatric Press, Inc; 2000.

Cohen D, Eisdorfer C. *Loss of Self: A Family Resource for the Care of Alzheimer's Disease and Related Disorders.* 2nd ed. New York, NY: WW Norton & Company, Inc; 2001.

Cohen S, Kamarck T, Marmelstein R. A global measure of perceived stress. *J Health Soc Behav.* 1988;24:385-396.

Costa PT, McCrae, RR. *The NEO Personality Inventory Manual.* 1st ed. Odessa, Fla: Psychological Assessment Resources; 1985.

Dawson P, Wells D, Kline K. *Enhancing the Abilities of Persons with Alzheimer's and Related Dementias: A Nursing Perspective.* New York, NY: Springer Publishing Company; 1985.

Duke University Center for the Study of Aging and Human Development. *Multidimensional functional assessment: The OARS methodology;* 1978.

Hellen CH. *Alzheimer's Disease: Activity-Focused Care.* 2nd ed. Boston, Mass: Butterworth Heinemann; 1998.

Hinman-Smith E, Gwyther LP. *Coping with Challenging Behaviors: Education Strategies for Work with Alzheimer's Families.* Durham, NC: Duke University Medical Center; 1990.

Khachaturian ZS, Radebaugh TS, eds. *Alzheimer's Disease, Cause(s), Diagnosis, Treatment, and Care.* Boca Raton, Fla and New York, NY: CRC Press; 1996.

Mace NL, Rabins PV. The *36-Hour Day.* 3rd ed. Baltimore, MD: Johns Hopkins University Press; 1999.

Mace N, ed. *Dementia Care: Patient, Family and Community.* Baltimore, MD: Johns Hopkins University Press; 1991.

Mahoney E, Volcifer L, Hurley A. *Management of Challenging Behaviors in Dementia.* Baltimore, MD: Health Professions Press; 2000.

McGoldrick M, Giordano J, Pearce JK, Giordano J, eds. *Ethnicity and Family Therapy.* New York, NY: Guilford Publications, Inc; 1996.

McKhann G, Drachman D, Folstein M, Katzman R, Price D, Stadlan EM. Clinical diagnosis of Alzheimer's disease: report of the NINCDS-ADRDA work group under the auspices of the Department of Health & Human Services Task Force on Alzheimer's Disease. *Neurology.* 1984;34:939-944.

Mittelman MS, Ferris SH, Shulman E, Steinberg G, et al. A comprehensive support program: effect on depression in spouse-caregivers of AD patients. *Gerontologist.* 1995;35:792–802.

Mittelman MS, Ferris SH, Shulman E, Steinberg G, Levin B. A family intervention to delay nursing home placement of patients with Alzheimer disease: a randomized controlled trial. *JAMA.* 1996;276:1725-1731.

Mittelman MS, Ferris SH, Shulman E, Steinberg G. The effects of a multi-component support program on spouse-caregivers of Alzheimer's disease patients: results of a treatment/control study. In: Heston LL, ed. *Progress in Alzheimer's Disease and Similar Conditions.* Washington, DC: American Psychiatric Press; 1997:259–275.

Olson DH, Portner J, Lavee Y. Family adaptability and Cohesion Evaluation Scales III. In: Fredman N, Sherman R, eds. *Handbook of Measurements for Marriage and Family Therapy.* New York, NY: Brunner/Mazel; 1987.

Pearlin LI, Mullin JT, Semple SJ, Skaff MM. Caregiving and the stress process: an overview of concepts and their measures. *The Gerontologist.* 1990;30(5):583–594.

Pfeiffer E. A short psychiatric evaluation schedule: a new 15-item monotonic scale indicative of functional disorder. In: *Proceedings, Bayer-Symposium VII, Brain Function in Old Age.* New York, NY: Springer-Verlag; 1979.

Reisberg B, Franssen E. Clinical stages of Alzheimer's disease. In: de Leon MJ, cd. An Atlas of Alzheimer's disease. *The Encyclopedia of Visual Medicine Series.* Pearl River, NY: Parthenon; 1999.

Reisberg B. Functional assessment staging (FAST). *Psychopharmacol Bull.* 1988;24.

Reisberg B, Ferris SH, de Leon MJ, Crook T. The Global Deterioration Scale for assessment of primary degenerative dementia. *Amer J Psychiatry.* 1982;139(9).

Ronch JL. *Alzheimer's Disease: A Practical Guide for Families and Other Caregivers.* New York, NY: The Crossroad Publishing Co; 1991.

Souren L, Franssen, E. *Broken Connections.* Royersford, Pa: Swets & Zeitlinger Publishers; 1994.

Stokes JP. Predicting satisfaction with social support from social network structure. *Am J Community Psychol.* 1983;11:141–152.

Tappen R. *Interventions for Alzheimer's Disease.* Baltimore, MD: Health Professions Press; 1997.

Yesavage JA, Brink TL, Rose TL, Adey M. The geriatric depression rating scale: comparison with other self-report and psychiatric rating scales. In: Crook T, Ferris SH, Bartus R, eds. *Assessment in Geriatric Psychopharmacology.* New Canaan, Conn: Mark Powley Associates; 1983:153–165.

Warner M. *The Complete Guide to Alzheimer's Proofing Your Home.* West Lafayette, Ind: Purdue University Press; 1998.

Yale R. *Developing Support Groups for Individuals with Early-Stage Alzheimer's Disease: Planning, Implementation and Evaluation.* Baltimore, MD: Health Professions Press; 1995.

Zarit SH, Orr NK, Zarit JM. *The Hidden Victims of Alzheimer's Disease, Families under Stress.* New York, NY: New York University Press; 1985.

# INDEX